The Crisis of Ugliness

Historical Materialism Book Series

The Historical Materialism Book Series is a major publishing initiative of the radical left. The capitalist crisis of the twenty-first century has been met by a resurgence of interest in critical Marxist theory. At the same time, the publishing institutions committed to Marxism have contracted markedly since the high point of the 1970s. The Historical Materialism Book Series is dedicated to addressing this situation by making available important works of Marxist theory. The aim of the series is to publish important theoretical contributions as the basis for vigorous intellectual debate and exchange on the left.

The peer-reviewed series publishes original monographs, translated texts, and reprints of classics across the bounds of academic disciplinary agendas and across the divisions of the left. The series is particularly concerned to encourage the internationalization of Marxist debate and aims to translate significant studies from beyond the English-speaking world.

For a full list of titles in the Historical Materialism Book Series
available in paperback from Haymarket Books, visit:
https://www.haymarketbooks.org/series_collections/1-historical-materialism

The Crisis of Ugliness

From Cubism to Pop-Art

Mikhail Lifshitz

Translated by
David Riff

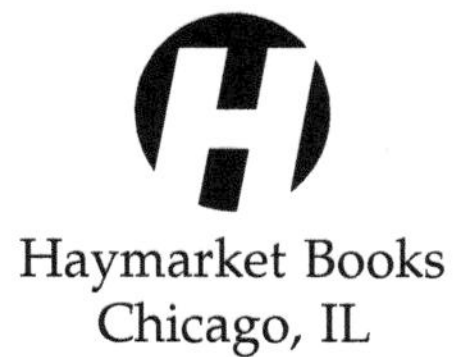

Haymarket Books
Chicago, IL

First published in 2018 by Brill Academic Publishers, The Netherlands
© 2018 Koninklijke Brill NV, Leiden, The Netherlands

Published in paperback in 2019 by
Haymarket Books
P.O. Box 180165
Chicago, IL 60618
773-583-7884
www.haymarketbooks.org

ISBN: 978-1-64259-010-4

Distributed to the trade in the US through Consortium Book Sales and Distribution (www.cbsd.com) and internationally through Ingram Publisher Services International (www.ingramcontent.com).

This book was published with the generous support of Lannan Foundation and Wallace Action Fund.

Special discounts are available for bulk purchases by organizations and institutions. Please call 773-583-7884 or email info@haymarketbooks.org for more information.

Cover design by Jamie Kerry and Ragina Johnson.

Printed in the United States.

10 9 8 7 6 5 4 3 2 1

Library of Congress Cataloging-in-Publication data is available.

Contents

Acknowledgement

This publication was funded by Garage Museum of Contemporary Art, Moscow as part of its Field Research project 'If our soup can could speak …', a three-year research project on Mikhail Lifshitz and his role in the Soviet Sixties.

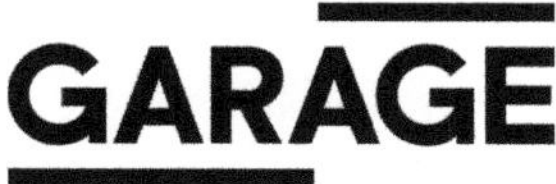

https://garagemca.org/en

List of Illustrations

All illustrations can be found in the separate Illustration Section following the Index.

Notes on Text and Illustrations

Footnotes and citations by Mikhail Lifshitz are numbered. Asterisk notes are translator's comments.

The original Soviet edition of *The Crisis of Ugliness* was generously illustrated with a set of black and white plates in the back of the book depicting classic works of Cubism and Pop Art mentioned in the text. In the USSR, illustrated books with an overview of modern and post-modern art were very scarce, so that *Crisis* was in high demand. The illustrations themselves were 'poor', inky, and heavily retouched, which gave them an intriguing artistic quality of their own. Their selection and positioning was undertaken by Lifshitz himself, who considered them an integral part of the book.

The present edition recreates these illustrations. Their translation into the present is not seamless, however. It proved impossible to reprint the Soviet reproductions due to legal stipulations of the various rights holders. Thus, the current body of illustrations follows the selection and ordering in the original book as far as possible, though using contemporary images supplied by the rights holders, in full colour and at the highest possible resolution.

Mikhail Lifshitz: A Communist Contemporary

David Riff

The year 1968 looks very different from a Soviet perspective than it does from a Western one. The newsreels and tv programmes made in the USSR at the time say it all: the student revolt in Paris receives no more than five seconds (as a trade union inspired strike), while hours of footage are spent to justify the invasion of Czechoslovakia. It was a fatal event that ended the socialist Sixties in all their ambivalence as a brief but intensive period of cultural and political liberalization and de-Stalinization from above. Soon afterward, stagnation would set in, so the story goes. For decades, the contributions of Soviet intellectuals and artists would be considered backward, or worse yet, all too eager to catch up to modernity. It was only after the fall of the Soviet Union that their importance to a global history of contemporary culture would come to be recognized.

This is one of the reasons why the Soviet aesthetic philosopher and Marx scholar Mikhail A. Lifshitz (1905–83) has remained largely unknown in the English-speaking world, aside from his early work *The Philosophy of Art of Karl Marx*, first published in 1938[1] and still used today to teach courses on Marxist aesthetics. It is only over the last ten years that scholars of philosophy and cultural history have begun to retrieve his singularity as a 'Marxist conservative,'[2] a 'creative' or 'Western Marxist'[3] trapped in the Soviet Union, an ultra-Hegelian at odds with the more heterodox and opportunistic totalitarian regime,[4] or as one of the founding figures of a secret socialist humanism whose potentiality has yet to be unlocked.[5] Recently, an entire issue of a scholarly journal was published devoted to different interpretations of his work.[6]

The Crisis of Ugliness has not yet been part of this new international reception, however. Published in 1968 only months before the Soviet invasion of Czechoslovakia, it is by far Lifshitz's most controversial book. As a phillipic

---

1   Lifshitz 1938.
2   Mitchell 2006.
3   Kasakow 2013.
4   Jubara 2010.
5   Chukhrov 2013.
6   Oittinen and Maidansky 2016.

aimed against the canonization of Cubism and Pop, it would finalize Lifshitz's reputation as a hardliner. Yet at the same time, it was one of the few sources on classical modernist and neo-avant-garde art widely available in the Soviet Union in the years to come. It was richly illustrated and served as a valuable source of information even if few agreed with its author's orthodox Marxist views.

The appearance of *The Crisis of Ugliness* was part of an ongoing scandal that first erupted in 1966 when the nationwide weekly *Literaturnaya Gazeta* published Lifshitz's manifesto-like essay 'Why Am I Not a Modernist,' the last text in the present volume. During the tentative 'Thaw' after Nikita Khrushchev's secret speech denouncing Stalin's personality cult at the 20th Party Congress in 1956, modernism had stood for de-Stalinization and democracy. It is exactly this link that Lifshitz called into question in his pamphlet. The idea that early twentieth-century modernism was inherently democratic was simply a myth, he argued. In fact, the campaign against reason waged by the thinkers and artists of the avant-garde opened the doors for the epoch's later barbarism. Lifshitz does not condemn this as complicity, but reads it in terms of tragic guilt and historical irony, central themes in his overall work. He admits that there might be 'good modernists', but there is 'no such thing as good modernism'. Instead, he votes for even the most mediocre academic art, though he winks and says that his faithful readers will know that this is not where he places his ideals.

In the essay's last sentences, Lifshitz dreams of raising Kafka from the grave to write a short story about the worshippers of modernist darkness, including his own. This mention of Kafka is a local reference for the benefit of the Czechoslovak readerships of the Prague-based journal *Estetika*, for which this text was first commissioned in 1964. But beyond a sympathy for one of the 'good modernists' it also suggests that there might be another, more subversive way of reading Lifshitz's polemic, though very few saw it at the time. Lifshitz's rejection of modernism was broadly interpreted as a demand for an unwanted return to Stalinist orthodoxy. That this demand seemed to come from an otherwise respected intellectual made it look like an act of betrayal.

Some still remembered Lifshitz as a prominent aesthetic theoretician of the 1930s who had fallen silent in the last decade of Stalin's reign. Right after Stalin's death, he had returned to the public eye with one of the first substantial criticisms of the vacuity, sycophancy, and superficiality of Stalinist prose with *The Diary of Marietta Shaginian*.[7] This article was one of the first signs of the 'Thaw',

---

7   Lifshitz 1954.

published in *Novy Mir*, a monthly literary journal edited by Lifshitz's wartime friend and former student, the poet Alexander Tvardovsky. 1954 proved too soon for such and similar critiques. Tvardovsky was dismissed for this and other contributions, though he was later reinstated in 1958, after which *Novy Mir* became the mainstay of institutional revisionism in cultural criticism. Perhaps the journal's most significant publication was that of Solzhenitsyn's Gulag novella *A Day in the Life of Ivan Denisovich* (1962). (Lifshitz wrote an internal review saying that it would be a crime not to publish it.)

Given these affiliations, no one was expecting Lifshitz to offer up any fundamental critique of modernism, and when he did, the negative response was overwhelming. Letters flooded in from all over the country.[8] A group of prominent academics wrote a public statement, former Stalinist hawks like Alexander Dymshits published rejoinders against Lifshitz's outburst of aesthetic conservatism, future dissident Lev Kopelev wrote to him imploring him to recant and give up his unflattering role at the 'Protopope Avakum' of a new sect of aesthetic Old Believers. Only the literary critic Efim Etkind came to Lifshitz's defence. Speaking at a public discussion of *The Crisis of Ugliness* in Leningrad, he pointed out that it was impossible to conflate Lifshitz with standard government issue anti-modernism. Instead, he was a 'tragic figure' who had made immeasurable contributions and upheld something like culture at the darkest hour. But now, he was out of step with his time.[9]

∴

Etkind was right to emphasize the importance of Lifshitz's earlier contributions. In the early 1930s, he had been the first to gather and systematise all references to art and literature scattered throughout Marx and Engels's writings and correspondence, a project that generated both the *Philosophy of Art of Karl Marx*, already mentioned above, and the anthology *Marx and Engels on Literature and Art*, often published under different editorships. Lifshitz's was the first work to examine in detail the implications of Marx's writings before 1848, showing how Marx the disappointed poet first became a radical humanist philosopher, how he developed an anthropology rejecting private property in its stupidity, one-sidedness, and hostility to all culture, and how he foresaw its positive sublation in a coming revolutionary humanism.

---

8 For more on the publication history of 'Why Am I Not a Modernist' and its scandalous reception, see Korallov 2008.

9 Fridlender 2008, pp. 334–5.

In the 1950s–60s, a new generation would massively tap into precisely this 'young' Marx. Especially Marx's manuscripts of 1844 and their use of alienation would become the mainstay of Marxism humanism in the 1950s–60s. Thirty years before, Lifshitz had been one of the first to work with precisely these texts, arguing that they clearly showed how Marx was heir to a legacy of aesthetics running from Schiller to Hegel and his ambiguous theory of 'the end of art,' whose traces could be found in the pores of his mature critique of political economy. Lifshitz's Marx is a defender of the classics who understands their impossibility under a capitalism hostile to art; he is a critic of Romanticism and its liberal alibi for maintaining a bourgeois autocratic status quo, a partisan of realism, understood broadly, and the forethinker of an art of truth to come once capitalism has ended. 'Art is dead! Long live art!' is Marx's slogan, according to Lifshitz.

There is clearly a link between this early work and Lifshitz's later anti-modernist writings, including *The Crisis of Ugliness*. In his introduction to the GDR-translation of his Marx-book in 1960,[10] he shows how his views took shape in the mid-to-late 1920s when he was a student and later a lecturer at the avant-garde art school Vkhutemas. In the 'classical period' of the 'negation of classical art,' Lifshitz would make the case for a Marxist interpretation of classical aesthetics. On the one hand, he opposed the productionism of the Soviet avant-garde, as in the group of artists and poets around the journal LEF. On the other hand, he would rebel against the sociological interpretation of art according to psychoideologies of class, which saw itself as a continuation of the 'sociology of art' developed by the father of Russian Marxism, Georgy Plekhanov. Such sociological art critics would include Vladimir Pereverzev or Vladimir Fritsche. Lifshitz's alternative was a return to Hegel and his lectures on aesthetics, read through Lenin (whose philosophical notes were only becoming known at the time), and brought to bear on the avant-garde's much fetishized negativity. Lifshitz's answer was 'the negation of negation', the Leninist conception of 'appropriating cultural legacies' that would later become so central to the entire Soviet aesthetic project under Stalin and beyond. In an interview in the 1970s, he says that he dreamed of a New Renaissance, brought about by the self-activity of the emancipated masses, a dream that, as he admits, was utopian,[11] perhaps even more so than that of his modernist colleagues.

---

10   Lifshitz 1988, p. 224 ff.
11   Lifshitz 1988.

In the late 1920s, at the height of the Cultural Revolution, Lifshitz was branded as a right-wing deviant, and he left his teaching position for a researcher's post at the Marx-Engels-Institute. It was here that he shared an office with philosopher György Lukács, who, though twenty years older, would later credit Lifshitz as a lasting influence.[12] Lifshitz and Lukács would become friends for life. Their collaboration was especially intense between 1933 (when Lukács definitively moved to Moscow) and 1940, in ever-darker times overshadowed by the rise of National Socialism in Germany and Stalinism in the USSR. Lifshitz's 1933 introduction to his Marx-book clearly positions his efforts as a comprehensive cultural counterproposal to the supposedly integral but actually wildly ecclectic fascist *Weltanschauung* that claims classical aesthetics for itself. This anti-fascist pathos resurfaced in a new form in 'Why Am I Not a Modernist' and subsequent texts, just as in Lukács' work from the 1950s–60s.

What also resurfaced through the discussion of 'Why Am I Not a Modernist' and *The Crisis of Ugliness* was Lifshitz's ambivalent role in intellectual life under Stalin. 'Somehow, I am guilty,' he would write in reference to his own participation in the fierce intellectual battles that continued right up to the time of the Great Terror. 'But of what? Of the fact that I made use of the [regime's] struggle against the opposition to effect a victory over an even greater evil, but the victory proved ephemeral'. That greater evil, to Lifshitz, was the class determinism and proletarian identitarianism that had grown rampant after 1928 in the 'class war' waged against bourgeois ideology and specialists during the Cultural Revolution. He himself had been a victim. But by 1930, the climate began to change with a series of campaigns in the intellectual world, first against the academic Marxist philosophers of the 1920s such as Deborin, Sten, and Luppol, then against the workerist literature of the literary organization RAPP, dissolved in 1932, ending with the readmission of non-Communist 'bourgeois' specialists into the intellectual world in the run-up to the Writers' Congress of 1934. In this time, he would rise to prominence as a critic of 'vulgar sociology',

---

12 For more on the relationship between Lifshitz and Lukács, see Ilés 1993 and Sziklai 1993. Lifshitz prompted Lukács to examine Marx and Engels's aesthetic writings, such as their polemic with Ferdinand Lassalle on his revolutionary drama *Franz Von Sickingen*, or Marx's reception of Vischer's Aesthetics, which then feed into his well-known theory of realism. Less obviously, Lifshitz also pointed Lukács toward the early works of Hegel and their connection to the French Revolution on the one hand, and that of materialism and economics on the other. Lukács would examine these links in his magisterial book *The Young Hegel*, submitted in 1939 as a post-doctoral dissertation, and dedicated to Lifshitz 'in devotion and friendship' in recognition of the former's contribution.

attacking the academic philosophers (many of them former Mensheviks) for not recognizing the significance of Lenin's philosophical insights into Marxism. But at the same time, he would begin to develop ideas fundamentally at odds with Stalinism's radical equalization, its deep-seated anti-intellectualism, and its constant tendency to nationalism and isolation.

Lifshitz would later characterize the period between 1931 and 1935 as a gap between two repressive systems in which he was able to make all of his most important theoretical breakthroughs. As cultural policy shifted, it partially embraced the kind of Marxist humanism he championed, and Lifshitz himself became more visibile, even if he never received an academic or permanent institutional post. He taught extensively at the Communist Academy until its closure in 1936 and in the period before World War Two, at the Chernyshchevsky Institute for Philosophy, Literature, and History (IFLI), where his lectures were remembered as especially powerful. Lifshitz was prolific as an editor for the publishing houses Akademia and Molodoya Gvardia, where he worked on the *Zhizn' znamenitykh lyudei* [*Lives of Famous People*] series. In 1936, he became involved with what today would be called curating as deputy director for scholarship at the Tretyakov Gallery. Here, he participated in the dismantling of the radical museological experiments of Alexei Fyodorov-Davydov, and provided the theoretical foundations for the rehabilitation of early 20th century Russian art and icon painting, which he read as a form of realism.

But most importantly, Lifshitz became known from the mid-1930s onward as one of the key intellectuals around *Literaturny Kritik*, a journal founded in 1933 in the run-up to the First Soviet Writers' Congress of 1934 to consolidate the literary community. Eventually, the monthly journal became a platform for the critique of 'vulgar sociology,' and for the articulation of a Marxist aesthetic opposed to the widespread officiousness and sycophancy of the era's culture. 'Under Stalin's shadow, the journal acquired the paradoxical status of a *fronde*,' writes Stanley Mitchell, and the place where Lifshitz and Lukács would develop their alternative to the normative notions of Socialist Realism. '[Combining] Hegel's aesthetic theory, Marx's early ontology and anthropology, Engels's definition of realism and Lenin's concept of reflection ... the two thinkers developed a model of aesthetics and realism that could be applied to the entirety of history, starting with cave paintings'.[13]

This realism would be far more than a heroic reappropriation of nineteenth-century naturalism, reassembled around a quasi-religious messianic expecta-

---

13   Mitchell 2006, p. 32.

tion; rather it would tap into the artwork's capacity for reflecting the profounder, more uncomfortable truth of outer reality in all its developing contradictions. This truth will not be the subjectivity of one particular class or nation, but the experience of society as a whole, Lifshitz proclaims in his key article 'Leninism and Art Criticism' (1936), also published in English in 1938. Class consciousness is not the egotism of one class; it is the consciousness of the totality of social relations, attained by overcoming the narrowness of class origin. In practice, this meant that the writers of *Literarurny Kritik* defended writers previously branded as class enemies. They endorsed the works of international writers like Thomas Mann, and gave very real support to the writer Andrei Platonov, whose dystopian novellas and stories of the ravages of the Civil War and rapid industrialization Stalin personally disliked, and whose frequent presence on the journal's pages eventually led to its closure.

Platonov's presence in the inner circle of *Literaturny Kritik* is a little like Lifshitz's mention of Kafka in his late 'Why Am I Not a Modernist'. It disrupts any facile critique of Lukács and Lifshitz's turn to classicism and realism as mere antiquarianism or even more to an idealistic form of art production suited to covering up the crimes of the regime, a 'personal Weimar – a cultural island among power relations unambiguously hostile toward any democratic culture,' as Ferenc Feher once put it in reference to Lukács.[14] Stanley Mitchell more generously speaks of a 'strategic withdrawal' of genuine Marxism to the aesthetic field in response to 'Stalin's suppression of revolutionary politics,' adding that this withdrawal's prototype was the 'reconciliation to reality' that Hegel had reached in the sobering aftermath of the French Revolution. Hegel did not give up on the critical insights or revolutionary ideals of his youth. Instead, he had realized that reason would not prevail on the strength of subjective ideas pitted against reality with willpower alone; if there was such a thing as reason, it was immanent to reality as a whole, even if that whole seemed 'wrong or unreasonable'.

Hegel's 'reconciliation' with reality and his recognition of the ideal immanent to the real set his philosophy apart from other German idealism. His realism allowed later readers to radicalize his philosophy, Lifshitz affirmed. In that sense, Hegel's seeming acquiesence to the state or bourgeois society was actually full of subversive elements, to be reclaimed by generations to come. Such subversive elements can also be found in Lifshitz's own texts. He characterises them as a form of ultra-sound, audible only to the trained ear of the thirties,

---

14   Feher 1979, p. 114.

and imperciptible to the repressive machine.[15] A brilliant stylist, he adopted the bombastic, lethal tone of the time's vicious literary polemics. 'But my task consisted in accepting [this tone as an] inevitable precondition, and in overcoming this element of crude directness with a highly developed literary form. I must admit that this was hellish work,' he later wrote in his notes.[16] The resulting style is very much like his characterization of one of his favourite writers, Nikolai Chernyshchevsky, usually known for the bluntness and even woodenness of his all-too-direct prose: 'It is time to finally recognize that Chernyshchevksy wrote intelligently, with a fine, sometimes nearly imperceptible irony, playing the fool while searching for the truth like Socrates, or goading his contemporaries with crass judgements to wake them from their protracted slumber'.[17]

∴

Lifshitz's characterization of Chernyshchevsky's bluntness – today one would call it political incorrectness – applies most of all to his anti-modernist texts. Most of his contemporaries and even his faithful readers proved impervious to their irony, especially vis-à-vis a preexisting and continuing anti-modernist discourse, and not only a pro-modernist one. One can already see this unusual combination in the title of the present book, *The Crisis of Ugliness*. Lifshitz did not invent it but rather lifted it from Georgy Plekhanov, the father of Russian Marxism, who had written about Cubism after a visit to the Salon d'automne of 1912. Plekhanov, in turn, was quoting the late nineteenth–early twentieth-century art critic Camille Mauclair. 'La crise de la laideur' appears in his *Trois crises de l'art actuel* (1906) in reference to the Fauves, whom he accuses of having gone too far afield from the last viable modern painterly practice, impressionism. Plekhanov translated this turn of phrase into Russian as *krizis bezobrazie*. Bezobrazie, in Russian, has nuances that the English ugliness does not, connoting infantile, even carnivalesque foolishness, leading far beyond the disfigured, the unattractive or the unsightly of the French *laideur*.

Lifshitz picks up Plekhanov's turn of phrase in his critical study of Cubism, the first and longest essay in the book, where he elaborates the attack on Picasso. By the early 1960s, Picasso had been fully rehabilitated as a friend of the Soviet Union, a communist party member, and the author of the dove of

---

15   Lifshitz 2007.
16   Lifshitz 2007.
17   Lifshitz 1979, p. 7.

peace and Guernica, symbols of pacificism and resistance to fascist aggression. His status as a normative classic was beyond question, his early radical work domesticated and considered 'beautiful' or 'expressive'. Lifshitz's study of Cubism rails against this consensus. 'Our yellow-pink drooling over Picasso deserves only a good Russian curse,' he would write in private correspondance.[18] Picasso, Braque, and the others were radicals whose work breathed burning kerosene to scandalize the last generation of aesthetes. To canonize them as a new aesthetic norm would completely miss their anti-aesthetic point. Lifshitz deconstructs the Western canonization of Cubism as a 'Copernican turn', showing how the same hackneyed, unquestionable stereotypes migrated from text to text, eventually making their way into the all-too uncritical writing of Western neo-Marxists.

Lifshitz opposes such admixtures of modernism and Marxism, and, in his blunt manner, declares the two utterly incompatible. But on a more subtle level, he also takes issue with the flat-out rejection of modernism in 'Eastern' Marxism, making it clear that censorship or worse are not on his agenda. These are not criminal proceedings against individuals or attacks on personal integrity, he emphasizes, echoing Marx's disclaimer that worker and capitalist are not concrete individuals but character masks. He seeks to complicate the widespread view of modernism as a mere symptom of bourgeois decadence through a critical reading of Plekhanov's 'Art and Social Life'. Plekhanov derides Leger's *Woman in Blue* as 'nonsense cubed' – Lifshitz clearly loves this blunt phrase – and sees it as an expression of decadent bourgeois idealism. But at the same time, Plekhanov ignores the Cubists' larger intent, their attraction to a new order of a wholly constructed, geometricized life, which politically corresponds to their drift to the right. Plekhanov thus bypasses what Lifshitz terms as the social or ontological utopia of all modernism, namely that of a hyper-personal, collectively organized life. Limiting himself to purely formal and logical aspects, Plekhanov infuses most later Marxist writing on Cubism with a heavy dose of 'vulgar sociology'.

Lifshitz proposes to think beyond Plekhanov and to apply Lenin's 'theory of reflection' to Cubism and modernism: to look at the total objective social relations as reflected in the truth-relations of the actual work. Cubism rejects Enlightenment values both in theory and practice; its grammar of primary volumes, passages, and prisms is a decomposition of the rationalist artistic tradition, where optics would strain to see truthfully past illusion. For Cubism,

---

18   Lifshitz 2009, p. 342.

vision offers no such path to truth; its multiple, simultaneous perspectives are hieroglyphs for the dream of attaining a true objecthood beyond vision – via the worship of materiality itself.

This activates another subtext in the Russian etymology of *bez-obrazie*, literally 'image-lessness', as in the lack of vision, images, or ideals. Lifshitz was probably not aware that the only equivalent to this etymological construct appeared in theological debates after the Second World War in Germany as *Bildlosigkeit*. But there is a (counter-)theological subtext in all of his writing that reaches one of its highpoints in *The Crisis of Ugliness*. In their iconoclasm and their search for a realm beyond images, the modernists resemble gnostic sectarians and mystics. They are true believers in hopeless times whose honest despair reflects 'the sigh of the oppressed creature, the heartbeat of the heartless world'. But their esoteric cults are adopted by the mainstream as opiates and ciphers for the dream of a world where the tortured spirit-mind has finally overcome itself, returning to matter in the form of a fast-moving mass commodity.

This is a new version of Hegel's legendary return of the spirit to matter from *The Phenomenology of the Spirit* (1807) that Lifshitz describes in his 'Phenomenology of the Soup Can' (1967), the shorter essay on Pop in this volume. Lifshitz, on the one hand, is making light of the deadly seriousness with which critics and philosophers considered Pop. But deeper down, the irony of his argument targets the conservative soft-modernist attitudes in the Soviet Union: he is mocking those proponents of classical modernism who support the decomposition of painting, but stop short of 'contemporary,' anti-formalist, conceptual practices, scandalized by their vapidity and emptiness.

In a situation generally starved for information, Lifshitz offers Soviet readers a brief history of Pop in an intricate digest-collage of French, German and English-language press clippings, up-to-date with happenings and performances that Moscow neo-modernist artists of the time did not know. He almost gleefully narrates Pop's ascendency over Abstract Expressionism from the price crisis of abstract painting in 1962 to the Venice Biennial of 1964, and its sprawl into the grey zone between high art and mass culture. Lifshitz's is a view at a remove; he never travelled to the West, compounding an already grandfatherly amazement at the antics – the *bezobrazie* – of the youth in distant lands. Lifshitz is not as scandalized by Pop as his modernist opponents: in fact, he at times even revels in drawing up an evocative narrative where 'the lovely Ingrid,' Batman, and Warhol's factory of superstars all beckon from across the sea. Yet at the same time, he is ruthless in his depiction of Pop's total, self-conscious commodification, its support by the state, but also its role in a society of 'bread and circuses', a massively expanding retail culture of increasingly atomized, alienated individuals. Lifshitz quotes contemporary American authors like David Riesman or Vance Packard, and there is also an overlap with Guy Debord's 'society of the spectacle', especially in a common sensitivity for what Debord calls the 'philanthropy of the commodity', which Lifshitz describes as the new social demagogy of a leisure society that pretends it has a new form of 'popular' art. Here, again, Lifshitz takes up the anti-fascist theme of his book, prefiguring the softer, post-modern authoritarianisms whose emergence we are currently witnessing.

The anti-fascist pathos of *The Crisis of Ugliness* is not the only link to Lifshitz's Marx-book of 1933. Another common motif is the role of unhappy or disintegrated consciousness (*zerissenes Bewusstsein*) in Hegel's *Phenomenology*, and the importance of this idea to Marx. In a disintegrating modernity, disintegrated, unhappy consciousness has an advantage. 'Since ignoble consciousness understands the "universally human" character of its own way of life,' he writes, 'it can rise to an understanding of how social relationships generally "disintegrate". Thus, it becomes immeasurably better than official society, which only pursues self-serving motives under the hypocritical guise of honesty and noblesse'.[19] For Marx, disintegrated consciousness had the chance to rise up in indignation, but in the case of Pop (and its predecessors), the indignation targets consciousness itself. This is why Pop is paradoxically flat, consciously dumbed down and intentionally vapid. It imitates the 'philanthropy of the commodity' – its conversion of leisure into a 'down-time' of non-binding, mindless pleasures – but it is made from a complex, fractured 'meta-position of the spirit' that dwells in the upper floors of consciousness and longs for self-oblivion. Today, such figures are still recognizable as the endless longing for the power of plain human stupidity in the age of technocratically accelerated artificial intelligence.

∵

The Crisis of Ugliness was at odds with the standard government-issue anti-modernist propaganda of its time, as we have seen. Taking up arguments and polemics from three decades before, it placed itself beyond both the outright rejection of modern art through Stalinist conservatives – on the grounds of its Western or non-proletarian nature – and its partial rehabilitation through the liberal Soviet intelligentsia. An attentive reader will see that this is only

---

19   Lifshitz forthcoming.

possible because Lifshitz's is not an external but an immanent critique of modernism. He is more than familiar with the logic of negation that far more benevolent critics in the West would fetishize. Its perfomative rejection of the modernist paradigm is at the same time a pastiche of avant-gardist criticism, belying firsthand experience of what it could mean to be a modernist or a contemporary artist.

Part of the historical significance of *Crisis* is that its publication coincided chronologically with a number of decisive cleavages in the art scene. After 1968, the bifurcation between 'official' and 'inofficial' cultures solidified. Both classical modernism and the local neo-avantgardes were increasingly pushed out of the public sphere into a domestic underground. Lifshitz now clearly belonged to the 'official' world, even if his writing and his positions were somehow alien to it. He had vehemently opposed the denial of publicity to modernist (counter)culture, demanding that Soviet audiences make up their own minds on Cubism or Pop. But now, that denial was almost complete. Just as modernism and contemporary art were excluded from the public, Lifshitz's theoretical position – that of Marxism-Leninism – was excluded from any serious debate about what it could mean to be contemporary, modern, or modernist until roughly two decades ago, even though his book was still there as a source.

After 1968, there was another split in the underground itself. Artists like Ilya Kabakov, Erik Bulatov, Viktor Pivovarov, or Komar and Melamid would articulate conceptualist practices, breaking with the 'expressionist' pathos of their neighbours, and rejecting their individual underground quests of metaphysical self-expression as false freedom. This rejection runs parallel to Lifshitz's argumentation against a reconciliatory, aestheticist modernism, but also resonates with his unmasking of its homemade theologies. There is not much evidence of Lifshitz's direct reception among the first generation of Moscow Conceptualists, however. One rare exception is a short enigmatic blank verse by conceptual poet Vsevelod Nekrassov, another is a recent interview of Alexander Melamid by art critic Andrei Kovalev, in which it turns out that Melamid was always familiar with Lifshitz in detail and even met him, because his parents knew him personally.

It is unclear how far thinkers like Boris Groys or artists like Ilya Kabakov were explicitly influenced by Mikhail Lifshitz's *Crisis of Ugliness*. It is highly suggestive, however, that the first generation of Moscow Conceptualists would be haunted by Socialist Realism and its central contradiction, the universal scope of its aesthetic ambition and its parochial lack of aesthetic means, its cosmic desires to reach the level of species-being – *Gattungswesen* – and its complete vulgarization and flattening of both classical and modernist means at its disposal. (Ilya Kabakov mentions this as the central drama of his artistic socialization, and one modernist practices could never fully overcome.) One could see this as the aesthetic version of the contradiction that Lifshitz – with Engels – sees at the heart of the revolutionary tragedy: 'the tragic clash between the historically necessary postulate and the impossibility of its execution in practice,' or as Lenin would put it in a marginal note, 'the gulf (chasm) between the immensity of the task and the poverty of our material and cultural means'. In Lifshitz's notes and essays, this 'gulf' resurfaces: 'Choleric revolt on the one side, fake communists on the other. How many bodies must we throw to bridge the chasm between them?'

As one can see, there is a huge difference between the Moscow Conceptualists and Lifshitz's positions. For the Moscow Conceptualists, the contradiction at the heart of Soviet aesthetics reflected little more than exhaustion and failure; Soviet aesthetics were interesting to them because they revolved around an 'empty centre'. Lifshitz's view of the revolutionary tragedy – and its possible reflection in aesthetic problems – is full of historical content, of an awareness of the fact that the Soviet experience was far more than just some semiotic construct of a propaganda machine. He would have dismissed the Moscow Conceptualists' obsesssion with linguistic conventions and hollow language as yet another post-modern version of the *nothing that nothings*. (Heidegger, not Lifshitz, Marx, or Hegel, was the philosopher the Conceptualists quoted and admired.)

In that sense, Lifshitz is a contemporary of the *contemporary* in the moment of its emergence in the Soviet Union, commenting on developments more and more limited in their relevance to the offworld of inofficial culture from the increasingly isolated vantage of his own, increasingly conceptual Marxist-Leninist aesthetic philosophy. His untimeliness in the Soviet Sixties, still lingering today, places him in proximity to the figure of the contemporary as described by philosopher Giorgio Agamben through Osip Mandelstam's poetic subject, who mends the broken backbone of the century with his own blood: one foot out of step with the present, yet able to see its darkness, and to understand it as a light from the future that has not reached us.[20] It is this 'darkness' that Lifshitz wants to show when he dreams of reviving Kafka, a darkness that extends far beyond the classics of modernist art or those of the Western or Eastern European neo-avant-gardes into our own present.

---

20   Agamben 2009, p. 42.

That is not to say that Lifshitz should be read as an anticipation of or contribution to contemporary theory, to be inserted seamlessly into a row of other neo-Marxist and post-communist thinkers retroactively. Even if many of his insights prefigure those of post-modern art criticism, he opposed the very idea of post-modernism vehemently in his lifetime. Instead, Lifshitz remains untimely. He stands out like a sore thumb in the world of contemporary theory, whose anti-essentialism and post-universalism cannot tolerate his insistance upon an art of apprehensible truth after the 'end of art'. In a post-colonial setting, his communist apology for Russian and Western European culture in its orientation toward Greco-Roman antiquity and Christianity as an alternative to the 'artificial barbarism' of modernity seems Eurocentric to say the least. Worse yet, his theories of the popularity of art as a criterion for its truth-value and his polemic against modernist elitism could be perceived as the historical version of today's attacks upon contemporary art and its infrastructure by the resurgent radical right.

In that sense, there may be a danger of reading Lifshitz naively as an argument against a 'globalist' contemporary art that encroaches upon national traditions and popular taste, and claiming that this is where his contemporary relevance lies. Such readings are deaf to the 'ultra-sound' of Lifshitz's writing, whose intention is more to overcome or to sublate modernism than to simply reject it, just as his intention was certainly not to embrace ordinary conservatism with all its variants of chauvinism. As for his purported Eurocentrism, it needs to be seen in the context of Russia as a 'subaltern Empire' on the margins of Europe, where the October Revolution offered a chance to take over and invert self-colonizing relations. One might read Lifshitz's appropriation of Hegel, Marx, Vico, or Winckelmann against the backdrop of Timothy Brennan's *Borrowed Light*, which points toward the reworking of Viconian-Hegelian thinking as an emancipative tool in the former colonies. Moreover, Lifshitz's very definition of realism has non-Eurocentric elements. He recognizes the realism of African or Asian art in its own setting, then de-realized, one might add, in its appropriation by Western modernists. Lifshitz envisions a new Renaissance in the underdeveloped East, but without the imperialist-national chauvinist elements he would oppose quite explicitly at the most dangerous of times.[21] That is ultimately the source of his counter-proposal to the global spread of modernist and contemporary culture as we know it today.

---

21   Lifshitz's lectures at the Chernyshchevsky Institute for Philosophy, Literature and History
      (IFLI) show him opposing the national turn of the early 1940s. See Lifshitz 2015.

In that sense, it seems crucial to read and translate Lifshitz in his tension as a communist contemporary of the contemporary, to place him into the context of the capitalist contemporary art he rejected, in all his untimeliness. Lifshitz acknowledges the ontological radicalism of an anti-aesthetic art and grasps the vector of its conceptual outcome. But he also continues to insist upon an aesthetic alternative to contemporary culture and its proposition-oriented conceptualism. To imagine that alternative today from the situation of a permanent legitimacy crisis – reflecting a very real epistemic uncertainty vis-à-vis an increasingly instable present – is more than intriguing.

At the same time, this alternative is like Agamben's light of some cosmic event in another galaxy that has yet to reach our planet. In Lifshitz's view of history, art will only shift from its ultra-modernizing mode of the eternal 'bad' present into true contemporaneity when the self-activity of the masses cleans the legacies of an oppressed humanity's cultural history, putting them to new use in the emancipation of consciousness from the narrow-mindedness of the past. For as long as this self-activity is absent, the crisis of ugliness persists, and Lifshitz's work stands out as an indictment of the art system and the subjectivity that keeps it intact.

Foreword

There is an old German fairy tale of three sisters, in which One-Eye and Three-Eyes pride themselves on their originality and laugh at Two-Eyes for looking like everyone else. They persecute and starve the poor girl, stealing the golden apples on her silver tree. Good always triumphs over evil in old fairy tales, so in the end, Two-Eyes marries a knight and lives happily ever after, the silver tree growing under her window. Her mean sisters sink into abject poverty, and when they come begging to the castle, she feeds them. This is how everything one-eyed and three-eyed comes to nought and finds itself eating from somebody else's table. Without a normal humanity, it cannot survive.

If some modern storyteller were to rework this edifying tale, he would have to complicate its original plot. The happy ending is too simple for our age. Today's storyteller would tell you that Two-Eyes was spoiled by too many golden apples and a life of ease. Some say that when her sisters turned up at the castle, the knight took to them with his cane. After punishing them for the wrongness of their 'worldview', he banished them from the keep, as Two-Eyes looked on, laughing merrily, munching on her golden apples.

The moral of the story will have changed, no doubt, but what will this moral now be? That is the question. Irritated by Two-Eye's actions, our storyteller might not know how to make ends meet, and could easily draw false conclusions. At any rate, many storytellers today, and their name is legion, will sympathise with One-Eye and Three-Eyes to the point of completely negating any difference between the three sisters whatsoever. Two eyes, they assert, have no advantage over other 'ways of seeing'.

From their point of view, only dogmatics and ignoramuses are capable of believing that there is any natural way of seeing the world. Two eyes see just as arbitrarily as one or three; they certainly aren't better, and they might even be worse, since they aren't as original. The new storytellers say that ordinary two-eyed people have always persecuted the one-eyed and the three-eyed, and that their conflict with overwhelming mediocrity means that they are the salt of the earth and the hope of humanity. Such conclusions will seem quite convincing, since readers tend to sympathise with the insulted and the abused.

In fact, the naïve reader is making a big mistake, having been led astray by incompetent or malicious storytellers. The only thing that follows from the modern version of the fairy tale is that golden apples can spoil even the most normal and healthy being. Other than that, one will naturally ask: why would a nice peasant girl marry a goonish knight? And, finally, if you own a cane, keep it for self-defence. There is no point in using it as an argument to prove your rightness, if only because such discussions often lead to exactly the opposite of their intended results.

Then again, how ordinary people see the world is entirely beside the point. One-eyedness and three-eyedness are still monstrous, even after taking a drubbing. A truth thus proven loses more than it gains – that is all. After seeing her better half cracking down on wrong 'ways of seeing', Two-Eyes won't laugh for long. In fact, she may well herself be scared silly, and that never helps to broaden one's perspective.

Such are the more or less truthful conclusions you might draw when you look at things as to their rationale and their morality, that is, from the perspective of the human will, its abuses and its mistakes. Needless to say, there is another side to the matter. If a child gets the measles, the parents or the kindergarten are to blame, because there is no absolute need to contract an illness. But the measles themselves are no mistake, and illnesses like these become more and more dangerous the older you get.

Let us now turn from fairy tales and allegories to real life. We hardly need explain that in our fable, One-Eye and Three-Eyes stood for the tendencies of modern art. Dominant in the West, they enjoy the unflagging attention of the international media. By now, any reader will have heard at least something of these trends. First, they were subject to all sorts of ridicule in our country, derided as 'idiocy', 'tomfoolery', and 'trickery', and such words often came with even stronger expressions. Later, under the sway of international relations, the tone turned more charitable, becoming restrained at the very least. Yet such silence is just as unhelpful in getting to the crux of the matter as those older taunts.

A certain re-evaluation of values is also underway in the Marxist literature, we should add. One trend has been particularly vocal, though hardly representative of all Marxist writing, in taking a new position on the problem of realism. This position is highly reminiscent of those modernist views considered bourgeois only yesterday. To these Young Marxists, believing that Two-Eyes is a normal being is tantamount to remaining in a state of 'dogmatic slumber', to use Roger Garaudy's term.*

Garaudy's books and articles tell us that 20 years ago, this 'dogmatic slumber' was especially deep, but that its beginnings actually lay in the epoch of the Renaissance, if not earlier, in classical Greek antiquity. In a word, the critique

---

* The term actually comes from Kant's famous *Prolegomena to Any Future Philosophy* (1783), where he thanks David Hume for his attack on metaphysics which 'interrupted [his] dogmatic

of dogmatism from this perspective demands the rejection of the figurative tradition in its classical form, of any 'way of seeing' the world as reality. Reading Garaudy's recent books and articles, one could conclude that the culture of the Renaissance is the principle source of the personality cult.

No conscious, modern person with an interest in public affairs could remain indifferent to the task of overcoming this affliction, especially after having first-hand experience of those delightful phenomena denoted symbolically by the name of dogmatism. However, many opponents of 'dogmatic slumber' only know about what we had to endure by hearsay. That might be one of the reasons why they solve these problems with such ease.

If you want to awaken from your 'dogmatic slumber', you have to get to the root of the problem and go to the end. You have to clearly imagine the essence of the things you are trying to negate without placing the whole story onto the game-board of liberal phrases that cost nothing and offer nothing, no emancipation, nothing at all but illusions, hypocritical or naïve. Because the experience of social life teaches that any critique of the past comes with a certain false criticism, ostentatiously freedom-loving, though it is little more than the same old filth in new raiments.

To take the fight with dogmatism to the Renaissance, to blame the realist tradition for all kinds of ugliness perpetrated by those who did not care whether they were doing it in reverse perspective or linear perspective, to identify the critique of dogmatic holdovers with an anarchic, decadent revolt against the old 'canons' and 'norms' that then occupies idle minds for nearly a whole century like a football game: all that amounts to a misdirection of social energy, wilfully or naïvely diverted away from real tasks to fighting ghosts. If you want to criticise society's 'dogmatic slumber', you have to be a democrat, not a liberal, as in any serious matter.

What does that mean? Let us try to explain. For the last ten to 15 years, Soviet literature has seen an intensification of realism of which one can honestly be proud. Without waiting for literary critics to open their eyes for them, thousands of people are finding the right books, the books they need. As long as a writer doesn't lie or deform life in the name of some arbitrary convention agreed in advance, as long as he refrains from speculating on commonplaces and doesn't distract the reader's attention with mannerisms of form, he can always count on society's sympathy. Such writers are enthusiasts, theirs is no easy effort, and it goes far beyond the mere retelling of hackneyed ideas in a

---

slumber and gave [his] investigations a completely different direction'. Garaudy appropriates the term in his *Realisme sans rivages* (1963).

more artistic language than that of the press. And it is thanks to this effort that literature can take on a greater social agency.

How was literature able to achieve such an influence over readers who see it as the mirror of their thoughts and vital interests? Only by telling the truth – to the extent of the talent and possibilities of its creators – and by looking around to see things as they actually are; in other words, seeing what anybody with two eyes can see, 'all jokes aside', as they say. This is the source of its truly innovative quality, and, if you will, the source of its artistic achievements, which are gains made in the struggle against insincerity, often including its own. It is a literature that conveys the dictates of reality to its readership, one that values nothing more than the interests of the people, that is, the development of Soviet democracy. It is a literature of ideas (*literatura ideynaya*) in the best communist sense of the word.

A different answer to the questions with which life faces artists is the fascination with modernism. It is another answer altogether, since here we are dealing with innovations whose character is more promotional than real. We are told that art can only carry out its emancipative mission by changing traditional forms, moving from the depiction of reality as it is to 'mythmaking'. We must deform what we see with our eyes in the name of the future, writes Roger Garaudy, the most consistent theoretician of that tendency.

We know, we've read it all before, and more than once! In the past, such methods were not called 'mythmaking'. Instead, one might have spoken of a realism with 'Romantic' supplements. However, the artist's putative responsibility to move away from reality – in the name of changing the world instead of simply interpreting it – was declared for over a decade in the most dogmatic of ways, especially when it was necessary to justify idyllic pictures of country life and other literary myths.

Of course, there is a difference. It is one thing to distract oneself from the real world through conventionally verisimilar paintings, and another to distract oneself through modernist attenuations of visible form. Yet from the perspective of a genuine realism expressing the living ideal of Soviet democracy and not liberal poses in the language of art, this difference is rather relative. Either way, both are cases of art that diverts attention from real life and objective truth as we see it in the past, present, and future.

If we are to believe the Young Marxists, turning your back on the real world as seen by two eyes is a means of struggling against 'alienation' and 'dogmatic slumber' in the name of individuality. From the perspective of Marxist theory, such fantasies have no value at all. They are, however, based on certain facts of modern life, a terrible tangle of spontaneous forces that the reader will have to navigate.

Imagine a young person who had 'the image of Tatiana'* pummelled into his head. Upon graduating from school, he promises himself never to read Pushkin again, and that decision might feel like an expression of his hard-won individual rights. Yet in fact, Pushkin never stopped being a great poet simply because he was taught by rote in school, so that the young person stands to lose a great deal through his decision. In his later years, he will certainly come to see that Tatiana was not to blame; rather the fault lies with educational methods that sadly often nip in the bud any interest in even the best creations of human genius as early as grade school. The same is true of realism when it is ingrained *argumentum ad baculum*, under the threat of force.

In those who claim an independent mode of thinking, openness to such spontaneous refusals is less forgivable than in yesterday's schoolboy. In the end, even when modernist games are played in earnest, they are reminiscent of Repetilov's 'infernal noise'.** As this 'infernal noise' becomes more significant in life, backed at a greater or lesser distance by real forces that you could hardly call progressive, it becomes necessary to draw a line between modernist 'mythmaking' and the real defence of the Leninist cause. Sooner or later, this demarcation line will emerge clearly for everyone to see, and the sooner, the better.

We take the term modernism to mean a system of devices for the creation of a moral alibi and a special pose that allows you to see yourself as cutting-edge and free, while continuing to do more of the same. When this system was first discovered, it expressed the real attempts of artists to emancipate themselves from an unfavourable social situation; several important personalities emerged in its wake. Today, it has become a token of good taste for the most affluent of philistines.***

---

*   'The image of Tatiana' refers to the main heroine of A.S. Pushkin's *Eugene Onegin* (1823–31), Tatiana Larina, who until today is a favorite topic for essays in Russian secondary school literature lessons.

**   Lifshitz is alluding to Lenin, who quotes Griboyedov's play *Woe from Wit*, using the loud-mouthed Anglophile Repetilov to characterise 'noisy' trends claiming to be revolutionary but actually seeking class rapprochement: '"At least we make an infernal noise" – such is the slogan of many revolutionarily minded individuals who have been caught up in the maelstrom of events and who have neither theoretical principles nor social roots'. Cf. Lenin 1964, p. 186.

***   One of Mikhail Lifshitz's favourite words is the untranslatable Russian *obyvatel'*, meaning the petit-bourgeois consumer and slave of convention who inhabits a world of standardised taste. The word 'philistine' in English, its standard translation, is a little too archaic to

The historical function of this phenomenon was nicely captured by the old Russian humourist Arkady Averchenko.* There is a Christmas tale in his anthology, *On Essentially Decent People*, in which the man-of-letters Vzdokhov and the painter Poltorakin** are on their way to an evening of festivities when they find an orphan freezing on the street. First, they want to warm him up and feed him, but then they understand that that will be just 'another little story', a Christmas cliché. So they leave the boy out to freeze. The story is very funny and it is also very sad. In fact, the uncompromising attitude to traditional forms and the panicked fear of 'clichés' easily turns into a readiness to reconcile with rather moderate, even retrograde content. History tells us that such forms of inner games with oneself always served as a pressure valve for 'essentially decent people', and that everything stayed as it was in the old days. If we don't want our orphan to freeze, we need to stay away from the games of an immature social consciousness.

You will tell us that any rejection of 'dogmatic slumber', even in its most awkward form, is justified as a spontaneous reaction to the perversion of great truths into banal 'little stories', hackneyed, hypocritical clichés. No wonder so many people striving for the most progressive social goals seek salvation in the aesthetics of modernism. After all, there was a time when even communist ideas expressed themselves in phantasmic religious imagery.

Such ways of thinking are rather popular today, though more in words than in deeds. While progressive ideas might carve their way in a contradictory form, let us note that they would be more progressive without these losses and complications. Spontaneous reactions like those of the schoolboy fed up with 'the image of Tatiana' – and especially the infantile thinking of the theoreticians who justify such spontaneity – ultimately never raise but rather lower the level of social engagement of 'essentially decent people'.

---

fully capture this word's everyday meaning, while consumer would flatten and neutralise the moral accusation behind this term.

* Arkady Averchenko (1881–1927) was a Russian playwright and satirist with liberal political views. He is best-known for his contributions to and editorship of the popular journal *Satyricon* in the years before World War I. In 1918, *Satyricon* was declared an anti-Soviet publication and Averchenko fled, first to his native Sevastopol, then to Istanbul in 1920, and on to Paris, Sofia, Belgrade, and Prague. His work includes several satires of early twentieth-century modernism, including the short story *Krysa na podnose* [Rat on a Tray] (1913), republished as a feuilleton in the newspaper *Pravda* in 1963 and later made into a short film in the same year.

** These last names might be translated as 'Sighly', and 'Oneandhalfer', respectively, and are jokes in themselves.

The larger part of human pursuits are born and shaped through contingencies. They do not correspond to the ideal demands of any system appropriate to their subject matter. To understand modernism as a social phenomenon of our time, one would have to write differently. Several lectures held at the Central House of Writers in Moscow in late 1956 were more systematic in that regard than the articles brought to the reader's attention in this anthology. However, life gave its own orders: a more extensive study of modernism and its problems in view of the entire evolution of social consciousness over the last century was placed in cold storage, and circumstances did the rest.

Bound by their shared position, both authors* hope their polemical approach to artistic questions with a broader bearing on life at large was more than a obstacle on the way to scientific analysis. Without real life urgency, science becomes false wisdom; it flickers and wanes rather than illuminating its surroundings, never mind all its imaginary freedom from the circumstances of its time. The authors also ask the reader to remember that for all its pointedness, their polemic is directed at ideas rather than people. Of course, people help to make the conditions that determine the direction of their intellectual interests and moral qualities. Which means they are responsible. One should not mix up social drama with criminal proceedings, however, since many factors are difficult to influence, and since the law of collective responsibility means people must often bear the burden of somebody else's guilt.

In the realm of ideas, on the other hand, even more responsibility is required. Comprehension itself is not everything by far, but it already contains the beginnings of freedom. As one wise man said in ancient times, 'everything can grow tiresome except comprehension'. The authors of this small book hope that people will soon tire of their present predilection for self-complacently blowing soap bubbles, and that the hour of comprehension is nigh. If anyone has a better or clearer explanation than ours, we will be happy to follow him and quote his words.

The articles in this book were published in Soviet periodica. A few exceptions aside, they were only subject to minimal literary editing.

---

*   The Russian edition of *Krizis bezobrazie* (1968) contained an article by Lifshitz's wife, Lidia Y. Reyngart, written in 1948 on abstract painting. It has been omitted from the present translation.

Myth and Reality: The Legend of Cubism

In recent years, contemporary Marxist thinking has encountered a new problem. Roger Garaudy and his followers in different parts of the world consider it crucial. The matter in question is Cubist painting. To Garaudy, 'the revolution effected by Picasso' is the greatest event of modernity, 'a Copernican turn, after which man became the center of gravity, a turn leading to an equally deep transformation of the object'.[1] Without arguing over this matter's importance in relation to other questions posed by the present, let us start by saying that its novelty is relative.

The scene of the action is Paris on the eve of the First World War. As the curtain rises, we see a crowd of philistines on a rampage, we hear jeering and mockery. But what is causing such a stir? The arrival of a new movement in art. 'Cubism' was born in 1907 or 1908. In the words of the French poet André Salmon, a friend of the Cubists, it was the beginning of 'a completely new art' on a mission to save the world.

Such a beginning predisposes us in Cubism's favour. We know that the new is born in throes; it clashes with the interests of the more conservative part of society, offending with its lack of regard for conventional taste. The reverse of this theorem, however, does not always hold true. The philistines of yesteryear may have shunned Rembrandt and Delacroix, but that hardly means everything they cast aside is as good as the art of those great masters. Theories or rather systems of words that find beauty in everything once rejected are hackneyed sophisms, and they are no less dangerous to social theory than the nightmare of tradition weighing upon people's minds for millennia. At any rate, this new danger is backed by a zeal just as fanciful, a mass hysteria of sorts. Legend has it that the inventor of the first bandsaw was thrown into the river with a stone around his neck and drowned for breaking ancestral law. In our day, the fanatics of 'the modern' are ready to drown anyone in a teaspoon of water if they refuse to worship the new as a god, as Lenin once put it. Their zeal manifests itself at the very first chance, in rather reckless practical acts against things and people. Sometimes, there is a clash between traditional philistinism and the new philistinism inspired by the fantastic, negative ideal of the future,

---

1   Garaudy 1963, p. 106.

and sometimes they fuse, as in official art under Mussolini and Hitler. Either way, reason suffers, along with society's level of aesthetic development.

A century ago, Marx wrote of modern mythology. To be sure, the idealisation of mythmaking has no place in Marxism, even if it has become so common in bourgeois theory after Nietzsche. Modern mythology in the Marxian sense implies the foul atmosphere of trivial clichés clouding the real facts of social life, produced on purpose at least in part through advertising and other suggestive means. Modern mythology in its contemporary phase also involves the personal drama of the artist as he clashes with a crowd of philistines, followers of conservative traditions. After the artist succumbs to this unequal struggle, there is an apotheosis of his genius in the minds of the next generation, and the price of his work soars at the Hôtel Drouot in Paris, one of the centres of the trade in paintings.

This story is half reality, half fairy tale. The real Golgotha of loners and tragic 'outsiders' like Van Gogh or Gauguin serves as the model for a mass of apocrypha from the vitae of other martyrs. The same cliché is repeated a thousand-fold in newspaper articles, monographs, novels, and movie scripts. Thus, there emerges something of a medieval town square mystery, only now played out for an audience of millions. Experiencing this sacred drama, the man in the street feels purified; he can now calmly go back to his everyday business, to life's unbearably boring routine. He needs a vent, to be found in the figure of the artist-innovator, his bold defiance of the surrounding world, and his condemnation to martyrdom. In the twentieth century, it is the painter who dons the saintly crown of thorns from the epoch of primitive Christianity to take on the sins of the laity.

One French author examines the myth of the struggling artist from the vantage of the psychology of a society bereft of even those pitiful forms of popular creativity* available in bygone ages. His analysis is as follows:

> Over the last century or two, as collective systems of labour and production asserted themselves, the dissatisfied and disobedient turned to poetry and painting. And over the last decades, it is more and more often painting that promises the possibilities of a free life, the possibility of finally getting a lungful of fresh air, 'authentically'. The success of 'artist's

---

*   The Russian *samodeyatel'nost'* is translated here as 'popular creativity', meaning non-professionalised artistic practices. The Russian term also has philosophical connotations: its more literal translation would be 'self-activity', in the sense of autonomous, non-controlled action.

hagiographies' rampant in our day is more than enough to determine the 'functional' character of this manifestation, that of 'damned artists' (*les artistes maudits*). Theirs are risky and solitary solutions of grandiose tasks, glorious services offered to the world at large, or, on the contrary, they describe chaos and express destructive emotions of the kind that would periodically and legitimately explode in the past. The artist is alone, but at least in his own eyes, he acts in the name of humanity at large when he does what he needs to do, following the most provocative, dangerous principles at his own mortal risk. It is precisely the personality of the artist that takes on this great role – to serve as a pressure valve, a fabulous expression, and an energy discharge, which it would make sense to introduce into the normal rhythm of collective life, of which it once was a part. Here, the twentieth century's paradox unfolds to the full. The figure of the artist attracts those injured by the oppressive necrosis and simplification of modern civilisation. To them, the artist's actions seem extraordinarily attractive and provocative, as do they to those who have trouble coping with the total absence of venues for 'voluntary' activity. It seems that the gulf between the artist and his audience so often cited as a characteristic of the modern age originates not only in the growing difficulty of artistic language but also in the disagreement between those who want the artist to initiate them into wondrous new world order and into 'the protocols of solemn service', and those who do not want any of that.[2]

The author of the lines cited above is at quite a remove from Marxism, as one can easily see in many of the nuances of his analysis. For example, he uses the vague and indisputably tendentious notion of 'collective systems of labour and production'. As if collectivism were to blame for the absence of voluntary activity, the mass of constraints imposed by dominance of large monopolies and the overgrown state machine disconnected from the people.

Still, there is much truth in the French author's deliberations. Most importantly, he does not place his trust in 'artist hagiography', the immeasurable body of writing that turns artists' lives into the vita of modern martyrs. Instead, he takes a rather critical view of this literature as a product of its social conditions. He notes that as illusory and fairy-tale-like as its common clichés may be, they still have some basis in reality, just as there is a basis in reality to the lives of ordinary Christian saints actually executed under Diocletian or in other ages.

---

2   Chastel 1955, p. 518.

He considers the legendary figure of the struggling innovator as a psychological compensation for people oppressed by the absence of genuine popular creativity; they thoroughly hate their forcibly allotted place in life and find themselves unable to escape this impasse in any other way.

André Chastel's writing betrays the influence of the Jungian school. He presents modern society with the positive example of previous archaic formations with their periodic 'discharges', explosions of wild social energy like the Dionysian orgies of ancient Greece or the more measured outbursts of late medieval passion plays and carnivals. These traditional forms of symbolic reconciliation with reality are lost to modern life, leaving a void or a vacuum. So now, the hollow soul is saved by a new mix of mysticism and mystification, the 'sacred' and the carnivalesque.

With its magical rituals, hypermodern art replaces those former outbursts of Dionysian madness now bound by the will. In other words, it serves up a special kind of soothing intellectual moonshine to the 'disobedient and dissatisfied', satiating them and making them obey. Chastel sees the existence of such a pressure valve or vent as a paradoxical fact of modernity, but he only studies this paradox, never doubting the legitimacy of its newly won mechanics of reconciliation with reality, for the lack of anything better.

It would be strange to expect our author to draw any other conclusion. The fact of the matter is that the only alternative to all kinds of 'discharges' and 'compensations' is the emancipation of modern humanity from capitalism, its fateful consequences and its metastases. A society like that of the Paris Commune or of Soviet democracy of the Leninist type are the only ones where the people's self-activity can find a reasonable, free way out of the economic and political barracks of the twentieth century. Only this type of modern rule by the people excludes both blind submission to routine and wild forms of protest.

Roger Garaudy calls himself a Marxist, so it would seem he should know that Marxism opens a real path for the emancipation of human energy. So then why does he take seriously this modern Ersatz for a religious outlet? Why doesn't he see what strikes even an author like Chastel?

In a rejoinder to the negative Soviet reviews of his book on realism, Garaudy invokes rather shaky arguments in the spirit of modern 'artist hagiography'. He recalls how in 1876 the bourgeois newspaper *Le Figaro* heaped abuse on an exhibition of the Impressionists, and cites a passage calling these artists madmen.

Of course, *Le Figaro* is a bourgeois newspaper with a yellow-press colouring. But what would Roger Garaudy say if we gathered and quoted all the insulting epithets that later, more radical artistic tendencies heaped upon the Impressionists?

As early as October 1912, the admirer of Cubism Olivier Hourcade was writing of the 'Impressionist's slipshod decadence',[3] and that was only the beginning. In the 1930s, Picasso's friend Christian Zervos dedicated an entire issue of *Cahiers D'art* to the denunciation of Edouard Manet as a man lacking imagination and what's more, as a simple plagiariser. We will not detail these clearly unwarranted attacks. It is enough to remember that Zervos ends his lead article with the following words: 'There is no serious reason to place the author of "Olympia" among the great future-oriented artists'.[4] No Soviet author, even the most vulgar, could have written on modernism as did the various representatives of hypermodern art's warring schools and sects.

To Roger Garaudy, however, anyone who disagrees with his praise of Cubism is perpetuating the tradition of *Le Figaro*. 'When the Cubists for their part demonstrated the arbitrary character of space as understood by the Renaissance, just as when the Impressionists showed the arbitrary nature of colour, they met with incomprehension and even abuse'.[5] This is a strong argument, of course, but it is enough to chase any player from the field, including Garaudy himself. His 'realism without frontiers' is broad enough to include even abstract art, but for reasons one can only guess, he excludes such celebrated or rather overexposed abstract painters like Jackson Pollock or Georges Mathieu from his enumeration of realists.[6] In that sense, it would be easy to say that Roger Garaudy, too, lies in the tradition of *Le Figaro*, since he disapproves of the senseless splotches, colourful bruises, and other symbols specific to these artists. After all, this is how narrow-minded people once treated the Impressionists and the Cubists.

In fact, if Garaudy runs the risk of coinciding with *Le Figaro*, it is from the other side. Actually, this newspaper has already changed its position. While it now heaps ridicule upon the more radical outbursts of so-called Pop Art and other tendencies of blessed fools, its position toward the generally recognised luminaries of the 'avant-garde' would satisfy even the proponents of a 'realism without frontiers'. When Garaudy's brochure appeared, heralding his turn toward modern painting, *Le Figaro* noted the fact with irony, but made no major objections.[7]

---

3   Hourcade 1912, p. 4.

3   Hourcade 1912, p. 4.

4   Zervos 1932, p. 311.

5   Garaudy 1965, p. 206.

6   Garaudy 1964.

7   *Le Figaro Litteraire* 1963.

The fact of the matter is that the 'Copernican turn' of the Cubists first seemed like a scandalous discovery, but it soon came into fashion in high society in the aftermath of the First World War. Today, it is accepted without question. When Georges Braque, one of Cubism's founders, died in 1963, his burial had all the hallmarks of a state funeral, down to a guard of honour in bronze helmets. In a word, challenging Cubism's significance today hardly means marching in step with the high and mighty of the West. Quite the contrary.

However, let us assume, improbable as it may be, that there is still some significant opposition in the bourgeois world to Cubism despite its general rise to acclaim. This assumption in no way lessens the chances for an altogether different, critical view of the Cubists and their art. From the vantage of logic, the argument of 'artist hagiography' rests upon a simple error. If Socrates was bald, that hardly means that every bald man is Socrates. Cubism might be subject to ridicule in the yellow press and even more serious bourgeois publications. So what? That alone is hardly proof of the aesthetic value and the revolutionary vector of Cubist painting. The bourgeois press laughed at them, but nowhere does it say that the Marxist press should do exactly the opposite.

Engels once called such deliberations *a contrario* 'Gribouille politics'. And who is Gribouille? He is a comic hero of folk tales (a 'trickster') who does everything out of sync. He laughs at funerals and cries at weddings. (A similar hero will be familiar from Russian folk literature.) However, today the logic of Gribouille is not just a memory of some primordial trickster, and also not just the mistake of a schoolboy who has forgotten Aristotle's rules. It is something far more dangerous and real. Lenin already criticised such thinking prominently in his 'Notes of a Publicist' (1922).

Writing on examples of repulsive international opportunism from Gompers to Serrati, he warns real revolutionaries of making a mistake that continued to cause harm even after this warning was issued. Lenin convinces the Italian communists 'not to yield to the very easy and very dangerous temptation to say "minus a" whenever Serrati says "a"'.[8]

Deliberations according to the 'minus a' method operate according to a negative logic of sorts, creating so many anti-worlds out of soapsuds. Then again, such logic has real root causes in our time. One could even say that it is the scourge of modern consciousness and the most reliable net through which the psychology of the old society, acting spontaneously, catches those souls who dare to flee its direct domination.

---

8   Lenin 1965, p. 211.

Everybody knows that capitalism today is nothing like it was in the previous century. All the more reason to admit that the social psychology corresponding to its practical movement has also undergone a considerable change. It is enough to remember that the idea of revolution has and had several different meanings. There is, for example, the notion of the 'revolution from the right', or, as they say in the USA, 'rightwing radicalism'. We should remember that the idea of several ultra-progressive anarchist tendencies such as 'the social myth' or 'direct action' had a great influence on the elaboration of the twentieth century's most reactionary political doctrines. The abstract opposition between 'old' and 'new', all the way to the deceitful demagogic utopia of the 'new order', is a presence in the ideological lexicon of our century's regimes, be they Bonapartist or far worse.

Long gone are the days when genuine revolutionary thinking drew sustenance from 'ideas of negation', as Belinsky put it. Now one far more frequently finds this idea harnessed up in a different team of horses. Nobody wants to admit that they are 'bourgeois', and, of course, everybody is against philistinism. Thus, for example, Malraux's fundamental *Psychology of Art* is completely saturated by the negation of the bourgeois character and the declaration of modernism as the most revolutionary form of all times and peoples. Garaudy's brochure did not escape the influence of Malraux's book, which itself, by the way, is not particularly original. The main ideas of his work were already articulated by German art criticism in the first years of the century.

Still, let us return to the 'minus a' logic. It is useful to have an understanding of who accepts and who rejects this or that point of view. It would be ridiculous, however, to turn this secondary orientation system, this method of repulsion into a universal skeleton key for all of life's most serious questions. The question can only be answered through independent, objective studies of its essence. Objective truth corresponds with neither conventional opinion nor its inversion, that is, with the mandatory infraction of commonly recognised canons or norms. Both are merely two sides of the same coin, two types of empty reflection at a considerable remove from concrete, dialectical thinking, which always rests upon the actual fullness of reality.

This is why neither Cubism's high standing in public opinion in the bourgeois countries, nor its negation by the same public opinion half a century ago, affect the real value of this phenomenon.

'Scandal in Art'

Having said all of the above, we might add that the legend of the artist's martyrdom at the hands of society's utter incomprehension is more well-meaning fantasy than actual historical fact. The outcome of the struggle between extreme innovators and conservatives was already decided in the century's first decade. It became a habit for artists to overthrow their forebears and to search for new, unprecedented styles, thus reducing the distance between persecution and triumph to a minimum. Even more, new tendencies are now already conceived with scandals in mind, fuelled by the 'aggression' of a new type of artist; he scorns the contemplative long-hairs; his intentional infractions of good taste are made for promotional effect, in short, as conscious provocations of 'conflicts with convention'. This conflict had its philosophical and economical justifications. These were the 'new barbarians', and they were preparing for war.

We should not forget the economic side; Cubism had business connections from the very beginning. The young Picasso's independence was sponsored by Vollard, while Braque had the backing of the German dealer Wilhelm Uhde. Yet it was Daniel Heinrich Kahnweiler who would become Cubism's main Minister of Finance; after the war, he would cede his place to Léonce Rosenberg. The whole business was set up on quite a scale. The possibility for speculating on rising trends had already been emerging in Durand-Ruel's day; now it took on a rather more tangible form. This involved private galleries (shops that sell paintings), international exhibitions (between 1909 and 1914, Picasso had a slew of personal exhibitions in England, Germany, Spain, and the USA, not to mention his participation in the Cubist exhibition in Russia), promotional publications like the series published by Rosenberg, or the way the Cubists occupied a favourable place in the Salon de Independents through their *pronuciamento* of 1911. All of this hardly looks like victimhood.

One can see what the other side of painting was really like by the early twentieth century in the account of Camille Mauclair, an art critic familiar with the life and mores of his milieu who thoroughly sympathised with the first generation of innovators, but not beyond. Describing how the discovery of unknown geniuses became a fashion and even a matter of sport, Mauclair bemoaned the consequences of the art world's infiltration through counterfeits. It had become possible to declare someone to be an artist independently of his actual talent, Mauclair writes. Success now depended more than anything on the interplay of forces, while the artwork was no longer itself; it had become a function, an echo of the artist's outer activity, or better yet, that of a certain group promoting its own.

There was such a fuss over the abuses of dogmatic criticism that now all criticism is based on personal impressions. The utter disorganisation of art criticism is the outcome. Each critic issues arbitrary directives and sets the value of an artwork according to his own acquired taste. Artists give orders of their own. There is one figure, however, who commands them all. Hidden but omnipotent, this figure is the art dealer. And it is not so easy to explain the psychology of this chief mechanic in charge of both art criticism and the Salons. Such explanations would deserve a book of their own. And even if this book were no more than a simple record of all the things people know and whisper without ever saying them out loud to the unsuspecting public – it would already be a terrifying document of human customs! Some naïvely imagine that in pre-revolutionary France, the artist was a hired hand serving men of note until he attained his freedom. Later people would rail against the tyranny of the academicians and high priests of painting, who would provide for their submissive students and thwart any independent effort. But in fact, the artist has only been in a state of real slavery since the day he fell into the hands of dealers who pay him, 'promote' him and hold a monopoly over his works. The artists of the eighteenth century enjoyed far greater freedoms. To make profit, the dealer requires publicity, and art criticism on the printed page is just what he needs. A few honest and discerning critics unwilling to put up with this kind of trade found a way to speak out in the press, but were avoided by a thousand miles. Art dealers enjoy the backing of rich collectors. Personal connections, self-interest, and exchanges of favours do the rest. People think of this as an art movement, while actually there is movement on the market of painting, where there is successful speculation with the art of unknown geniuses. To succeed here, one must act in secret, quietly convincing those collectors who understand nothing – and to be honest, these are no rarity – that they are doing something great in buying the work of an unknown genius. Subtlety is required in dosing the process of the chosen artist's 'discovery', until the day the carefully prepared fanfare finally sounds. Heretofore, the unknown genius takes his place among other geniuses, always risking replacement by the next of his kind. The value of artworks becomes less important than the perfection of methods for making artists fashionable. We see many masterpieces of that kind, because the art dealer is a miracle worker, and his system is exceptionally well-organised.[9]

---

9   Mauclair 1906, p. 320.

Thus, the intrusion of capital into art history so apparent over the last decades was already well underway in Cubism's time.

The highpoint of the Cubist's persecution came when the municipal councillor Lampué wrote a letter of complaint to the Deputy Minister of Culture Bérard, published on 16 October 1912 in *Mercure de France*. It was on the basis of this letter that the socialist Jean-Louis Breton made a motion to prohibit the exhibition of new 'Cubicist' (sic!) painting in the Salon d'Automne in the National Assembly. Breton said: 'It is absolutely inadmissible that our national palaces should be used for manifestations of such an obviously anti-artistic and anti-national kind'. However, this protest was not carried by the socialists, all the more so since it was opposed by the famous opportunist leader Marcel Sembat, who sympathised with modernist painting. His answer to Breton was rather sententious: 'When a painting seems bad to one, one has an incontestable right, that of not looking at it and going to see others. But one doesn't call in the police'.[10] And that was that.

Formally, Sembat was right: you should never call the police when art is in question, and it is unbefitting for socialists to take responsibility for administrative measures imposed by the bourgeois state, even if these demonstrations of a new taste have the quality of hooliganism, are saturated with pornography, and are accompanied by all kinds of anarchist gestures. Surrealist exhibition openings almost always involved someone firing a revolver, naked women on tables with champagne bottles and other, spicier attractions. In such situations, someone might inevitably call the police. But who should call them, that is a different question. The task of socialists, if they truly oppose bourgeois society, is to reveal the social conditions that lead to such wanton forms of self-expression.

That said, it would still be ridiculous to justify these antics as a struggle against the dominance of conventional taste. You cannot stay wholly neutral in the face of such ludicrous excesses of protest, be they false or genuine. You cannot simply turn away and go someplace else. After all, the matter in question is that of a worldview and its resulting practices, which in this case offer a re-evaluation of all values, demanding society's approval or rejection. In short, we need an answer that goes beyond the bounds of formal law. It is one thing not to support police repressions, but another entirely to justify erroneous methods of protest against the bourgeois state, especially since they

---

10   Golding 1988, p. 14.

are often so advantageous to life's proprietors. To confuse a disgust at their goons with neutrality in ideological questions is a hallmark of opportunism.

In that sense, Sembat was wrong. At the very least, his rejoinder to the socialist rank-and-file was not well-founded, since the formula 'there is no accounting for tastes' will not solve the social problems that emerge along with the appearance of Cubism and other similar movements.

Many bourgeois newspapers commented negatively on the extravagant new painting; however, its adepts were hardly defenceless – they had protectors of their own in the press. The writers involved with Cubism were the kind of people who are never at a loss for words, and at that time, a strongly spoken word already had more weight than thinking weakened by the well-fed liberalism of the second half of the nineteenth century. Advertising and suggestion can do anything: that is the main rule of the new tendencies promoted by the seekers of the modern. Cubism was backed by a circle of poets and critics of an active bearing, to put it mildly. Their activism was principled. It resulted either from their embrace of Henri Bergson's philosophy or emerged organically from the same literary field. They were often called Cubists, though such terminology makes less sense when applied to literature.

The uncontested leader of this movement was the poet and publicist Guillaume Apollinaire, who supported the new painting with his articles in the newspaper *L'Intrasigeant*. Another critic who sympathised with the Cubist was the aforementioned Hourcade of the *Paris Journal*. The modernist monthly *La Section d'or*, published by Pierre Dumont, presented a mix of articles by writers close to Cubism such as Raynal, Reverdy, Jacob, Salmon, and André Warnod. The Lyon-based journal *L'art libre* featured exhibition reviews by Roger Allard, another heated proponent of the new painting.

Finally, 1912 saw the publication of the first gospel of this trend, *Du cubisme* by Albert Gleizes and Jean Metzinger, which was immediately translated into Russian. The poet André Salmon's *La Jeune Peinture française* appeared in the same year, Apollinaire's anthology of articles *Les Peintres Cubistes* went to print in the next. The first book in English on Cubism was published in 1914, its author the American Arthur Eddy. Further enumerations would be impossible, considering the broad flood of literary effusions in honour of 'the Copernican turn'. We should only note that the managers and dealers of Cubism Kahnweiler, Uhde, and Rosenberg also had literary-philosophical aspirations; Kahnweiler's *Der Weg zum Kubismus* (1920) is considered a classic on the subject.[11]

---

11   For more see Golding 1988, Sérrulaz 1963.

In that sense, allusions to smear campaigns in papers like *Le Figaro* are hardly enough to present Cubism as the victim, may the reader rest assured. The new painting was bound to cause a scandal when it emerged, not because it so far outstripped human understanding, but because without this scandal there would not have been any new painting in the first place. Its content was not the art itself, but rather the artist's behaviour. The activity of the man with the easel became a symbol for the negation of all conventional norms. In a word, this was not so much painting as a programme designed to provoke scandal.

Why 'the conflict with philistinism' was to become the century's mythological cliché par excellence is a complicated question. To explain such features of our time, we would need to consider the entire rhythm of economic and social life under late capitalism, and we would need to study the process of how all its pores have been flooded by conventionalism and bureaucratic routine. We would also have to examine the constant revolt against these in the frame of capitalist production from the side of new, more aggressive economic and political forces. This all is linked to the obvious growth of coercion and the development of anarchistic forms of protest that later become different, far more terrible manifestations of modernity. Such a broad analysis lies outside the scope of the present sketch, however. Suffice it to say that spreading thick the myths of the suffering Cubists and other methods of legendary historiography cannot satisfy even the most rudimentary demands of independent, objective study.

Despite the high-sounding claptrap dredged up to the surface under high pressure by such powerful pumps, the Western literature still sometimes produces articles and books with more realistic contents. Despite the influence of dominant life conditions, there is honest thinking everywhere. It is worth drawing the reader's attention to an interesting book published in the Principality of Monaco by the French critic and expert Robert Lebel with the characteristic title *The Other Side of Painting*.[12]

Lebel shares the secrets of his guild. His pamphlet contains a multitude of facts revealing the mores of the 'tableauistes', as he calls that special breed of people who produce paintings and participate in their sale. This stratum consists not only of artists and art dealers, but also includes collectors who invest capital into artistic treasures, museum workers and experts in art history, confirming that canvases on stretchers have a certain value convertible into a

---

12   Lebel 1964.

certain amount of bills and coins. This is an entire 'state within a state', and even an international Masonic society of sorts. Of course, Lebel cannot part with some of the traditional attitudes that this influential corporation imposes upon consciousness. But he is honest enough to acknowledge the doubtfulness of its principle undertaking.

There is a special chapter in Lebel's book called 'Scandal in Art'. Considering this subject in its historical aspects, the author draws the following conclusions:

> It is precisely by openly declaring their right to dissent in the artistic field and by claiming this right, never mind all the obstacles, that modern artists became forerunners of the future. In that sense, one cannot deny their revolutionary role; their moral position has earned them a brilliant rehabilitation in our day, far more than have their artistic achievements, with regard to which the last word has yet to be said. Their works were controversial trophies whose beauty depends foremost on the vivid memories to which they are connected.[13]

Amidst all the drum rolls in honour of 'modern art', these are sober words of caution.

Whether we see the work of ultra-leftist artists as revolutionary depends on the meaning we vest in the term. Considering the matter from a purely formal point of view, the fold of revolutionaries would then have to include not only Schopenhauer, an unacknowledged loner in his lifetime, embittered against the revolution of 1848, or Nietzsche, rejected by all the priestly brethren, but also Oswald Mosley, the leader of the British Fascists, who until now has gotten off lightly with a few bumps and bruises. Of course, you cannot compare ultra-leftist artists with abominations like Mosley; that would be insulting. However, many of them wouldn't stop identifying as Nietzscheans. At the same time, while not every follower of Nietzsche is necessarily a reactionary, his philosophy is still openly opposed to the ideas of democracy. This means that a formal conflict with the dominant psychology, ethics and aesthetics does not make someone a revolutionary in the actual, historical sense of the word. The notion of 'revolutionary' can only have any kind of meaning if it has a concrete content. This is especially true in our time, when you come across misuses of the notion at every step.

---

13   Lebel 1964, pp. 89–90.

Even if we agree with Lebel in thinking that the efforts of the ultra-leftist artists deserve moral approval, however, we still face the question of so-called modern art's actual positive achievements. As the reader can see, doubts in the value of this art can visit even people with a practical interest, members of that international corporation of *tableauistes*, people who work professionally to spread 'a completely new art', an art that has been raised, in the words of the same Lebel, 'to the heights of the social establishment thanks to half a century's praise'.

The truth is that the innovators owe this great fame, unknown to the most official, gilded academics of yesteryear, not to art in the proper sense of the word, but to social conflict, if not scandal in the direct sense. This is the conclusion Lebel draws from his sober analysis. It may well be that this is what the bourgeois audience deserves, once it has been conquered by bold travesties of itself, to the point of being enraptured with the spittle so masterfully lunged its way. But even dried up spit cannot become the pearl of creation, and when the trophies of bygone scandals are sold as real painterly achievements equal to those of the Van Eycks or Delacroix through unprecedented psychological attacks upon conventional taste, you involuntarily begin to appreciate the somewhat inconsistent and all-too-careful but still honest confessions of authors like Lebel. Indeed, the last word has yet to be said on what these achievements mean from a purely artistic angle.

By the way, the recently deceased famous artist Yves Klein expressed the same idea, though not in words, but in practice. Toward the end of his life, he was no longer selling paintings but the pure action of innovation without its realisation on canvas. Upon receiving payment, Klein would give out a certificate that the collector could hang up in his sitting room. From a logical perspective, this is consistent and deserves respect: if you are doing something, do it fast and to the end. Klein's magical gesture completes a long series of similar gestures, gradually liberating 'modern art' from the duty of being a real activity, connected to draughtsmanship, chiaroscuro, or colouring, that is, liberating it from the duty to be art in the previous sense of the word. This is already the beginning of something completely different.

Still, let us get back to Lebel. 'Such an interpretation', he continues, 'can provoke the protests of connoisseurs, who will hardly excuse our disregard for the artwork's independent value, to which we might answer that they were the first to ignore it altogether'.[14] And really, the honesty of *The Other Side of*

---

14   Lebel 1964, p. 90.

Painting and its author did provoke the ire of his colleagues, confirming that the emperor only seems naked because he is wearing clothing made of the most subtle fabric.[15] Still, Lebel's answer contains a sound thought that cannot be deflected by empty words, since it is based on the real history of the matter. It is enough to remember Mauclair's account. Despite more than half a century's difference, it is highly reminiscent of what Lebel has to say. Since then, the situation has not changed for the better; on the contrary, on the strength of some strange paradox, the more people write on the 'autonomy of art', the less they are interested in the actual work and what lies within its boundaries. Erotica, nervous pathologies, political innuendo, civilisational critique, the latest scientific discoveries, outer space, and all kind of other strong irritants, always new and unexpected, any kind of outer symbol, anything but painting!

So, it was the crowd of innovation enthusiasts that trampled underfoot any criteria for assessing the artistic value of a work, ascribing to art absolutely extraneous goals. Above, we could see that the painting of the Impressionists serves as proof for the 'arbitrary nature of colour', while the painting of the Cubists demonstrates 'the arbitrary character of space'. Such are rhetorical commonplaces and systems of words accompanying the victory parade of artistic devices. They turn the artist into a dropout art historian, writing his dissertation on canvas with the intention of proving this or that. Is this really what painting is supposed to do? Such explanations are based on an exaggerated historicism gone sour as a weakness of the soul. It assumes that a few apples on a white tablecloth were painted to occupy a certain place in the history of art and to clarify the true meaning of light or space, and painting.

At the very most, such doubtful constructs confirm a fact long since recognised by Hegel. Namely, the art of modernity is gradually overtaken by reflection and abstract thinking, so that the line between art history and artistic practice becomes all too fine. And this really is the case, if we remember the role declarations and manifestos play in so-called modern art. 'The whole art world is poisoned by the battle of programme against programme', Wilhelm Hausenstein already accurately noted.[16] There is too much false philosophising, swallowing up all real feelings and unencumbered relations to the visible

---

15 Cf. Berne-Jouffroy 1962. This article is one answer to the part of Lebel's book previously published in the same journal. Opinions differed, however. 'Of course, today's scandal is no simple repetition of what came before. It has taken on a solid, sometimes even a high bourgeois quality. But "tableauism" still bears the burden of guilt, since its utility remains doubtful in the eyes of others'. Cf. Hoctin 1964, p. 84.

16 Lunacharsky 1941b, p. 331.

world! But this is a disorder, not a justification, and if the Impressionists were only interesting as proof for the arbitrariness of light or other theorems, in a word, for the validity of their own doctrine, one could hardly speak of their paintings having any value of their own. Thankfully, they were artists. Cubism is a later and more ambivalent phenomenon.

Turning to the question of what has taken the place of the artwork's independent inner value, Lebel continues:

> We might also be accused of exaggerating the prestige that freedom enjoys in the eyes of our contemporaries. Really, looking at their way of life, one might rather think that they thirst for exactly the opposite. However, it is precisely in modern art that they find the paradigm of a free behaviour of which they themselves admittedly are incapable. Thus believers venerate saints for virtues that they themselves lack. In this sense, modern art becomes a religion of freedom with its own martyrs – the unrecognised masters of this art. These people receive the more veneration, the more they have suffered and the greater a scandal their efforts provoke.[17]

In this way, Lebel reaches conclusions close to those drawn by André Chastel in his analysis. For some, the fascination with 'modern art' is the sigh of the hopeless creature; for others, it is an inwardly hypocritical self-discharge.

> That the most rigid philistines are interested in these thoroughly non-philistine paintings pays testimony to their own lack of freedom, and appears as a good way of getting in touch with their own good intentions of yesteryear. It is as if they were buying freedom in its finished form at a high price, though one still less than the one they would have to pay for actual freedom. Thanks to the rising curve of value, they often even make financial gains.[18]

To show how the actual church sees this new possibility of quasi-religious compensation, we would have to expound the views of the prominent proponent of Catholic 'sacred art', Father Régamey. That, however, would take us too far afield. We have already heard enough to draw some conclusions from

---

17   Lebel 1964, p. 90.
18   Lebel 1964, p. 90.

the objective eye-witness accounts above as they sketch out the transition from art proper to something else – a psychological compensation for the real lack of individual freedoms, now replaced by the professional boldness of the artist who sells a slow-motion picture of his tragic experience as a cellophane-packaged scandal. His protest against modern civilisation is bought up retail and sometimes even wholesale, as was the case with Georges Rouault's entire future work, with the goal of reselling it bit by bit after the inevitable and pre-calculated rise in the market value of this underground genius's paintings.

Thus, the dominant philistines adopted the spontaneous forces of revolt and even turned them into an area of capital investment, as one can see today. Sadly, all of this is brutal irony in light of the scorn for the bourgeoisie and the desire to offend it so characteristic of modernism beginning with Baudelaire's times. That past tragedy has long since become a farce.

Lebel writes:

> Indiscernibly, the function of art itself has changed. First the artist served as a paragon of social order, then he became its bogeyman; now, he once again becomes a supplier of easy outlets for all the repressed instinct of the ruling class. At the same time, this ruling class tries to keep its conscience politically clean without ever learning the lessons offered by painterly liberalism.[19]

It ultimately proved beneficial to these new mechanics when a new form of scandal in art emerged with Hitler and Goebbels's persecution of the 'degener-ates'. The social standing of the ultra-leftist artists only grew stronger as a result. They found official refuge in the so-called Western democracies, which, accord-ing to Lebel's altogether justified comment, opened their arms 'not without their own propagandistic ulterior motives'. All the more, since there was now a chance to draw analogies between the attitudes of the *Reichskulturkammer* and Socialist Realism. 'Thus there emerged a strange and silent alliance under the banner of "cultural freedom"'.[20]

And really, it is strange. Despite total prosperity and easy chances for capital gains without any loss of innocence, and even more – in supercilious know-ledge of one's own moral superiority – this whole boom has placed 'modern art' into a position that is dubious if not obscene. Reconciliation with the bour-

---

19   Lebel 1964, p. 91.
20   Lebel 1964, pp. 90–1.

geois audience has a bitter taste to an art that sees its mission in the constant conflict with the surrounding world and elevates this conflict to an eternal law of artistic life.

> Even if circumstances seem to have changed in their favour, many artists have anxiously noted that their works are no longer any cause for scandal. Did they understand the true meaning of this hiatus? No, they rather saw it as a bad omen, a warning and a threat, and their masochistic intuition sounded the alarm.

To make it one's job to wear a crown of thorns is rather ridiculous than pitiful. But there still is something sad about all of this – some people understand or almost understand deep down inside the social function of such public symbols, yet they continue to serve the new cult nonetheless. Such cases, too, have not been uncommon in the twentieth century. You come to an arrangement with an inwardly dead cause out of material necessity and life habits controlled from on high, or better yet, out of fear for interrupting a routine sanctified by all the powers of the dominant order. You are free to break with this false freedom – just as you are free not to work at an office or on an assembly line.

Here, we see yet another page in the history of the individual's enslavement to a contingent world order's material forces, a final ironic reply to the haughty paltriness of his protest. Especially if those forms of protest can be turned into comedy so effortlessly. What a shame that people who in practice stand for other forms of struggle more dangerous to this routine fall prey to the same illusions and even support mythologies that have already survived themselves as things of the past.

Two Appraisals of Cubism

Science begins where essentials separate from the forms of their manifestation. Actually, even the most modest seeds of a scientific outlook are impossible while we are blinded by an object's exterior, as brilliant or polished to a shine it sometimes is by ignorance and popular superstition. False aureoles often emanate from the very essence of the matter, and it is characteristic for many phenomena to be something very different from what they seem. In short, real and nominal value often fail to correspond.

However, it is hardly enough to reveal the 'captivating idol' for what it is. Phenomena may be insignificant on their own, but they can play a huge role under the right circumstances. Properly speaking, nothing exists on its own.

And if there is still some objective measure of a phenomenon's significance, it cannot be understood abstractly, without transitions from great to tiny and back. When an off-duty petty officer of the guard consoles a woman, it is a small real-life situation, a simple matter of contingency. If the action is set in Spain, however, writes Marx, in the epoch of absolute monarchy, and if this woman is a queen, the petty officer's personal qualities may well influence the course of history.* In other words, each phenomenon's degree of significance is historically concrete, though that does not rob it of its objective content or us of our ability to tell the difference between silly and serious. There is such a thing as abstract criticism, like the refutation of religion through the eighteenth century's Enlighteners, who saw no further than the deception of the clergy, and then there is dialectical criticism, which goes far beyond the boundaries of abstract truth, utility, and morality, entering the world of history.

It would be naïve to believe everything said and written about 'modern art' by people in the thrall of this mythmaking and its snowballing growth. Much of it is silly. Still, no matter which verdict history ultimately passes, we are dealing with a phenomenon of no small import.

First of all, we need to acknowledge that artistic antics like the Cubism that emerged between 1907 and 1908 have by now entered academic art history. There are many exultant books on the Cubists, printed on glossy paper with illustrations of the highest technical quality. Understandably, the average person cannot remain indifferent to this landslide of enthusiasm.

Slowly but surely, even people we consider specialists in criticising the art of the decadent bourgeoisie begin to think that they understand something of the new painting's riddles, as the border of recognition moves further and further to the left. In the West, this is already an accomplished fact. Today, the obscure language of abstraction is already understood as academic, while its admirers mourn the demise of this painting, now displaced by Pop Art. Will this happen here as well?

There is something astonishing about the reputation enjoyed by these fits of artificial savagery, but on the other hand, there is no reason to be so surprised. We know that even miracles, real medieval miracles, are possible in

---

*   There is no footnote or citation in the original, but Lifshitz seems to be referring to Maria Christina of Bourbon, Princess of the Two Sicilies, Queen of Spain as the wife of Ferdinand VII. When the latter died in 1833, she secretly eloped with Agustín Fernando Muñoz, a sergeant of the guard, and continued to act as regent for her daughter Isabella II. Marx mentions her as 'Madame Munoz' on several occasions in his writings on the Spanish Revolution (1854–6) for the *New York Daily Tribune*.

the twentieth century, and they too are the subject of newspaper articles and books printed in the most modern way. The formula 'the whole world recognises' means absolutely nothing. After all, this world is a little crazy – it has gone out of joint, as Shakespeare's famous expression has it.

There is no small measure of comedy when the American ambassador places the entire weight of his nation onto the scales to make sure that the first prize of the international exhibition in Venice goes to Robert Rauschenberg, the founder of Pop Art. It shows that the interplay of social forces can ascribe symbolic meaning to even the most insignificant phenomena. Yet comedy is still comedy, even when acted out on an international scale.

All of this goes for Cubism to a degree – no more or less than is actually the case. The scholarly scrupulousness of art historians, the technical effects of publishing houses, hypnosis through an already-established new tradition – nothing can transform that painting famous as the 'Demoiselles d'Avignon', conceived as a parody of a sign board for a brothel, into anything more than a sign of the times, a trophy of a bygone scandal.[21] Still, read the bombastic art-historical analyses! The artist himself must be laughing at them deep down inside. How could a humanity capable of understanding Marx or Einstein seriously read this hogwash, written under the assumption that nobody will complain since all resistance has been quashed? Here, there is cause indeed to scoff at society's stupidity, but you won't make this epidemic go away with mockery or vulgar phrases. Still, a respectful academic tone itself is already a compromise with fashion.

The fact of a given phenomenon's ludicrousness hardly means that it holds no power or that we should consider it a simple anomaly. Marxism as a doctrine has never claimed that history is only governed by forces rational from an economic or a spiritual point of view. It is enough to remember the wild superstitions and rituals that consumed all of society's attention for centuries.

History has not yet ended; it continues, wearing its suit of armour and its shaman's robes. The success of modern artistic fantasies, however ludicrous, is no more irrational than other quirks of our time, if even just in the economic field, not to mention the political brutalities, senseless from all sides, the extermination of entire peoples, chauvinism, Bonapartism and all the other social crimes that have left so deep a mark. Genuine reason in history only manifests itself on the basis of negative experiences, as a result of the objective irony of the facts themselves, humbling the blind will of interested classes

---

21   Cf. the chapter 'Scandal in Art' in Lebel 1964.

and parties. The world's only hope lies in the development of the conscious element, capable of comprehending and taking control of the laws behind these spontaneous forces. Now, let us return to the miracles of 'modern art'. First, let us look at how the scholarly if not scientific literature of art history reflects upon this subject. John Golding, author of a fundamental monograph on the topic, writes:

> Cubism was perhaps the most important and certainly the most complete and radical artistic revolution since the Renaissance. New forms of society, changing patronage, varying geographic conditions, all these things have gone to produce over the past five hundred years a succession of different schools, different styles, different pictorial idioms. But none of these has so altered the principles, so shaken the foundations of Western painting as did Cubism. Indeed, from a visual point of view it is easier to bridge the three hundred and fifty years separating Impressionism from the High Renaissance than it is to bridge the fifty years that lie between Impressionism and Cubism. If social and historical factors can for a moment be forgotten, a portrait by Renoir will seem closer to a portrait by Raphael than it does to a Cubist portrait by Picasso.[22]

In the unanimous opinion of authors like Golding, the Cubists introduced a new general type of visual art, and thus made a big step forward:

> Feeling that traditional painting was exhausted, they took each of the elements that comprise the vocabulary of painting – form, space, colour, and technique – and substituted for the traditional use of every one of them a new interpretation of their own. In short Cubism was a completely new pictorial language, a completely new way of looking at the outside world, a clearly-defined aesthetic. As such it has shaped the course of almost all twentieth-century painting.

Here are some examples of those radical changes brought on by the new aesthetic.

> To the system of perspective which had governed European painting since the Renaissance the Cubists had opposed the right of the painter

---

22   Golding 1959, p. xiii.

to move freely around his subject and to incorporate into his depiction of it information gathered from previous experience or knowledge. For the first time in the history of art, space had been represented as being as real and as tangible, one might almost say as 'pictorial', as the objects which it surrounded ...[23]

And so on in the same vein – outstanding merits, incomparable discoveries and achievements. We will return to these later on. For now, let us note that in the conclusions it draws, Golding's monograph presents a broad collection of commonplaces belonging to the Cubists themselves and their earliest patrons.

To help the reader imagine the enthusiastic expressions used to write on Cubism, let us quote a few more phrases from another book published in England, where, as we know, there is great appreciation for moderation and tradition.

There are moments in the history of art when the genesis of a new and major style becomes so important that it appears temporarily to dictate the careers of the most individual artists. So it was around 1510, when the diverse geniuses of Michelangelo, Raphael, and Bramante rapidly coalesced to create the monumental style of the High Renaissance; and around 1870, when painters as unlike as Monet, Renoir, and Pissarro approached a common goal in their evolution toward Impressionism. And so it was again around 1910, when two artists of dissimilar backgrounds and personalities, Picasso and Braque, invented the new viewpoint that has come to be known as Cubism.

From our position in the second half of the twentieth century, Cubism emerges clearly as one of the major transformations in Western art. As revolutionary as the discoveries of Einstein or Freud, the discoveries of Cubism controverted principles that had prevailed for centuries.[24]

The author will not settle for less.

In his newest synoptical work, Maurice Sérrulaz writes: 'As we can see, Cubism boldly breaks with the larger part of traditions that worked infallibly

---

23   Golding 1959, p. 197.

24   Rosenblum 1966, p. 9. Mikhail Lifshitz is mistaken as to the author's British origins. He seems to have been using a British edition of New York art critic Robert Rosenblum's *Cubism and Twentieth-Century Art*.

since the time of the Renaissance'.[25] We should note that Sérrulaz's small book is quite apologetic with regard to its subject, and that it was published in the *Que sais-je?*, a popular series presenting latest discoveries of science.

It is astonishing how monotonously the same phrases migrate from book to book and article to article, not to mention the underlying ideas, if one can even call them that, since we are rather dealing with the unprovable formulas of a new faith. This faith has its adepts everywhere, crossing borders and social orientations. It is a faith that rich proprietors with big collections of modern art share with people of the most progressive mindset, as if they were members of one and the same community of believers who see the light shining at them from the other world. In a book by the British writer John Berger, who is more critical of Picasso than Garaudy, but also very left-wing both in the good and bad senses of the word, we read: 'It is almost impossible to exaggerate the importance of Cubism. It was a revolution in the visual arts as great as that which took place in the early Renaissance'.[26]

Finally, to supplement the testimony of art historians and critics, we might cite Arnold Gehlen, one of the most influential representatives of contemporary philosophical anthropology. This author is erudite and far from untalented, but he pays obeisance by writing on 'Cubism's glorious artistic revolution', on the 'astounding innovation of introducing multiple aspects of the same object'. He compares all this hurly-burly in art with the reformation of scientific thought undertaken by Descartes in 1637, which consisted in turning from sensual experience to the elementary data of consciousness, to *idées simples*, simple ideas.[27] When a German professor like Arnold Gehlen picks up his pen, he can supply a shade of absolute necessity to any intellectual or artistic regression.

It would be easy to further expand this overview of the newest literature on Cubism and related tendencies, filling not one but many quires. To help the reader grasp this coin's nominal value on the world market, however, these examples are more than enough. A few rare exceptions aside, all aesthetic theory in the West views the acts of the Cubists as a great intellectual revolution, linked to changes in the worldview and way of life of twentieth-century humanity.

Cubism's 'Copernican turn' was welcomed with a choir of praise from thinkers representing the most modern varieties of philosophical idealism. We

----

25   Sérrulaz 1963, p. 30.

26   Berger 1965, p. 73.

27   Gehlen 1965, pp. 73–101, 188, etc.

should not forget the field of philosophy has its own 'avant-garde'. The critique of the materialist tradition of the Renaissance and the noticeable turn toward a religious contemplation of the world are both commonplaces in all the fashionable philosophical literature that considers itself to be the last word of modernity. The more sharp-sighted of this intellectual movement's standard-bearers could immediately see Cubism's mystical, otherworldly colouring. The Cubists themselves did not hide their sympathy for the ideas of the deepest Middle Ages, especially for scholasticism of the 'realist' type under the influence of Plato. There is more on this topic below. For now, let us bring up two examples that show clearly enough in which stream of ideas the new aesthetics found its place.

Jacques Maritain, an influential leader of neo-Catholic philosophy, combining the tradition of scholasticism with refined innovation, wrote the following of Cubism:

> Art opened its eyes on itself at the time of the Renaissance. It may be said that for the last half-century it has been seized by another fit of introspection, giving rise to a revolution every bit as important. Work such as Picasso's reveals a frightful progress in self-awareness on the part of painting. Its lesson is as instructive for the philosopher as for the artist, and therefore a philosopher may be permitted to say a few words about it from his own point of view.

Jacques Maritain sees the practice of the Cubists as the manifestation of 'an heroic will, [...] courageously [confronting] the unknown'. Painting now 'advances a step in its own mystery':

> As Cocteau has rightly pointed out, Picasso's works do not despise reality, they resemble it, with that spiritual resemblance – 'superreal' resemblance, to use a word very true in itself – of which I have already spoken. Dictated by a demon or by a good angel – one hesitates at certain moments to decide which. But not only do things become transfigured in passing from his eye to his hand; at the same time there is divined another mystery: it is the painter's soul and flesh endeavouring to substitute themselves for the objects he paints, to drive out their substance, to enter in and offer themselves under the appearances of those trifling things painted on a canvas, and which live there with another life than their own.[28]

28	Maritain 1962.

We will soon see the equivalent of such eloquent, unctuous and utterly non-committal phrases. For now, let us note that the French thinker's comfortable mysticism stands out in its calm comeliness. It clearly attempts to smooth the devilishly sharp edges and hellish irony of Cubist painting, whose origins are with Satan rather than with God. However, there is a possibility for other interpretations, just as mystical, but more saturated with the turmoil of the time.

In Russia, Cubism was hailed enthusiastically by Nikolay Berdyaev, that famous proponent of reactionary thinking. In 1914, this prophet of the new Middle Ages wrote:

> Picasso mercilessly lays bare the illusions of personified, material, synthetic beauty. Behind captivating, fascinating female beauty he sees the horror of disintegration and decomposition. Like a clairvoyant, he sees through all veils, outer garments, and intervening layers to the depths of the material, where he perceives his composite monsters. These are the demonic grimaces of the pent spirits of nature. If we go any deeper there is no longer any materiality but already the internal harmony of nature, the hierarchy of spirits. The crisis of painting inevitably leads to the abandonment of physical, material flesh and entry into another, higher sphere.[29]

Yet not everything in this contemporary's testimony is fanciful artifice. Still, even if one accepts some of Berdyaev's observations, there are different ways of assessing their object. To begin with, the appraisal of Cubism in the Marxist literature was always negative. We know why: 'the abandonment of physical, material flesh' to the 'hierarchy of spirit', and then 'into another, higher sphere' is not what Marxism seeks. It does not even approve of attempts to do so. Berdyaev might have sympathised with the Cubists' eagerness to reject the realist tradition of old art, and to turn to the other world. Yet it was only natural that the revolutionary milieu would receive it as a retrograde sign of the times, yet another symptom of the bourgeois intelligentsia's turn from Voltaire to the Jesuits, from the free worldview of older days to reactionary idealism.

A variety of arguments are made to justify the 'completely new painting' as an inevitable, obligatory feature of modern artistic culture. They should be considered per se, without reference to the force of authority, since such argumentative methods only weaken the proper cause. However, we are not

---

29   Berdyaev 1982, pp. 111–12.

indifferent to the existence of the Marxist tradition. It is a tradition with which one cannot play hide and seek; it cannot be ignored. Maybe it needs to be overturned? That is a different question. The proponents of new perspectives in Marxist literature should prove the necessity of abandoning our classical tradition in the appraisal of phenomena like Cubism's 'final revolt' without hiding behind a polemic against Zhdanov or other literary inventions.

In any case, there are two appraisals of Cubism. On the one hand, there is philosophy like Berdyaev's; on the other is the old Marxist thinking. Its negative verdict is still in force, and requires that we make a choice, one way or the other.

G.V. Plekhanov and Cubism

Such a negative verdict is to be found in the works of Georgy V. Plekhanov, where it appears clearly and without any doubts. A loyal defender of Marxist ideas from inundation through bourgeois attitudes and decadent taste, Plekhanov proved the overpowering strength of his polemic in the struggle with Bernsteinianism and various attempts to water down Marxism with the help of loans from fashionable philosophical tendencies. He also penned articles and pamphlets against decadent 'rulers of men's minds' like Ivanov-Razumnik* as well as the 'god-seeking' theoreticians of 'proletarian culture' with their anarcho-syndicalist political orientation such as Alexander Bogdanov and his school.

Cubism emerged in years of intense ideological struggle, in the course of which the opponents of Marxist socialism, liberals, 'vekhovtsy',** and anarcho-

---

*   Razumnik Vasilyevich Ivanov-Razumnik (1878–1946) was a Russian, Soviet author, philosopher and literary critic, best known for his book *The History of Russian Social Thought* (1907). During World War I, Ivanov-Razumnik was the leader of the literary group *The Skyths*, whose members included Alexander Blok, Sergey Yesinin, and Andrei Bely, among others. A left-wing Social Revolutionary, Ivanov-Razumnik initially stayed in the USSR and was vice-president of the Free Philosophical Society, closed down in the 1930s. During World War II, Ivanov-Razumnik found himself behind enemy lines and eventually settled in Regensburg, where he died a year after the cessation of hostilities.

**   *Vekhi* [Milestones] was a landmark anthology of social and intellectual criticism edited by Mikhail Gershenzon and liberal philosopher-qua-politician Peter Struve. Its contributors included Nikolai Berdyaev, Sergei Bulgakov, Alexander Izgoev, Bogdan Kistyakovsky, and Semyon Frank, as well as Struve and Gershenzon themselves. Five of the contributors were former Marxists who had tried to participate in the formation of a liberal political

decadents often posed as progressives, accusing social democracy of conservatism and philistinism. The actual philistinism of the Second International's dogmatics famously offered ample cause for such masquerades, though that hardly justifies them. Most of these campaigns against Marxism have been forgotten by now, though their old patterns often reappear with new names. It is quite indicative that in bygone days, such schemata were often expounded to demand an even newer modernity. Plekhanov's paper *Art and Social Life* is an early reaction to the first attempts at mixing socialism with modernism, a phenomenon more than familiar from our own time.

Plekhanov draws a comparison between the fascination of educated people in Tsarist Russia for the social, philosophical and aesthetic doctrines of the Western European bourgeoisie in the epoch of its decline, and the Russian eighteenth-century aristocracy's interest in the ideas of the Encyclopedists. Plekhanov sees both as 'pre-emptions' of their respective ages. Under Ekaterina II, Russian society was not ready for the practical implementation of the enlightening theories of Diderot and Helvetius, just as there was no basis in Russian society under Nikolay II for the assimilation of retrograde ideas from the age of Western capitalism's decline. After all, the Russian bourgeoisie had not yet undergone the social development already completed by the Western bourgeoisie.

Plekhanov's deliberations display a certain weakness characteristic of his understanding of the historical process in Russia. Of course, the reactionary ideas of Russia's liberal bourgeoisie had their national roots, though this did not prevent them from taking on an imitative quality. Still, Plekhanov was right to maintain a negative attitude to such ideas; later, Lenin would condemn the attempts of Bogdanov and Bazarov 'to smuggle in old and reactionary philosophical rubbish disguised as a criticism of Plekhanov's tactical opportunism'.[30] It seems useful to remind some of our time's own Marxists of these circumstances as they repeat the old mistakes of 1908.

Concerning his historical parallel, Plekhanov writes:

> The infatuation of Russian aristocrats for the French Encyclopedists had no practical consequences of any moment. It was however useful, in the sense that it did clear certain aristocratic minds of some aristocratic

---

party but withdrew to the exploration of the self as an alternative to populist and nihilist programmes. The anthology was widely read and discussed and drew a broad neo-idealist literature in its wake.

30   Lenin 1963, p. 34.

prejudices. On the other hand, the present infatuation of a section of our intelligentsia for the philosophical views and aesthetic tastes of the declining bourgeoisie is harmful, in the sense that it fills their 'intellectual' minds with bourgeois prejudices, for the independent production of which our Russian soil has not yet been sufficiently prepared by the course of social development. These prejudices even invade the minds of many Russians who sympathise with the proletarian movement. The result is that they are filled with an astonishing mixture of socialism and that modernism which is bred by the decline of the bourgeoisie. This confusion is even the cause of no little practical harm.[31]

Of course, Plekhanov could not foresee the scale this 'astonishing mixture of socialism and modernism' would reach in the years of great upheaval after World War I, let alone today. He largely limits himself to the logical side, proving that such mixtures are inappropriate since modernism in art is clearly contiguous with bourgeois theory's general tendency toward reactionary ideas. Matters are not so straightforward, however. The fact is that this mixture of the darkest sentiments with revolutionary and even socialist phrases is very widespread, and that requires an independent historical analysis. We are not just dealing with a simple misunderstanding, but a really existing contradiction, no matter how obvious its inappropriateness.

In that sense, Plekhanov's critique is not enough. Still, one cannot take away two of its obvious merits. First of all, Plekhanov comes close to the truth in his dissection of the ideological content of the newest artistic tendencies and their link to philosophical idealism. Second, he sees perfectly well that these tendencies contain bursts of wild 'innovation' related to the psychology and theory of anarchism; under the right circumstances, they easily turn into their own opposite and are no stranger to the restoration of the most banal forms of reactionary philistinism.

Plekhanov delivered his paper *Art and Social Life* in 1912 at Paris and Liège. It is the first response to the emergence of Cubism in Marxist writing, and, admittedly, one that came without delay. The 'completely new art' had only just been baptised. Plekhanov writes on the basis of his own personal impressions; he saw these paintings in the Salon d'automne and heard the laughter of its most naïve visitors, and he also read Gleizes and Metzinger's programmatic book *On Cubism*, published in the same year.

---

31   Plekhanov 1956, p. 205.

Plekhanov's paper considers the newest excesses of Parisian fashion in connection with the history of art and literature, against the broadest possible social backdrop. The conflict between the artist and the crowd can have a tragically serious quality, as was the case, for example, in Pushkin's age. The great poet did not want to serve the social aims of the regime under Nikolay I, and he was right. Plekhanov offers a sharp-witted proof of this correct thesis, thereby countering Pisarev's view* – popular in the revolutionary milieu – of the illusory gentility that supposedly lay at the root of Pushkin's poem 'To the Poet' (1830). Yet gradually, the ambivalent character of such circumstances gained the upper hand, as one could already see clearly enough in the theory of 'art for art's sake' of the French Romantics, the Parnassians, and the first Realists (meaning 'realism' as a literary tendency in the second half of the nineteenth century.) As the conflict between the artist and his surroundings lost its broader social meaning, proud individualism increasingly poisoned the noble solitude of the creative personality, until it yielded something like a parody of Pushkin:

> *Exacting artist, are you pleased with your creation?*
> *You are? Then let the mob abuse your name*
> *And on the altar spit where burns your flame.*
> *And shake your tripod in its childlike animation.*

'The amusing thing about the parody is that in this case the "exacting artist" is content with the most obvious nonsense'.[32] As an instructive example, Plekhanov mentions Fernand Léger's *Woman in Blue* and its 'form of several haphazardly arranged cubes, or rather, parallelipids', coloured in more or less densely with blue paint. Contemporary admirers of the 'Copernican turn' are accustomed to rather different appraisals and will of course be indignant to read Plekhanov's paper. '"Nonsense cubed!" are the words that suggest themselves at the sight of these ostensibly artistic exercises'.[33]

The difference between Plekhanov's jibes and Berdyaev's exaltation is truly huge, but both points of view are quite consistent, and, to be sure, more deserving of respect than any familiar 'astonishing mixture of socialism and modernism'. Eclectic poses produce nothing but pathetic confusion. Of course,

---

*   Dmitry I. Pisarev (1840–68) was a radical Russian writer and social critic. His article 'Pushkin and Belinsky' (1865) presents a thoroughly negative view of Pushkin as an outmoded, aristocratic author.

32   Plekhanov 1956, p. 216.

33   Plekhanov 1956, p. 214.

one can deride Plekhanov's appraisal as outdated, dogmatic, and in need of creative revision. One could argue that public opinion has long since changed as to Léger and other artists who turned women into collections of geometrical figures. Today's exhibition-goers no longer laugh at such 'exacting artists', even when they are caught up in pursuits far more fantastic than Cubism. On the contrary, they look at them thoughtfully, trying not to show that the worm of doubt is wiggling inside of them.

Yet none of this can make much of a dent in Plekhanov's position. In 1912, the audience was laughing, and now it is not. That's life. But does this speak in favour of the audience, at least one that considers itself up to date on modern culture? That is still an open question. Plekhanov might have ascribed the progressing seriousness of such matters to the further decline in the level of intellectual culture, connected to the agony of the old world order. When such unhealthy processes drag on for decades, people become capable of god knows what. Plekhanov probably would have seen the solemn dances of today's crowds around the altar of the 'exacting artist' as the most amusing act in the historical parody on the old theme of 'the calamities of the author', a genius's conflict with an underdeveloped, hostile environment.

By the way, this change in audience attitudes was already apparent enough when Plekhanov gave his paper, so that the negative appraisal of these new tendencies now in turn became a protest against the psychology of the crowd. For a contemporary account, we might cite A.V. Lunacharsky's contribution to the newspaper *Kievskaya Mysl'* on the Salon de Independents of 1911:

> The general public wanders through the 27th pavilion in utter perplexity, never daring to tell the good from the bad. This might be foolish, impudent smearing, but god forbid, don't laugh or shrug your shoulders, only a reckless daredevil would do that. Or have you forgotten that your father laughed at 'The Poor Fisherman' by Puvis de Chavannes or shrugged his shoulders at Manet's 'Olympia'? And aren't these suddenly masterpieces now? No, it's better not to be surprised at anything, but to go from hall to hall with a serious and concentrated face 'reflecting nought but calm derision'! The audience is terrified. Rail at an innovator, they'll say you're a 'conservative'; praise him, and they'll call you a 'snob'. The general public is lost for good, much to the bane of talent, benefiting the hooligans of the brush.[34]

---

34   Lunacharsky 1941a, p. 200.

What a familiar scene! It shows that the thought behind Pushkin's poem 'To the Poet' applies at least in part to the art critic's independent aesthetic judgement; it too should not sacrifice its exactingness to the vacillations of fashion, ruled by spontaneous laws of imitation and antithesis.

However, Plekhanov hardly limits himself to jibing at 'nonsense cubed'. He recognises that Cubism has its cause: 'Calling it nonsense raised to the third degree is not explaining its origin'.[35] Indicating the direction in which this cause is to be sought, Plekhanov cites Gleizes's and Metzinger's book. These thinkers of Montmartre justified the artist's withdrawal into fruitless scrambling with vacuous personal experience and morbidly fantastic concoctions in that they were somehow similar to philosophy or rather, 'sophistical distortions of the idealist theory of knowledge'.[36]

There is much that rings true in Plekhanov's writing on these 'sophistical distortions'. He had an excellent grasp of the subjective-idealistic themes wandering through the minds of those participating in the famed 'Copernican turn'. Plekhanov's other writings on to purely philosophical questions had often dissected those bookish sophisms, and now they were entering the consciousness of artists poorly prepared for independent thinking.

'There is nothing real outside ourselves', write Gleizes and Metzinger. They later make the reservation that they do not doubt the existence of the outer world. Its existence granted, they hasten to declare it unknowable. Attempting to unravel this tangle of contradictions, Plekhanov jokingly proves the total helplessness of Cubism's theoreticians in the obvious tendency of their philosophy of art to 'make every individual person the measure of things'. That is why he calls the Cubists' position 'sophistical' in contrast to other forms of idealism that ascribe a super-individual character to human consciousness as the beginning of any and all reality.

Unfortunately, Plekhanov left aside the new aesthetic's distinctive tendency from purely subjective 'sophistical deformations' to false objectivity, to a Platonising and medieval metaphysics of ideas, which means that Cubism has something in common with more modern forms of idealism. The author of *Art and Social Life* did not appreciate this transition, which at least in part explains the enthusiasm with which Cubist painting was met by the luminaries of the newest bourgeois philosophy, disappointed as they were in the subjective tenuity of thought. They thirsted for a strict new order, for geometrical

---

35   Plekhanov 1956, p. 214.
36   Plekhanov 1956, p. 217.

constructions of the human pneuma, where there is nothing but commands and blind obedience.

Of course, in those days it was not so easy to recognise this tendency and the danger it posed not only to painting, this desire to replace the visual principle of art with the hyperbolic activity of a strong will, subordinating everything alive to the cold geometry of abstract form. Still, Plekhanov's analysis of literary decadence contains a profound idea, capable of shedding light on the strange fractures of such a psyche. The fact of the matter is that the dominance of pure individualism – close to anarchist revolt and characteristic of the first stage of the 'completely new art' – easily turns into its own opposite. Moribund subjectivity's complete self-denial favours the flattest system of patriarchal, antiquated ideas of heavy-handed discipline and everything the Germans call *Zucht*. The veneration of blood and soil, blind obedience and petit-bourgeois routine now gain the appearance of intellectual depth and become the last refuge of decadents in disguise.

Plekhanov writes:

> Anarchism, generally, is only an extreme deduction from the basic premises of bourgeois individualism. That is why we find so many bourgeois ideologists in the period of decadence who are sympathetic to anarchism. Maurice Barrès likewise sympathised with anarchism in that period of his development when he affirmed that there is no reality save our ego. Now, probably, he has no conscious sympathy for anarchism, for the ostensibly stormy outbursts of his particular brand of individualism ceased long ago. For him, the 'authentic truths' which, he maintained, were 'destroyed' have now been restored, the process of restoration being that Barrès has adopted the reactionary standpoint of the most vulgar nationalism. And this is not surprising: it is but a step from extreme bourgeois individualism to the most reactionary 'truths'.[37]

Of course, such flights to Tushino* are much older than the doings of Barrès and other nationalists. In the early nineteenth century, European Romanticism experienced a similar evolution from the subjective negation of reality to a full

---

37   Plekhanov 1956, pp. 207–8.

*   This untranslatable ironic-derisive expression refers to those boyars who fled from Moscow in 1608–9 from the Czar Vasily Ivanovich Shuisky to the camp of the imposter False Dmitry II at Tushino.

reconciliation with its most conservative traditions. Yet even here, there was still plenty of serious content, and this experience entered the history of culture with more than just its limited side. In the second half of the nineteenth century, the self-denial of the newest subjectivity in favour of 'unimpeachable truths', hard 'knowledge' (instead of fluctuating visual 'apparition'), strict architectonics and discipline can already be felt in many aesthetic tendencies, anticipating the crisis of bourgeois culture. In a word, this is a phenomenon both widespread and diverse, and no doubt full of deceptive allure – a happy mirage where the individual and its 'strain', to use Dostoevsky's famous expression, dissolves into a thoughtless unity with objective principles and blind collective volition. In our own time, such ruptures, turns, and shifts are especially characteristic of bourgeois thinking, and what's more, they now lack any historical justification or spiritual value compared with older, more naïve forms of similar mythology.

This, by the way, also offers an explanation for facts that until today haunt people's minds and serve as fertile ground for various political intrigues. Why did the totalitarian regimes in Italy and Germany stand for 'the classics' and 'realism'? That question is often hurled at the Marxist philosophy of art by its opponents as a challenge.

For the same reason (one might answer) that led Barrès and other French chauvinists to the false restoration of the most vulgar 'unimpeachable truths' long before Goebbels or Mussolini. Only one step separates anarcho-decadent aesthetics from the sham restoration of classical art. Yet all of that certainly has nothing in common with genuine realism, although it logically follows from the paradoxical vacillation of the 'modern spirit', in which it spontaneously blends together with ordinary blackhundredist* demagogy geared toward popular prejudice. That is the old logic of bourgeois mythmaking and its fluctuations between ultra-leftist fanfares and the 'revolution from the right'.

The return of the Cubists Gleizes and Severini to the Catholic Church is a typical example of inordinate 'leftism's' turn to traditional philistine values. Cubism is a sibling of Marinetti's Futurist aesthetic, dominant in Fascist Italy, at least in the early years of that regime. Other tendencies influential in Italian art in the 1920s–30s – 'metaphysical painting', neo-classicism, 'Novecento' –

---

*   The Black Hundreds gang was an early twentieth-century ultra-nationalist movement in Russia. It staunchly supported the monarchy, stood for extremist Russian nationalism, xenophobia, and anti-Semitism. The Black Hundreds incited pogroms against the Jewish population as well as terrorist violence and assassinations of anti-Czarist revolutionaries.

would have been unthinkable without Cubism, as was the 'new objectivity' of Alexander Kanoldt, who became one of the official maitres of Hitler's Reich.* It would be a simplification to link the Cubism of 1907–14 to totalitarian ideas. There is no direct link, of course, but the ambivalences are obvious.

To show the ideological chiaroscuro in which Cubism first emerged in the run-up to World War I, let us hear the account of a friendly witness, Ilya Ehrenburg's excellent novel *The Unusual Adventures of Julio Jurenito*. Ehrenburg no doubt had sympathy for the modernist movement (more or less up to abstract painting), but that makes his testimony all the more valuable. His novel centres round a teacher of the new faith, the mysterious Mexican Julio Jurenito. He is surrounded by a group of apostles and the novel's author is one of them. This new faith apparently consists in the belief that the entire hypocritical world of old must be destroyed to its foundations to allow the rise of a new life, strong in its primordial freshness.

Of course, Julio Jurenito did not 'fall from the sky', as they say. His new faith is composed of themes from the 'life philosophy' popular in the beginning of the century. There is nothing very original in his anarchist idea of 'the worse, the better', that is, in the Great Provocateur's striving to push modern civilisation toward complete senselessness and collapse. Yet the author is not answerable for his hero's thoughts, thoughts that have coagulated in life to the point of being ripe for embodiment, so that the figure created by Ehrenburg has rather objective features, its arbitrary nature notwithstanding.

Consciously or unconsciously, Julio Jurenito's apostles were helping to renew the world by intensifying its negative forces. One of them was a certain Karl Schmidt. Even as a student before the world war, he stood out through his fantastic thirst for the violent reorganisation of life. Here, the idea of destruction becomes an idiotic mania for order.

> The main thing is organise the whole world, just like one's life; after all, he, Schmidt, was convinced that he was living more rationally and beau-

---

*   Alexander Kanoldt (1881–1939) was one of the major representatives of the German New Objectivity (*Neue Sachlichkeit*) movement and its 'magical realist' wing (along with Max Beckmann and Georg Schrimpf). Although the conservative wing of the NSDAP considered his paintings 'degenerate', his work found favour with several leading personalities of the regime. Kanoldt became professor and then director of the Berliner Kunsthochschule. He was also given a post as a senator of the Prussian Academy of the Arts. He retired in 1936 on grounds of ill health. In 1937, during the crackdown on degenerate art, his works were removed from public collections but remained popular among the Nazi elite.

tifully in his doghouse on sixty marks than any millionaire. He could be a nationalist, a supporter of the Kaiser, and a socialist all at once. After all, it was all one and the same, since both Kaiser Wilhelm and any socialist understood that the world is disorganised. It requires organisation by force.

Indeed, Karl Schmidt is absolutely sure that anarchy is evil, while organisation is good. He knows no other dimensions. To him, the notion of organisation is a general form of order, the negation of everything concrete, alive, and thus disorganised.

It is easy to see that the writer's imagination here is probing the broad spectrum of half-scientific, half-mythical ideas of our time, from Alexander Bogdanov's 'universal science of organisation'[38] to Pere Dubarle's terrifying cybernetic utopia.[39] Abstract order *à toute outrance* and the opposite reaction of irrational life forces are two spectres of bourgeois ideology, and such false consciousness sometimes has also infected socialist thinking.

When Julio Jurenito and Ilya Ehrenburg meet Karl Schmidt again after the war, this apostle of forcible organisation is already working for the Comintern. He has come a long way from being a general of the German army, becoming a dour Spartakist. But his goal in life is still the same. The walls of his Moscow

---

38　Alexander Bogdanov (1873–1928) was a revolutionary, rival to Vladimir Lenin, physician, philosopher and science fiction writer. 'Bogdanov attempted to develop a universal science of organization ("tektology", the Greek word for "to construct") that would encompass "practical and theoretical methods as the methods of conscious man and spontaneous nature." He contended that heretofore organization had been studied only in separate and specific areas – in reference to things, people, or ideas. [...] Bodganov assumed there was a continuous process of organization-disorganization – indeed that all human activities consisted of ordering, sorting, and organizing. The "task of tektology" was to systematize those activities [...] through inductive and deductive methods, through which "spontaneous, accidental, anarchic, trial and error methods" could be eliminated in favor of planned organizational activity' (Sochor 1998, p. 44).

39　Dominique Dubarle (1907–87) was a Dominican friar and philosopher who published his review of Norbert Wiener's *Cybernetics* in *Le Monde* in 1948. Here, 'he contemplated the possibility of an all-powerful "machine à governer" that would make the state "the only supreme co-coordinator of all partial decisions." "In comparison with this," wrote Dubarle, "Hobbes's Leviathan was nothing but a pleasant joke. We are running the risk nowadays of a great World State, where deliberate and conscious primitive injustice may be the only possible condition for the statistic happiness of the masses: a world worse than hell for every clear mind"' (Cf. Gerovich 2002, p. 100).

office are now covered by different plans, drawing up the future of social organisation on the testing ground of the city of Tula. The wild, senseless chaos of the old world and the rule of incongruous coincidence must disappear. Now everything will be different. There will be so and so many engineers, so and so many poets, all according to plan. The total number of births is strictly metered in accordance to tasks allocated by the centre. The family is no more. There are children's homes, schools, and work communes, all with unvarying nutrition. A special entertainment distributor rations out doses of aesthetic feeling and other emotions. The central medical commission is working to organise the sexual life of every individual.

Ehrenburg was well ahead of Aldous Huxley in drawing this paradisiacal picture of a 'brave new world'. Then again, the apostle of universal organisation Karl Schmidt had plenty of predecessors of his own. It is enough to recall the character Shigalev from Dostoevsky's *Demons*. The trouble is that such caricatures can have and sometimes do have real models. One could meet dangerous crackpots like Karl Schmidt in the early days of the October Revolution. A.V. Lunacharsky once called them 'Futuro-Communists'.

Exaggerated ideas of planning and forcibly realised utility are infantile disorders of any social revolution. The deeper the revolution, the greater the danger of such disorders; the more people it affects, the stronger its own administrative apparatus grows, and the longer this disorder lasts. However, the ideas of Karl Schmidt are neither socialist nor revolutionary taken by themselves.

Instead, we are dealing with one of the sides of the old social order, embodied through a forcible state-capitalist organisation from above, hostile to the people. Ruling over the majority's minds and imposed by the force of things, ordinary bourgeois consciousness constantly vacillates between two poles of modern mythology, long since expressed by its rhapsodists in the form of 'Apollonian' and 'Dionysian' principles, principles of organisation and chaos, neat order and spontaneity. Of course, socialist thinking can slip down this old, welltrodden path, but in that case, it will be theoretically and practically infected with the crudest bourgeois holdovers. Karl Schmidt's presence in revolutionary Moscow is historically possible; its true place is not here, however. The emergence of totalitarian states in the West would have probably forced him to change colours yet again, because genuine socialism, based on the selfregulatory organisation of the population, does not coincide in any way with the forcible utility of a Karl Schmidt, inculcated by a few organisers knowledgeable in that science. Here, one can only speak of an 'astonishing mixture of socialism and modernism' that sometimes takes a very practical form.

What seems important for our purposes is how Julio Jurenito explains Schmidt's activities to Ilya Ehrenburg, who is perturbed by the approaching boredom. The world is moving from anarchic volition to soulless order. Even in chess, combinations are displaced by positional play. 'Instead of unexpected combinations and the noble sacrifices of gambits, there are precise, sparing, carefully calculated plans'. People have parted ways with all those abbots, madonnas, and royal highnesses, breaking with the motley, painterly, chaotic romance of the old, rotten to the core. The removal of all this vivid multifariousness is an irrefutable, principle feature of our epoch.

> Have you seen paintings by contemporary futurists [Cubists]?* After the 'divine caprices' of the impressionists, you have the precise, synthesised construction of forms which are closely akin to Schmidt's graph.
>
> Were you in the war? What did you see there – Napoleons and Davids and the exploits of heroic standard bearers, or Mr. Cool's exemplary management?[40]

Thus, in Julio Jurenito's opinion, if not that of Ilya Ehrenburg, Cubism expresses the idea of the world's cold-blooded organisation, triumphing over the past's painterly diversity at every step, with same inevitability as the spread of corporate conglomerates and the twentieth century's world wars. Modernity! The new automatism becomes a social ideal, the norm of taste and the object of fashion, architectural style, the psychology of the automobile owner, and so on, all the way to organised, simplified sex.

This all is true to a degree, but not entirely. On the one hand, Cubism really does reflect the growing 'over-organisation' of life, which, according to the testimony of many Western writers, has become the real scourge of contemporary humanity, a force out of control, irrational for all its idiotic rationality. However, neither Karl Schmidt nor the theoreticians of Cubism can be taken so seriously. Their illusory power over their own inner anarchy is pure rhetoric or verbal magic. Their strict organisation of the spirit is endlessly formal, shaky, and based on a monstrous inner chaos, just like some of modernity's prophets praise and others mourn this 'over-organisation' in real life. The despotism of dead order is the flip-side of anarchy and spreads chaos in its own right.

Plekhanov left aside or simply did not notice Cubism's connection to 'Mr. Cool's exemplary management', though this is not the problem of his critique.

---

*   Usik Vanzler's 1930 translation substitutes the Russian original of *khudozhniki Kubisti* [Cubist artists] with 'contemporary futurists'.

40   Ehrenburg 1930, p. 339.

The parallel between the turn to geometric taste in painting and the development of trusts, monopolies, or 'organised capitalism' was drawn more than once by quasi-Marxist vulgar sociology both in our own country and in the West. But all these analogies are beneath Plekhanov's point of view. They elevate the myths of Karl Schmidt's hot-headed fantasies to the level of unimpeachable truth. Here, modernity is still the arena of the battle between two mythological divinities – Organisation and Chaos.

The real deficit of Plekhanov's critique lies elsewhere. He did not notice that Cubism is a social or an ontological utopia, if one can put it that way. This utopia is based upon the ennui of subjective thinking that has lost its faith in itself and now thirsts for salvation under the roof of hyper-personal, 'collective' reality. Barrès's evolution from contempt for the barbarian philistines to full idolisation of their persistent and monumental barbarity is one example of such psychological shifts. These are simply different forms of regressing into art's most primitive modes. The banal shop sign and the thick delirium of the consumer, his dreams of tropical jungles and the moonlight's glow are a further form of such self-denial. The principle of Karl Schmidt, that is the socialisation of the spirit and the retention of its technical organisation, the flight from reason to empty rationality, is a third form, especially widespread in all kinds of 'purisms' and 'constructivisms' after the First World War.

No doubt these ideas are connected to the real subordination of man to machine and the intrusion of an uncontrollable mass of technical means into human life. Yet this link is not direct but oblique. Contemporary technological civilisation, even in the form of 'Mr. Cool's exemplary management', has no need for Cubist painting. That need comes from modern bourgeois consciousness, in constant conflict with itself, from the individual's disgust at his own ideal aspirations once they lose their force, from the desire to insult oneself, to abuse one's own empty aesthetic broadness, to kill off one's own decrepit inner freedom in order to resurrect it, creating an additional source of excitement with the help of a specific masochism, taking pleasure in one's own pain.

These are complicated psychological mechanisms, generally based on self-denial as the true road to paradise. The same purpose can be fulfilled by 'machine-worship', to use Lunacharsky's witty expression, and by the unnatural love of the sterile ideal of organisation in the spirit of Karl Schmidt, as well as just those arbitrary, crudely smeared abstract forms that tear and crowd out life in the Cubists' early experiments.

Of course, the individual's self-disgust and his attempts to break out of his cell into another, truer world can ultimately be explained by the absence of genuine self-activity and the unbearable pressure of external forces, and those include technology's dominance over humanity. Still, though art-historical writing often purports a direct correlation between contemporary technology and the fantasies of the Cubists, this is ordinary academic drivel. It only starts to look like truth through endless repetition. Such is often the case with commonplaces.

It is just as clear that there is no direct correlation between geometrically oriented taste and the planned development of society or its conscious organisation. One can however say that in the epoch of late capitalism elements of this organisation, limited to the formal side, take on especially superficial, violent, alienated qualities. Wherever this infection is present, the ailing mind seeks an exit to a freer world, finding nothing but the cult of its own torment and the high-flown veneration of dead forms. This is how true believers make something godlike of the alien forces of material necessity, revelling in their own suffering.

While treating the views of Gleizes and Metzinger in their dissatisfaction toward the manner of the Impressionists as an example for capricious subjectivity, demanding a stricter, more objective painting, Plekhanov might have recalled his own analysis of Barrès's career. We already said that the turn to the tradition of French nationalism is but one of the utopias thrown up by spontaneous, that is, bourgeois consciousness, one of a thousand. This thousand also includes the restoration of 'authentic principles' declared by Cubism and expressed through a rather chaotic system of abstract forms. Despite all the differences between personal and social shades of all these subjective daydreams of a new, lasting life order, they are more or less one of a kind, and conform to the general law of statistics.

After a drawn-out period of unhappiness with one's surroundings, and its negation from a position of subtle aesthetic individuality, after that pose of decadence, now comes self-negation. The guilt for the general breakdown of life is now ascribed to overdeveloped individual consciousness, its scepticism, its critical attitude to the world, its anarchy of taste, and its overall instability. Now you have to exterminate that inner hydra and to train with the most primitive archaisms, to be found in those epochs of healthy barbarism when people only knew what they knew, and didn't want to know anything more. How good it is to be an ancient Iberian! In the prehistoric world, people expressed their uncomplicated ideas with explicit, crude symbols, and not through visual images artificially induced through academic proficiency. Ignorance once was artistic; it follows that art itself now must be ignorant.

This is how the weakened reflections of an enfeebled consciousness give rise to the utopia of mindless force and strict mental discipline. 'The completely new art' of Salmon is a chapter from the history of utopian thinking; it combines the idea of a return to primordial crudeness with the pursuit of the most modern form. This mixture is original, of course, and it has a specific colouring unknown to previous epochs. Despite the specifics of its time, it still has something in common, for example, with the primitivism of the different sects of late antiquity, with the mystical propensities of the Gnostics. Cubism's apocalypse is not just 'nonsense cubed', a mere symptom for the general decline of bourgeois culture. It is a phenomenon of social impotence, a search for a fantastical way out of a rather difficult situation, a savage form of protest reflecting the presence of a huge stratum of people hungry to see a new heaven and a new earth. In that sense, some of the objections voiced by Lunacharsky after Plekhanov's lecture in 1912 are not groundless. As one can see from Plekhanov's answer, the matter under discussion was the problem of 'waverers'.

I have no desire to assess the modern artist's activities from the moral standpoint, Plekhanov says, or to prescribe him this or that direction.

> I do not say that modern artists 'must' take inspiration from the emancipatory aspirations of the proletariat. No. If the apple-tree must bear apples, and the pear-tree must produce pears, artists who adhere to the standpoint of the bourgeoisie must revolt against the aforesaid aspirations. In decadent times art 'must' be decadent.[41]

Of course, such words are not to be understood in the sense of a total fatality of class position. Plekhanov allows for the possibility of a crossing-over of 'waverers' to the side of the working class, and he writes that such a crossing-over can have a huge positive significance for the work of any artist.

> Only these ideas must become part of his flesh and blood, and he must express them precisely as an artist. He must be able, moreover, to form a correct opinion of the artistic modernism of the present-day ideologists of the bourgeoisie. The ruling class has now reached a position where, for it, going forward means sinking downward. And this sad fate is shared by all its ideologists. The most advanced of them are precisely those who have sunk lower than all their predecessors.

This thought is brilliant and valid in many ways, if, of course, it is understood dialectically. There are situations in which moving forward means taking a downward path, but people who descend before the others are also an 'avant-

---

41   Plekhanov 1956, p. 223.

garde' of sorts. They aren't just descending; they are going forward in the opposite direction. In other words, bourgeois ideology also undergoes an upgrade of sorts. It now obliquely reflects capitalism's general decline and the ripening necessity of a new social order, which cannot be realised for this or that reason. The luminaries of this modernism in all fields have a greater presence than the simple epigones of the bourgeois worldview's old forms, although, generally speaking, the latter are better. Such questions cannot be generalised. Concrete history creates complex combinations of movements 'forwards' and 'backwards'.

In some fields, for example in philosophy or the historical disciplines, modernism is not uninteresting despite the obviously reactionary nature of its general trend. In some epochs, for example in that of Baudelaire, Verlaine, and Rimbaud, principled decadence could push great poetic characters to the fore. Seemingly, these possibilities exhausted themselves quite early on in the field of painting, and here the leaders of the new modernist tendencies are figures rather prominent than significant. Their demonic work of visual art's sequential self-destruction increasingly takes place under the minus sign.

Yet even here, 'nonsense cubed' is not just simply the decline of bourgeois ideology. As a symptom, these morbid fantasies do not characterise bourgeois ideology in the narrow sense of the word as much as the spontaneous moods of the 'wavering' strata that effect its renewal. In short, pear-trees do not bear pears in times of change, but who knows what. Their outlandish fruit might not be tasty on its own, but it proves that in society there are neither 'apples' nor 'pears'. There is only the objective course of history, a general process of development of which bourgeois ideology is only a transitory form, its present meaning fully defined by the content of that process.

Plekhanov's notion of class ideology is too 'sociological'. He imagines bourgeois ideology as the hermetic self-consciousness of a class, and not as a mirror of objective reality, however limited and wrong it might be. The theory of knowledge behind this analysis lacks a dialectical quality of the kind that characterised Lenin's articles on Tolstoy. To be sure, if we speak of applying reflection theory to phenomena like Cubism, it is not our intention to justify them or to place them on an equal footing with Tolstoy's practice. Quite the contrary. By applying one and the same method, one can reach very different results, depending on the object of study.

A further deficit of Plekhanov's critique of Cubism is that it limits itself to the logical side and to the formal-aesthetic field. Plekhanov thinks it possible to compare the painting of Monet and Renoir to the literature of French Realism from the second half of the nineteenth century, but at the same time, he notes that realism here only touches upon the surface of things. The

Impressionists specialised in lighting effects – something necessary in painting, but less important than ideological content. Hence, the turn to fantasising in the Cubist vein is inevitable, in Plekhanov's opinion. Artists of this tendency felt the need to go beyond the 'outer rind of phenomena', they wanted to return to ideological content. Matters were not quite so simple. Wherever consciousness is limited by its 'self', it is impossible to think one's way to serious ideas.

> And just as people, when they have no bread, eat dockweed,* so when they have no clear ideas they content themselves with vague hints at ideas, with surrogates borrowed from mysticism, symbolism and the similar 'isms' characteristic of the period of decadence.[42]

In such epochs, the philosophy of subjective idealism becomes more than an egoistical rule defining interpersonal relations; it becomes the basis for a new aesthetic.

Plekhanov's thinking would have a lasting impact upon the general direction of the Marxist critique of Cubism. However, as correct as its point of departure might be, it has a deficit whose dimensions become ever grander, the more it is repeated and spread. It is true that there was still a strong realist sub-current in Impressionism, partially even strengthened by new turns of perception. Impressionism is no simple fascination with effects in the absence of ideas, however. Instead, it is a position taken by consciousness in relation to the world, even overloaded with ideas, albeit ideas that only concern reflection and the artist's inner self-consciousness. But that is another question. In any case, there is enough philosophy in the art of the Impressionists, and the final conclusions drawn by this school bring us straight into the world of symbols and intentional simplifications.

As for the Cubists, it was not subjective idealism that confused the founders of the 'completely new art', despite their propensity for naïve philosophical phraseology. Their position was derived from their own rendition of the situation of life in their time and from the previous development of art. Moreover, if there are philosophical parallels and justifications in Cubism, the parallel with the philosophy of subjective idealism hardly exhausts the essence of the mat-

---

*   The Russian original is more colourful than the 1957 translation of Plekhanov: 'when people have no bread, they will eat a swan'.

42   Plekhanov 1956, p. 213.

ter, as we already said above. In general, the position of artistic consciousness cannot be explained in purely logical terms. It is rather the propensity for certain philosophical constructs that determines a position, which in turn reflects one possible aspect of reality, be it true or false.

Plekhanov's thinking follows that of Camille Mauclair, at least in part. An admirer of Impressionism, Mauclair lifts his hands in dismay when faced with the strange caprices of taste driving younger artists to everything ugly and dead. Plekhanov also speaks of a 'crisis of ugliness'.* Arguing with him after his lecture in Paris, Lunacharsky seems to have noted that the definition of a 'crisis of ugliness' presupposes absolute criteria for beauty, when in fact taste is historically relative and connected to certain social situations. Everything changes, as do people's notions of beauty.

In his conclusion, Plekhanov answers the objections of his opponent, who carried the problem over into the broader field of the theory of knowledge. There are no absolute criteria for beauty, but we do have the possibility of judging whether the execution of an artistic idea is good or bad. If instead of a woman dressed in a blue dress we see some geometrical figures painted blue, the spectator might say that the painting is no good.

> The more the execution corresponds to the design, or – to use a more general expression – the more the form of an artistic production corresponds to its idea, the more successful it is. There you have an objective criterion. And precisely because there is such a criterion, we are entitled to say that the drawings of Leonardo da Vinci, for example, are better than the drawings of some little Themistocles who spoils good paper for his own distraction. When Leonardo da Vinci, say, drew an old man with a beard, the result really was an old man with a beard – so much so that at the sight of him we say: 'Why, he's alive!' But when Themistocles draws an old man, we would do well to write underneath: 'This is an old man with a beard' – so that there might be no misunderstanding. In asserting that there can be no objective criterion of beauty, Mr. Lunacharsky committed the sin of which so many bourgeois ideologists, up to and including the cubists, are guilty: the sin of extreme subjectivism. How a man who calls himself a Marxist can be guilty of this sin, I simply cannot understand.[43]

---

*   Camille Mauclair's 'crise de laideur' is translated into Russian as *krizis bezobrazie*. *Bezobrazie* has a dual connotation of disfiguration and foolery, while its literal meaning is perhaps closer to 'imagelessness'.

43   Plekhanov 1956, p. 226.

Today, all we have to judge this discussion by is its written retelling in the printed edition of the lecture *Art and Social Life*. Still, Plekhanov's critique was probably fair enough. It is valid with regard to the relativist theory of truth, which exaggerates the historical relativity of social consciousness. Plekhanov was familiar with this indisputably negative feature from his polemic with Alexander Bogdanov, and Lunacharsky was more or less in the thrall of Bodganov's tendency at that time. Hence, the purported shade of 'subjectivism' in his deliberations on the impossibility of absolute criteria of truth. Then again, Plekhanov's position is also not entirely without fault.

It is as if he were factoring out the unity of execution and design, form and content. In explaining famous artistic phenomena through their social causes, we follow Spinoza's rule: not to weep or to laugh, but to understand. Apple trees produce apples, and pear trees produce pears, but there remains the question of how to judge the phenomena of taste in their historical necessity. And from this point of view, they all lie on the same common plane. All notions of beauty and all forms of taste are measured by the same yardstick, be it Leonardo's drawings or the smearing of Gogol's character Themistoclius,* a sculpture by Phidias or an African fetish. Did the artist convey the thing he wanted to convey correctly or incorrectly, that is an objective criterion. We can see this with our own eyes; there is no point in doubting our judgement, and no labels or other incidental recognition aids can fool us.

However, many works of Medieval painting have all kinds of labels, and that does not prevent them from being works of art, and what's more, to an immeasurably greater degree than other formally realistic paintings of later times, where we see everything clearly with our own eyes, without written explanations. Of course, Plekhanov admitted that such contradictions were possible. Resemblance with the object is the last foundation of visual art, as of all human consciousness in general, but this truth cannot be applied in the abstract, otherwise the result will be nonsense. It could be that the bearded man, drawn by Leonardo himself, cannot compete with an academic work from the nineteenth century.

---

*   Lifshitz quotes and continues to quote Plekhanov's reference to the character Themistoclius, Manilov's eight-year-old son in Nikolai Gogol's *Dead Souls*. Themistoclius knows that Paris is the greatest city in Europe and that Russia's grandest cities are Petersburg and Moscow; in Manilov's eyes that qualifies him for diplomatic service, even when he later tries to bite off his brother Alkid's ear. There is no mention of his artistic exploits or his spoiling paper for fun in Gogol, however.

To correct matters, we need to introduce other parameters into our artistic criteria, for example, the depth of the artist's understanding of the depicted object. This already alters such a simple yardstick as the one Plekhanov suggests, taking the initial idea to its end. Indeed, the archaic sculpture of ancient Greece is far less similar to the living human body than later works of the Hellenic period. Yet Greek archaic art amazes us with its mysterious depth. As one can see from the further deliberations of Plekhanov himself, he grants that the correspondence between an idea and its execution in turn depends on the content of this idea. A false idea cannot find a truly artistic expression, since all inner falsehood pushes art into decline. This is already something other than the simple difference between Leonardo's drawings and Themistoclius's smears. The artist's desire to represent an old man with a beard so that everyone would exclaim 'he's alive' must also be placed among the possible ideas tested according to the inner value, their content, their depth. Then it could be that the exclusive striving for the verisimilitude of visual images is also a phenomenon in the history of human consciousness and its relation to the objective world, and not an unconditional yardstick applicable to all the other phenomena of its history.

The formal correspondence of an intent with its execution is often the result of dexterity, not art, and then it deserves no more than a bucket of peas, which is what Alexander the Great gave to an entertainer who tried to impress him with his dexterity at throwing small peas through the eye of a needle. Virtuosity can be empty. There can be too much of any merit, including that of verisimilitude. It has long since been noted that an excess of verisimilitude gives pictures a vulgar note. Why is this so? Because realism is not the basis of painting? Hardly. Only because even realism can take on a formal, one-sided character, and everything one-sided diverges from the truth at the base of what we call realism. That's all.

Thus, Plekhanov's criteria require concrete development, lest they fold under the onslaught of relativist aesthetics. This task cannot be achieved by dividing the objective from the absolute. On the contrary, the application of our objective criterion to all times and peoples will only be just in its concrete dimension, in the frame of absolute content. That includes all of art history and the entire breadth of aesthetic truth, and rejects all one-sidedness, even one-sidedness created in the name of the basis of any art – its verisimilitude.

In a word, without falling prey to 'the sin of subjectivism', one can and should see all intent and all forms of execution from a historical point of view. The main thing is that history should not lose its absolute content in our eyes. Of course, the intent of the author of 'Woman in Blue' cannot be measured by the same yardstick as the intent of Titian's *La Bella* in her blue velvet dress, but by the same token, one cannot say that Léger is a second Themistoclius, spoiling canvases because he simply cannot draw. Yes, the 'Woman in Blue' at the Salon d'automne is ugly, but it does not bother the author in the least that he has rendered an ugly pile of dead forms instead of a woman; on the contrary, he is happy and considers his painting a job well done. And really, its execution corresponds to its intent.

By the same token, one cannot agree with Plekhanov that ugly forms are the spontaneous consequences of an artist's erroneous ideas, that he failed as a result of his decadent predilection for subjective idealism. Hardly. He failed because he wanted to. We will be ignoring the heart of the matter if we leave this paradox aside, that is, if we consider 'the crisis of ugliness' as a simple lack of beauty.

Plekhanov's words on the 'crisis of ugliness', justified in and of themselves, can lead to dangerous misunderstandings. They force us to remember those forms of criticism often levelled and still applied to various forms of philosophical and aesthetic modernism. After citing one of the many modern calls for a 'new barbarism' or examples of literary amorality, the critic thinks he has already accomplished his mission. In fact, the crux of the matter is that authors with such claims are not ashamed of their barbarism in the least; on the contrary, they see it as the height of refinement, the last word for the mind and the senses. If a Marxist critique wants to succeed in the struggle with such unquestionably reactionary phenomena, it cannot see them as the simple result of intellectual inadequacy, since such a point of view is beneath its opponent. In general, the bad is not simply an absence of the good; likewise the negative pseudo-value worshipped with such enthusiasm by those who go forward in reverse, would be utterly insignificant if they didn't hold some attraction, if they didn't have some misleading side.

The same goes for the formula of 'the crisis of ugliness'. It may be true by itself, but we still need to explain why so many people strive to the side of everything ugly, if it is not talent they lack, and if so many of them are oppressed by and unhappy with bourgeois society that they desperately hate. On what grounds do these 'flowers of evil' grow?

If Lunacharsky wanted to say that there is no difference between the beautiful and the ugly, because history is constantly changing, he was wrong. Yet when people paradoxically choose the ugly, this hardly means that they are like Themistoclius spoiling paper or because of some other personal weakness, such as the inability to 'think their way' to a higher goal. Just as an extremely lifelike, verisimilar picture can be false art, so false art that makes this falsehood its credo can be a mirage of the truth, a surrogate for realism, a deceptive utopia attracting the artist's spontaneous consciousness. This does not make such forms of consciousness any better and does not vindicate them from the vantage of reason and beauty, which have a universal world historical content and cannot be fully dissolved into a multitude of tastes and points of view. To ensure that our appraisal is made in the name of this absolute content without becoming a one-sided point of view, it needs to base itself on an understanding of the social and psychological causes that give rise to these by-now familiar oddities in art. A court of law acts in the name of higher principles when it shows the causes of evil and the paths to its elimination, and not just when it punishes and forgives. In a word, our appraisal must have a concrete, dialectical character.

The formula of the 'crisis of ugliness' introduced by Mauclair and taken over by Plekhanov, aptly expressed the turn emergent in European painting from its first steps into the new century. However, when one reads Mauclair's *Three Crises of Modern Art* today, one can only wonder at the French critic's inconsistency. His book is made up of separate articles printed in magazines over the course of several years. In this time, Mauclair could see for himself just how fatally art was affected by principles he had defended so enthusiastically. It is not so easy to draw such conclusions, however. Understandably, one finds no such verdict in the pages of Mauclair's book, although the bankruptcy of his point of departure is striking. Can one really be surprised at the efforts of the 'avant-garde's' most desperate representatives to ugliness after setting up an inevitable art-historical law according to which previous canons of taste are overthrown by younger seekers of the new? In practice, there is nothing inevitable about this historical pattern. The gain of something objectively valuable is a sure sign of progressive development. The new is good when it contains this unconditional element. To say that the new is good in itself would be a complete perversion of the dialectical meaning of history, one that, by the way, is rather widespread and even attractive under certain circumstances.

If there is such a thing as this doubtful law created by critics like Mauclair to justify modernism's first steps, and if this indeed has become a banal commonplace ever since, the Fauves or the Cubists were absolutely right to trample underfoot whatever their predecessors considered beautiful and whatever was really still beautiful. This is why we have so little sympathy for the complaints of the last representatives of a more refined taste like Mauclair or Remy de Gourmont. There is no point to the justified rebukes they address to a younger generation. There is no stopping now, no holding back, up to the total victory of negative principles, to the point of total Nothingness.

The author of *Three Crises of Modern Art* writes that the new must be recognised even if that means suppressing one's own aesthetic inclinations which one should 'force into silence'. This introduces into art history a principle fraught with great consequences. The reader might recall Lebel's book. In the modernist pattern, the work's immediately perceptible artistic quality steps into the background as the demand for the unconditionally new comes to the fore. Neither taste nor any special talent on the part of the artist can live up to their former roles. Inventiveness, hypnotic power, and an unstable psyche turn the personality into a membrane sensitive to the smallest changes in moral climate; they now mean more than a true eye capable of apprehending beauty and the character of real forms. What emerges is a notion of aesthetic appraisal against one's own convictions, suppressing the inner voice of taste. Beautiful forms must now be subjected to calculated torture. The 'crisis of ugliness' is an invisible presence in all of this, it is already at hand.

The Terms 'Reactionary' and 'Bourgeois'

Thus, there is not only a growing wave of positive responses to the 'Copernican turn' effected by Cubism's founders, but another, largely negative appraisal of this event. One can disagree with the Marxist tradition of placing Cubism among the phenomena of reactionary ideology in the epoch of the bourgeois order's decline. But one should not forget that such an appraisal exists, nor should one simply replace it with a 'strange mix of socialism and modernism'. One shouldn't lie.

This question is too deeply linked with the common system of views to emerge in the struggle of many generations of proletarian revolutionaries; its decision cannot just be changed for tactical reasons, which clearly play a large role in contemporary attempts to reassess Marxist aesthetics, or because of any other historical circumstances. Even if Cubist painting is now considered a museum piece, we have no reason to suspend the old verdict pronounced by the working class.

The people who created the revolutionary Marxist tradition believed that the downfall of world capitalism was imminent. The real course of history turned out to be more complex – the epoch of the bourgeois order's decline and decay drew itself out for an entire century. It gave rise to a mixture of highly developed science, technology and organisation with barbarity and stupidity that the world had never seen before. This age will not only go down in history for its achievements in physics, but for its world wars, its revival of medieval torture, its brutality, and its superstition. Though the streets of the cities are not overgrown with grass as they were in late Roman times, a habituation to the phenomena of decline and even a kind of pride taken in new barbarism runs likes a red thread through the entire intellectual lives of the most highly developed capitalist countries. It is no surprise that the criteria have changed, and that yesterday's decadence today is crowned with academic laurels. The caretaker's cottage looks like a castle when the actual castle has been razed, a field of potatoes growing in its place.

The fatal logic of having to go down to go forward, deeply rooted in modern bourgeois civilisation, meets with a simple lack of culture, with Asiatic* mores, or those even more ancient, and this meeting does not only take place in backward, poorly developed countries, but also in the world capitals of Europe and America.

Taken in sum, all of this paints a special intellectual-historical backdrop for the twentieth century. Actual movements forward take place under difficult circumstances, meeting on the way with specific conditions that the classics of Marxism did not and could not foresee. This is why even the notion of 'decline' customary to the old Marxist literature, is now more complicated. All zigzags and complications of the historical path aside, however, its principle contour is still clear, and the 'strange mix of socialism and modernism' is still inexpressibly tasteless.

Let them call us 'petit bourgeois' for not wanting to reconcile ourselves with this kind of innovation. All the Merezhkovkys, Berdyaevs, and Ivanov-Razumniks already discovered this mode of anti-Marxist polemic before 1917. Let modern philistinism bow down to what was dragged through the dirt yesterday. Neither curses nor paeans of joy produced by one and the same culture mill can influence history's objective court of law, the only one that counts in this case.

If, however, we want to hold onto a sturdy system of orientation in a changing world – a crucial task for contemporary Marxism – we must deal with the other side of the question. We must defend theory from its transformation into a simple scheme, easy to use for practical purposes. Marxism's vulgarisation was already a dangerous force during the lifetime of its founders. It is always closely connected to the declining level of activity of the practical working-class movement; this is something one can see in the example of many socialists from the time of the Second International.

Another form of this vulgarisation, especially noticeable in our time, is the false sharpening of political appraisals and formulas known under the rubric of 'dogmatism'. One cannot fail to see the damage done to revolutionary theory

---

*   Here Lifshitz refers to the Marxian concept of the Asiatic-despotic mode of production to precede antiquity, rather than any geographical or cultural notion of Asia.

by wooden straightforwardness, the banishment of dialectical fullness and concrete content (usually connected to loud-mouthed demagogy and exaggerated, would-be utility), to the huge detriment of the communist cause. And now we face a great complication, since words like 'bourgeois' or 'reactionary' awaken vivid memories of unjust accusations, loutish barking and other abuses. But it would be stupid and even dishonourable to blame them on Marxism.

Still, a word dropped from a song makes it all wrong. This is why it is necessary to explain in which sense the terms 'reactionary' and 'bourgeois' are applicable to the aesthetics of painting and to manifestations of art. First and foremost, we generally need to drop the habit of interpreting these terms in their moral and juridical senses. They do contain an element of personal responsibility, but this responsibility has a historical character; it is only beyond a certain point that it applies to individual personalities in the narrower sense of the word. This, in fact, is what sets apart Marxist socialism as a scientific theory from socialism based on moral-sentimental or juridical ideas, bourgeois socialism; it departs from historical, social, and class-specific notions.

It was already in the preface to the first volume of *Capital* that Marx saw the need to make the following clarification:

> To prevent possible misunderstandings, let me say this: I do not by any means depict the capitalist and the landowner in rosy colours. But individuals are dealt with here only in so far as they are the personifications of economic categories, the bearers of particular class-relations and interests. My standpoint, from which the development of the economic formation of society is viewed as a process of natural history, can less than any other make the individual responsible for relations whose creature he remains, socially speaking, however much he may subjectively raise himself above them.[44]

The exaggeration of the idea of personal responsibility results in the transfer of any question into the world of criminal law, utility, and abstract morality ruled by a battle of good and evil geniuses. It is a holdover of 'dogmatism' and 'the personality cult'. It can be understood in part but not justified as a reaction to the early social-democratic perversion of Marxism, which consisted in a similarly heavy-handed emphasis on the notion of natural-historical necessity. This notion was to serve as a convenient justification for one's own inaction.

---

44   Marx 1976, p. 96.

The negation of this system of perspectives led to another extreme: the habit of seeing everywhere the work of the devil, the traces of the unholy will of dangerous persons. By the way, all vulgar Marxism shares these qualities, because it strips this worldview of its principle component, its revolutionary dialectic.

It is not our job to depict the founders of Cubism in rosy colours. Yet this does not mean that a Marxist critique of such phenomena with their matrix and their objective forms in the social life of late capitalism should become an indictment of individuals. It would be the same as accusing the gnostic Carpocrates of immorality for teaching that carnal sin is necessary for the saviour of one's soul. The Cainites who exclaimed 'Hail Cain! Hail Sodom! Hail Judas!' were probably far more honest than any bureaucrat of the Roman Empire. But where do these wild forms of social consciousness come from? That is the main question. What makes up their inner logic, prepossessing a thinking bound by the force of circumstance? Here, we are not dealing with personal weaknesses – one can subjectively raise oneself above one's situation and still follow its invisible orders. 'The mistakes of the able-minded are always great', said one Arabic writer.

Generally, all other conditions being equal, personal culpability rises along with the objective possibility of a different, more conscious understanding of things. This is why, in our case, such responsibility primarily rests upon the shoulders of those who speak in the name of Marxism and uncritically repeat commonplace bourgeois ideas. It is another matter entirely to consider people of art, passively or if you will traumatically touched by the flood of such ideas. Here, we need a different yardstick, though there is no Wall of China between art and philosophy.

From a historical point of view, Cubism is a reactionary movement, but it hardly follows that its founders were reactionary in terms of their politics, their intentions and their personal lives. Are such contradictions possible? – Yes they are. History is full of reactionary movements and reactionary ideas, their participants and proponents do not always deserve to be despised as reactionaries. For example, the Narodniks'* ideas about the peasant commune

---

*   The Narodniks were a social movement of 1860s–70s involved in social agitation against the Tsarist regime. Its common slogan was for the progressive intelligentsia to 'go to the people' to rediscover the positive values of the traditional peasant commune and to incite the peasants to revolt, a project viewed with suspicion by the peasants themselves. This social movement later produced Russia's first organised revolutionary party *Narodnaya Volya* (The People's Will), founded in 1879, which advocated conspiratorial terrorism as a chief means of struggle. In 1881, they succeeded in assassinating Alexander II.

were clearly reactionary, but the Narodnik movement included personalities like Andrei Zhelyabov and Sofia Perovskaya.*

This comparison is very flattering to Cubism, when in fact there is little more than a general analogy. It consists in the fact that even great revolutionaries can have reactionary ideas; they can even be present in Cubism, a rather harmless tendency from the vantage of the dominant order. This hardly means that representatives of these movements are evil geniuses, in need of exemplary punishment. Our critique is aimed against Cubism, not against individuals; it is a critique of ideas, a critique of art, and not a criminal trial.

This needs to be said because the rather common vulgarisation of Marxism in our country has led to a complete lack of understanding for the difference between historical and personal reaction. Some, for example, will construe the existence of reactionary and revolutionary romanticisms, referring to the political views of its various representatives. In fact, as is completely clear in the works of Marx and Lenin, Romanticism is a historically reactionary tendency, that is, a turn to the past. It expressed the opposition to bourgeois society of those classes perishing under the iron heel of the historically progressive capitalist mode of production. It hardly follows that the early nineteenth-century Romanticism was not a great page in the history of art. Nor does it follow that the spread of Romantic ideas among the peasantry and the petit bourgeoisie – such as the agrarian utopias of the Russian peasantry between 1861 and 1905 – reactionary in and of themselves, could not serve as a banner for the revolutionary upsurge of the masses. They deserve a thousand times more respect than the pitiful slogans of liberal sobriety and moderate progress. (Lenin points at this historical dialectic with the greatest possible precision). Finally, it hardly follows that the writers of the Romantic tendency did not include real defenders of the people, of the working majority. They were only mistaken in their choice of the path for struggle, in their understanding of historical life, and even these errors contained a great deal of truth.

As for their membership in definite political parties, an ordinary summary division into revolutionary and reactionary Romanticism does not yield much in the face of concrete history. Among the Romantics, we meet representatives of various political tendencies of their time: they included outright reactionar-

---

*   Andrei Zhelyabov (1851–81) and Sofia Perovskaya (1853–81) were both key members of Narodnaya Volya, and among the chief organisers of the assassination of Alexander II in 1881. Both were tried with their co-conspirators, known as Pervomartovtsy (the March First group) and executed.

ies, defending the interests of the landed aristocracy, feudal socialists, liberals and manifold representatives of vacillating petit-bourgeois spontaneity, as well as those with a revolutionary-democratic cast of mind.

On a personal level, it also makes sense to differentiate important nuances. There are more progressive views adopted by the dishonest or by simple philistines, and there are errors made in good faith that weigh down the work of people with great hearts and minds who deserved a better fate, so to speak. Authors usually labelled as reactionary Romantics include Friedrich Schlegel, Zhukovsky, Wordsworth and Carlyle. Giving them short shrift with the aforementioned accusatory formula of 'revolutionary Romanticism' would be humiliating especially to Marxism as a scientific theory.

None of this suspends the danger that reactionary ideas pose in all fields, even those far from practical interests, science, for example. Lenin says: 'For mistakes are made in this sphere too, and there are examples also in Russian literature of the obstinate advocacy of, for instance, reactionary philosophical views by people who are not conscious reactionaries'.[45] In short, calling something 'reactionary' is not just a simple insult and does not always imply personal guilt. This quality can be the historical tragedy of an exceptional individual or even an entire social tendency.

In defending Sismondi, the excellent democratic writer of the early nineteenth century, from accusations of being reactionary, Lenin writes:

> The wishes of the romanticists are very good (as are those of the Narodniks). Their recognition of the contradictions of capitalism places them above the blind optimists who deny the existence of these contradictions. And it is not because he wanted to return to the Middle Ages that he was regarded as a reactionary, but because, in his practical proposals, he 'compared the present with the past' and not with the future; because he 'demonstrated the eternal needs of society' by referring to 'ruins' and not by referring to the trends of modern development.[46]

Narodniks such as Ephrucy, for whom the terms 'petit bourgeois' or 'reactionary' only implied a desire to say something especially caustic, and meant no more than a simple polemic turn of phrase, did not understand the historical content of such appraisals.

---

45 Lenin 1965, p. 186.
46 Ibid.

> This mistake of Ephrucy's was due to the very same narrow interpretation
> of the terms 'petty-bourgeois' doctrine and 'reactionary' doctrine referred
> to above in connection with the first of these terms. They by no means
> imply the selfish greed of the small shopkeeper, or a desire to halt social
> development, to turn back: they simply indicate the given author's mis-
> taken point of view, his limited understanding and narrow outlook, which
> prompt the choice of means (for the achievement of very good aims) that
> cannot be effective in practice, and that can satisfy only the small produ-
> cer or be of service to the defenders of the past.[47]

Again, in the case of Romanticism from the first half of the nineteenth century,
the analogy with the aesthetics and the painting of the Cubists is flattering,
even though late Romanticism directly turns into decadence, so that there
is even some genetic connection here. Such comparisons will limp, however,
and to keep ours here from falling over, we should remember that despite all
the contradictions of its theory and practice, the Romantic school belongs
to the happy time of the bourgeois order's intellectual ascent. This is why its
retrograde aspects find a far greater level of compensation through the real
achievements of theoretical thinking and artistic practice, meaning that there
is a far greater distance between the historical and personal senses of the word
'reactionary'. All caveats aside, we should keep this distinction in mind with
regard to the modernism of our own time.

Again, we are dealing with a movement of ideas that is reactionary in the
historical sense of the word, even if it is quite possible that its proponents are
personally pure. However, the general level of historical being corresponding to
these ideas is lower in modernism, which is why the freedom of personal development, intellectual strength and talent is more limited, despite appearances
to the contrary, that is, with the subjective claims of the individual heightened
to an extreme.

There is nothing more unpleasant than passing judgement on artists, even
in those cases when these artists err. After all, an artist – if he isn't simply an
executor of commissions or a charlatan (as can be the case under any social
order) – puts a part of his own life into his work. It is all the more unpleasant to
pass judgement when we are dealing with people like Picasso, not just artists
but public figures, fighters for peace and democracy. But it would be empty
quibbling or dishonesty to circumvent the fact that Cubism is, in fact, Picasso,

---

47   Lenin 1960, p. 243.

Braque, and Léger ..., though clearly at a certain stage of their past practices and in the aureole which now surrounds that time.

The founders of Cubism had the best intentions, and their social honesty is beyond doubt. The crux of the matter, however, is that Cubism is a decisive juncture on bourgeois modern art's way from the realist legacy of previous centuries to the complete collapse of artistic culture into the ridiculous and dark jokes of abstract painting, Pop Art and other similar schools. That argument is impossible to counter.

Why do we call such art bourgeois? Are its representatives men of property or lackeys at least? Not necessarily. Often, the opposite is true. In our day, however, the less life demands that the inventors of new tendencies wear a crown of thorns, the more the proprietors of the bourgeois world pat them on the head. Even when sects like Cubism suffer persecution (the policies of Goebbels have been a frequent point of reference in this regard), it changes little in the matter. Anarchists were thrown into prison or executed by hanging, yet anarchism is still the bourgeois character turned inside out, to use Lenin's expression. There are plenty of instances in history when precisely the boldest protest against the dominant forms of life leads in the opposite direction, to its affirmation. Such cases obviously present any honest Don Quixote with a huge personal drama.

This is the sense in which Cubism is bourgeois, along with the other aesthetic tendencies in the course of which it was born and carried out its ostensible feats, opening the doors for a cavalcade of even more extremist schools. Let us see what was so special about its position.

The Revolt against Things

Since we are dealing with artists and not political activists or creators of philosophical systems, let us try to take a more positive approach. To do so, we might consider the historical circumstances from which Cubism's arcane symbols emerged. History may not suspend our judgement of facts, but it can still soften our verdict.

Our century's first decade was a time of the 'sweet life', as a senile Europe grew fat as a parasite feeding on the rest of the world. This was an epoch of decay and decline for the bourgeois nations, a classical age of parliamentary windbaggery and yellow socialism, a strange calm before the storm already rising among the gigantic, heavily armed imperialist powers, with colonial conflicts and the first breaking rays of revolution in the East. Few anticipated the coming of the terrible catastrophe that would drench Europe in blood, throwing it far back into savagery and hunger. Still, there was an air of approaching death, a tense expectation of something about to happen. Mistrust of well-fed prosperity could be felt everywhere: in the crisis of science, in Sorel's revolutionary phrases on *l'action directe*, 'direct action', and in the bold grimaces of the new French painting that so astonished the world.

These grimaces contained it all – scorn for the official good looks of 'cultivated capitalism', a sense of dread in the face of civilisation's mechanical forces tormenting the human eye and ear, the body and the soul, and, finally, a horrible revulsion at life itself. The new painting seems to tell the rest of the world: 'Your vile civilisation makes us want to get down on all fours like animals amidst the skyscrapers, the glinting showcases, and the roaring cars. We will rain down the ugliness of all ages, we will unleash primal instincts of destruction, we will trample your logic and your rationality underfoot and throw all your warmth to the wind!'

Yes, Cubism is a demonic protest against the kitschy degradation of customary forms that once gave a political and moral shape to human life, a life of passions. The living eye now sees a disgustingly familiar mask; it beholds a boring, grey world that already took shape in the nineteenth century, the world of the petit bourgeois in coat tails, in the face of which an artist's brush is powerless, to use Herzen's expression. And now, the artist takes his revenge on such a picture of the world. He does so by creating monstrous deformations of visible things, turning the world into a ruin, a pile of rubble of a fossilised culture; meting out brutal punishment to everything warm, hypocritically beautiful, and hypocritically alive, he exults over this world in his mind.

Though the artists themselves may not always be aware of it, this is the actual inner meaning of the revolution that the apologists of the new painting consider an art-historical turning point. In a way, it really is a turning point – from positive aesthetic values to negative ones, from a beauty poisoned by the venom of a dying world to an ugliness in which artistic thinking now seeks salvation. Such are these ghastly women, cut to pieces by parts of straight lines; composed of different geometrical figures, with crudely emphasised sexual traits, they are a slap in the face of the Louvre. The paintings of the Cubists were made in a state that could be expressed in Braque's words: 'It looks like you're drinking boiling kerosene'.*

---

*   Lifshitz slightly transforms Braque's comment, made at the Demoiselles d'Avignon. In most English-language sources, it reads: 'It's as if you wanted us to eat tow and drink kerosene in order to spit fire'. Cited in Everdell 1997, p. 248.

In his typically paradoxical style, the poet Apollinaire called this feeling 'lyricism'. The publishers of the journal *Espirit nouveau* Ozenfant and Jeanneret would also later write about the 'lyrical' tone of the new movement. In their famous book *La peinture modern*, they supply a short definition of the Cubist aesthetic:

> Its theoretical import could be summed up as follows: Cubism considers the painting as an object creating lyricism, and this lyricism is this object's only goal. The painter is permitted all liberties, on the condition that he evoke this lyricism. The Cubist sees that the painting has nothing to do with nature, and he uses forms and colours not for their imitative power, but for their plastical value.[48]

Such annotations to diametrically opposed phenomena are a typical example of the newly discovered method of provocative mystification so typical of the Cubists, the Dadaists and other radical movements. The truth is that painting from the time of 'boiling kerosene' takes lyricism to its extreme and turns it inside out. This is the general tendency of a dying art; it consciously strives to provoke nausea and revulsion toward everything once deemed beautiful in life, and in the end, toward life itself as the basis of beauty and poetry.

Oppressed by the petrified order of social relations, bereft of its customary self-activity and freedom, the artist's consciousness looks for a way out through a purely inner triumph over the vulgarity of its surroundings. Instead of fighting to change the real forms of life's ongoing process, he breaks the forms in which it is perceived. In that sense, Apollinaire's lyricism is not merely a bold joke or a mystification; no, it is a mystery, a description of how the 'completely new art' emancipates consciousness from its slavery to the material world, liberating it through a purely subjective, inner victory over evil.

If the reader says that such a revolt against things is a sure sign of one's own powerlessness, the sigh of the oppressed creature, as Marx put it, he will be drawing the right conclusion. Yet for some reason, the thinking of many people with no lack of talent went precisely in this direction. By the late nineteenth and early twentieth century, the creators of 'the completely new art' were overcome by a feeling of tedious stuffiness and a thirst to break everything to the point of total negation, to absolute Nothingness (as Mallarmé almost literally put it in one of his poems). Life – a life that channels the

---

48   Ozenfant and Jeanneret 1925, p. 82.

flow of human material, its plans and orders unknown to the blind masses, a life sometimes poor and sometimes rich but always lacking inner meaning – becomes unbearable for the artist. The more life's iron assembly line besets him, the more he thirsts for freedom or at least an outlet, never suspecting that such outlets have a certain spontaneous utility from the vantage of the dominant bourgeois order that he so despises.

Such an outlet is to be found in the *espirit nouveau*'s discovery of ways to break free from the chains of necessity through an illusory victory over the material world. 'As long as art does not free itself from the object, it condemns itself to slavery'.[49]

Braque expressed this quixotic idealism even more vividly:

> There is no reason to imitate things that are in fact transitory and constantly changing, though we mistakenly take them for something unchanging. Things do not exist for themselves. They only exist through us.[50]

The complete emancipation from the power of objects is Cubism's main historical achievement, according to its earliest theoreticians Gleizes and Metzinger:

> For the partial liberties conquered by Courbet, Manet, Cézanne, and the Impressionists, Cubism substitutes an indefinite liberty. Henceforth objective knowledge at last regarded as chimerical, and all that one crowd understands by natural form proven to be convention, the painter will know no other laws than those of Taste.[51]

It is a paradox but also completely natural that once the artist's taste detaches fully from any objective content and dominates him completely, this unconditional pure taste takes on a purely negative value. The entire matter runs down to getting rid of what was once known as taste in older times, inseparable from the commonplace existence of the philistine crowd in the eyes of the Cubist artists. According to Gleizes and Metzinger, the artist's mission, his cherished goal is to free himself and others from the 'banal appearance' of things, yet the only way he has of pleasing the crowd is to restore the banal appearances of the surrounding world.[52]

------

49   Cited in Gantefährer-Trier 2004, p. 54.

50   Hess 1956, p. 54.

51   Gleizes and Metzinger 1992, p. 195.

52   Gleizes and Metzinger 1992, p. 195, n. 53.

An even greater paradox is the belief in the magical role of so-called deformation in the Cubist aesthetic. Painting deals with the visible side of the surrounding world. The relation between the artist's eye and the face of the things he depicts has a historical character, however; it changes from epoch to epoch. For several centuries, the artist has lived in constant conflict with the outer appearances of the objects surrounding him. His aesthetic conscience cannot accept the world of vulgarity and prose, and prohibits him from justifying such a life by depicting it. The artist's eye has found many different solutions to this painful conflict. This is why he is an artist, a visual being, and it is not his fault that this struggle is hopeless for as long as art only has its own means at its disposal. At the end of the bourgeois era, the artist concludes that these possibilities have exhausted themselves. He no longer wants to hide his defeat and rejects all further compromises; he tries to free himself from the derivative forms that justify the old world's vulgarity.

Even today, this position is completely understandable. Its irreconcilable honesty deserves the highest praise. On the other hand, it can give rise to a new type of reconciliation with the rejected world of banal forms. Intransigence is a great thing, but it can be exaggerated, for example, to the point of negating the rules of orthography or street traffic. Will this illusory freedom ever be anything but an empty, feeble pose? Philistines strictly adhere to the rules, afraid to break them no matter what; but there is another kind of philistine who constantly breaks the rules, trying to prove to himself and others that he is above philistinism as such.

Just as an anarchist is a liberal with a bomb, so the artist-destroyer wrecks traditional pictorial forms to leave behind life's actual revolutionary content 'for other, higher spheres', to use Berdyayev's expression, or to put it differently, into emptiness. He begins to play games, or, in the words of the same author, to pull 'the demonic grimaces of the shackled spirits of nature'. Yet no matter how hard he tries to jump out of his own skin, he would rather soothe his demons than try to solve the conflict so deadly to art. Because his battle against appearances is the policy of an ostrich hiding his head in the sand, the rage of a child, taking out its sense of injury on an innocent object, simple hysteria. It could be that this sad experience is something art requires before the transition to a new social content can clearly bring the old forms back to life, divesting them of their temporary sluggishness, and thus allowing artistic culture to develop further. In expectation of this turn, our thinking grows more certain; even the most inventive taste will not go far if it assumes the negation of realistic images. The negative charge of the 'completely new art' comes down to a few very simple, crude formulas. Two or three generations of modernists really exhausted them to the full – all that is left are variations, made with commercial intent. Wherever matters run down to simple inventiveness, that is, to new combinations of formal elements given in advance, machines do a better job than people. The depiction of the real world is a different matter altogether. This is the only source of positive, synthetic (in the Kantian sense) gains that add something to the already existing stock of idioms and images. Everything else has a more or less spectral character and exists through negative reflection, repulsion, irony, and paraphrase.

In art, and especially in painting, these moments can play no more than a subordinate role. Their emancipation as independent forces is a dangerous game. At first, it creates a feverish excitation and pulls you into the nocturnal realm of false dreams. But in broad daylight all that remains is the bitterness of lost illusions. This path has already been taken, and the poisonous swamp-flowers on its side have withered; it's time to take the beaten track.

Of course, every field has its craftsmen and its sell-outs. When realism has society's protection, they are realists. When the bread is buttered on the other side, they are the first to see that the times are changing. All kinds of imitation, 'Ersatz' or mimicry are especially widespread in our day because the formal elements of culture are so easily attainable, and for a host of other reasons. This is not our concern here, however. Rather, we are dealing with the content of the matter, which has a significance of its own.

From this vantage, 'mimesis', that is, the depiction of reality, is primary, principal and essential to art. Everything else is derivative, including the negative freedom of style breaking the visible image of things. This is real museum art with a minus sign, since it has no power source of its own. It is only on the basis of realism that there is an endless possibility for new work, even in the field of form, just as endless and inexhaustible as life in its development, and its manifold reflections in the invaluable mirror of our eye.

If it doesn't work out so quickly or easily, should we blame those old forms of art connected to the human eye's interest in the visible side of things? The flowering of art is the task of an entire historical period and not a wonder cure for all illnesses; no one can make those kinds of promises. If we are dealing with a weak work painted in the spirit of the realist tradition, we can still ask whether its content is really that advanced and new, or if it is in fact just a shop sign. There is still some hope here – the possibility for concrete verification. Still, we probably know that the revolution against the real semblance of things declared by Cubism is no more than a semblance of revolution, one of the most ridiculous and lamentable forms of self-deception that people could invent under the difficult circumstances of our century. That the circumstances of our century have not been easy for artists lies beyond any doubt.

Fusion with Objects as an Ideal

Cubism drew mountains of fanciful conceptualisations and commonplaces in its wake, and they all require strict verification. One often hears: 'I like this still-life, even if it's made up of fragments of objects. It's decorative, it's beautiful, and I don't care about the rest!' We know how easily the consumer submits to herd instincts when prompted to destroy something or another and especially when flattered as capable of unconditional inner freedom from all 'canons' and 'norms'. He has heard that educated people have to understand Cubism, so he tries to force the strange impression made by this still life to fit the frame of a taste accustomed to admiring pretty things.

As for the Cubist himself, there is nothing more insulting than such a verdict. If his painting retains an element of decorativeness, even elegance (as one could easily find, for example, in Picasso's oval still lifes of 1912), all of this is a remnant of simple healthy sensibility within the artist, unsuccessfully muted by the imaginative system he has otherwise adopted.

Is this really what it's all about? Decorativeness and beauty are easier to find in ordinary painting that doesn't break objects into tiny pieces, that is, outside of Cubism, while here, obviously, the goal of art lay elsewhere. It is enough to remember the honest indignation of the Cubist theoreticians Gleizes and Metzinger at the attempt to derive 'the spirit of the new painters' from decorative preoccupations. 'Enough decorative painting and painterly decoration, enough confusion and ambiguousness'. Any merits a painting might have – claimed the authors of *Du cubisme* (1912) – were very much its own. It expresses a certain conception of the world, which the artist conveys through visual signs, nothing more. 'Cubism', says one of this movement's participants, Juan Gris, 'is simply a new means of grasping things'.[53]

Thus, in the opinion of the Cubists themselves, paintings are philosophical treatises of a sort, expounded on canvas through paint and lines. This already comes closer to the truth. However, such interpretations of Cubism's mysteries generated new heaps of rhetoric, now more scholarly though possibly even more pitiful than the prejudices of the philistine. The apologists for Cubism will see who knows what kind of philosophical content in these strange hieroglyphs. Cézanne's art already seemed to contain 'a critique of the theory of knowledge, written in paint' to one of his commentators.[54] It is not surprising

---

53   Kahnweiler 1946, p. 289.

54   Novotny 1932, p. 278.

that people find the ideas of Plato, Kant, or Hegel reflected in Cubism. When a scholarly author, writing in any language, wants to express a special level of profundity inherent to his object, he will use the German word *Weltanschauung*, worldview. One example can be found in Christopher Gray, the author of an extensive study of Cubist aesthetics. To him, the coup carried out in the painting of Picasso and Braque heralds the onset of a new era and a new worldview.[55]

One could cite many similarly enthusiastic accolades on Cubism's profundity, but it would be vacuous and naïve to place any belief in these loud words. Distorted beyond recognition, the image of the outer world in the paintings of the Cubists bears no relation to any rational philosophy, even that of an idealist ilk. If we are talking about parallels to the development of theory, we can merely mention modern philosophical tendencies occupied with arbitrary deformations of the world and the production of fantastic symbols, visions, prophecies, just like the factory of the 'completely new art'. In a word, we will only be dealing with mystical constructs clothed in the uniform of philosophical terms, with modern mythmaking. From this point of view, Cubism really does present an important milestone, since its example illuminates some aspects of a certain view of the world.

In terms of the formal constellation of ideas, Plekhanov's analysis comes close to the truth. In its initial position, the philosophy of Cubism appears as an extremely superficial subjective idealism, as assimilated by people like Braque, a Norman farmer's son and hardly a professor of philosophy, in the table talk of the early twentieth century, when it was all the rage. The negation of 'naïve realism' based on the indications of our senses, the transferral of things from the outer world into ourselves, into our imaginations, is no slip of the tongue, but the first thesis of Cubist aesthetics, which, in fact, is what they wanted to express on canvas. The worldview of the Fauves (Matisse, Vlaminck, Derain and others) was more concerned with the moral side; it presents a doctrine of active Nietzschean freedom in life. Cubism, on the other hand, is characterised by its incursions into the field of the theory of knowledge.

It sees the greatest danger in the visual perception of the real world. If the world is bad, it is vision that is to blame for reproducing it to us again and again. In its assumption that visual perception gives us images of the real world, the old painting attempted to convey these images with the greatest possible fidelity and fullness. The modernist schools reach for exactly the opposite result: all their discoveries are a 'sum of destructions' aimed against the perception of

---

55   Gray 1953, p. 3.

the ordinary person. Things-in-themselves do not exist or are unknowable to us; truth consists in the artist's subjective experience. Properly speaking, this false axiom was already found by the predecessors of the Cubists, who now only had to make the next step: from the simple negation of 'naïve realism' to the total rejection of vision as the basis of painting.

To Cubist aesthetics, the principle source of evil is to be found in the principle of the outer world's reflection in our eye and on our retina. In the end, all we see are appearances; the semblance between visual images and reality is based on illusions, that is, on deception, *trompe l'oeil*. The literature of Cubism has had much to say about this pitiful, hypocritical, deceitful illusion poisoning contemporary humanity, which now serves as a scapegoat for all of bourgeois civilisation's sins. One could say that Picasso and Braque deserve a sad respect for the consistency with which they were able to take this strange logic to the point of absurdity, understandable only as a rhapsody of savage despair. Closing your eyes not to see the dragon won't save you or anyone else.

Living in Paris in 1904, Picasso became close with such doomsday prophets as Apollinaire, Jacob, and Salmon, poets 'boundlessly worshipping strength and action, the anarchism of thought, and the revolt against reason'.[56] These admirers of Rimbaud and Mallarmé were seekers of pure form. They stood at Cubism's cradle, though they weren't the ones who invented it. 'When we invented cubism', says Picasso, 'we had no intention of inventing cubism but simply of expressing what was in us. Nobody drew up a program of action, and though our friends the poets followed our efforts attentively, they never dictated to us'.[57] Other than Braque (considered the father of Cubism along with Picasso), the emerging trend attracted artists like Fernand Léger, Robert Delaunay, Juan Gris, Henri Le Fauconnier, and others.

The word 'Cubism' seems to have first appeared in 1908. Legend has it that Matisse said that Braque's painting *Houses at l'Estaque* reminded him of cubes. In the same year, art critic Louis Vauxcelles noted that Braque's painting showed nothing but cubes in the end. Hence, so the claim, the name of a new school was born, even if it initially was intended as mockery.[58]

One cannot say that this name was a matter of pure contingency, since the artists who joined forces in the struggle against the old aesthetic under the banner of Picasso and Braque really did like to distort soft surfaces through geo-

---

56   Klemperer 1957, p. 81.

57   Zervos and Picasso 1968, p. 51.

58   Golding 1959, pp. 20–1, 26.

metrical faceting reminiscent of cubes. Examples of this manner of painting include Picasso's *Portrait of Fernando, Harlequin's Family*, and *Seated Woman* (1908), as well as Le Fauconnier's *Abundance* (1910), Metzinger's *Woman with a Coffee Pot* (1911), Gleizes's *Portrait of Jacques Nayral* (1912) and others. However, the term 'Cubism' is too narrow to encompass the entire programme of this direction, as founded in the spring of 1907.

The group of artists in their old house on Rue Ravignan in Montmartre dreamed of something more – with the wonders they worked, they wanted to renew the earth and the heavens. As for the cubes, their appearance in the first, so-called 'analytical' period of Cubism (1907–12) was only the first step in the dissolution of form. Further on, these cubes fell apart into facets, anatomic slices, or simply body parts.

There have been attempts in art theory to justify this experiment through the artist's desire to strengthen the role of volume in painting. This view has its source in the Cubists' eloquent phrases on 'the study of the structure of primary volumes', on the perception of space through kinetic and tactile sensations, etc. Such verbal hypnosis often accompanies the emergence of a new sect. We should note that for reasons it is impossible to detail here, all modernist trends and schools appear as antitheses to their closest predecessors. Hence the special formal characteristics of Cubism, as mysterious as they may be from the vantage of an uninitiated eye. They are the 'sum of destructions'.

At first, the task of modern painting consisted in the negation of relief and light-dark modelling. This feature of real visual perception seemed like nothing but a spectre of academic mannerism, chiaroscuro subjected to anathema. Everything was flooded with a more or less regular mass of light. At the next stage, light separates out as a special force of nature in post-Impressionism and demands the transition to flatness. In the work of the Fauves, flat painting as the antithesis of modelled relief already reaches its fullest development. Now it is time for the next negation, so that flatness and surface are called into doubt. In a new antithesis, they are replaced by the spectre of volume.

Of course, the essence of the matter runs down to more than a simple to-and-fro of the pendulum. A return to the academic relief was the last thing on the new generation's mind. On the contrary, Matisse's painting seemed unacceptable precisely because it had not yet fully lost its link with the flatness of old painting, in turn connected to the modelling of real forms, that is, to the depiction of the world as it appears to our eye. The 'primary volumes' of the Cubists are a further step on the way to a non-pictorial art.

There are many contradictions in Cubism's literary documents, no fewer than in holy scripture, but one cannot fail to acknowledge that the greatest authorities of this school decisively rejected the aesthetics of volume. Thus,

Gleizes and Metzinger begin their book by affirming that 'the understanding of volumes' does not exhaust their movement, 'striving to an integral realisation of painting'. In one of his theoretical statements, Picasso does not accept the theory of formal experimentation as a transitional stage to a future art that will be able to use the Cubist's laboratory experiments in the study of 'primary volumes' (in a conversation with Marius de Zayas, published in the journal *The Arts*, 26 May 1923). In another statement (a letter to the editors of the journal *Ogonek*), he makes light of his own epigones and their mania for volume. They wanted to make Cubism into something like a cult of the body. 'And so then we saw the sickly swell with importance. They got it into their heads that building everything in cubes makes them strong and powerful'.[59]

Actually, in Cubism as such, that is, in its original version according to Picasso and Braque, there was no emphasis on volume in the sense of the usual perception of massive forms. Looking at Cubist painting, it comes to mind that fractures are more important than mass. The authors of many articles and books have laboured to decipher these mysterious figures. One cannot say that all of this is a waste of paper. But still, well-meaning attempts to pretend that Cubist paintings are analytical etudes in stereometry necessary to strengthen the volumetric basis of a painting destabilised by impressionism are threepenny claptrap.

Whoever wants to attain a proficiency in depicting real volumetric bodies will not find anything of use in these roughly daubed edges of cubes or cylinders (as in Léger), mixed up with remainders of human faces, arms, and legs. Cubism never set itself the task of depicting real volumes, but had another goal entirely.

This is why the differentiation of the Cubists from their closest predecessors proceeded along other lines. As the most consistent seekers of 'modernity', the innovators of Rue Ravignon saw the flat painting of Matisse as something outdated since it was still too closely linked to visual sensation. It is true that the Fauves already fought against the *pittoresque* but they only did so through the simplification of contours while dreaming of style. 'And since they only address the outer appearance of objects, the artist can only provide an impression for the sense of vision'.[60] The Cubists' goal consisted in ending painting's shameful dependency on vision once and for all. The war against vision, taken to its utmost victory – that was Cubism's battle cry.

---

59   Picasso 1926.
60   Gleizes 1920, p. 18.

Painting, excluding vision if possible, that was the essence of 'volumetric' or 'stereometric' Cubism. Vision gives us a picture of the world in perspective. This is why perspective is one of the 'new spirit's' most dangerous enemies. It flatters the eye with a deceptive illusion of depth and the reduction of figures through foreshortening, but all of this smells like the temptation of the visible world. 'The eye quickly interests the mind in its errors'.[61]

The Cubist must be as faultless as a puritan. No wonder André Salmon compared the geometrical mysticism of his friends with the religion of the Huguenots. After Picasso and Braque, there really did appear a sect of the pure, the so-called Purists, who saw themselves as even more consistent proponents of the geometrical method and enemies of any compromise with the multiplicity of life and the charms of its visible images.

This also explains why much modernist painting gravitates to the reverse perspective, incomprehensible as it is to the naïve eye. To end the 'deceit of vision', Picasso of the Cubist period dumps the entire inventory of his painting onto the viewer. He does not move from visual flatness to depth, but from a dark, opaque background to different parts of his presentation of forms. Léger once said that the paradigm of such constructions is the shop display, so arranged that the exhibited commodity is visible to the observer from all sides.

The new sect felt that its system was more scrupulous than the depictions in perspective found in ordinary painting. The Cubist visionaries assured themselves and others that this system would finally bring humanity not a spectre or a deceptive semblance, but the object as such. 'Respect the object', says Picasso. It was Cubism's dream to convince the world that the new painting does not depict the object but simply presents it to the viewer. One should create new, self-sufficient objects, 'object-paintings', *peinture-objet* instead of 'nature-objects', *nature-objet*, pictured on canvas through illusions of perspective.

Now we see why there was such a need for Cubism, precisely. In the gibberish of the 'new spirit', the cube is a symbol for forms that exist beyond the limits of deceptive appearance. That, in fact, is pure form, reality 'in itself', which our opponents of hypocrisy wanted to catch in its natural shape before it was wrapped in the radiant veils of *maya*. Leave the enjoyment of this radiant veil to the Impressionists. The elusive multiplicity of outer appearance hides the most important thing. What might that be? Volume? In the end, it isn't even volume. 'For us lines, surfaces, and volumes are only modifications of the notion of fullness'.[62]

---

61   Gleizes and Metzinger 1968, p. 213.
62   Ibid.

Only this mysterious 'plenitude', an abstract expression of that which is not the object's outer appearance, this is all that matters. One should not think that the Cubist artist is trying to penetrate into the objective construction of things, to depict them in anatomic vivisection, or to create an explicit model of their microstructure, and so on. Though its obsequious defenders might say otherwise, Cubism never pursued such scientific-popular goals. No, all we are dealing with is a negative abstraction of objective existence, of that which is not appearance. To escape the dubious world to the object as such – that is the goal. 'You don't simply want to depict objects. You need to penetrate them', says Braque, 'you yourself need to become a thing'.[63]

Thus, we have the painting's transformation into an object, an 'integral realisation of painting' effecting the final removal of the painful disharmony between the artist and the world of things. The task is quite difficult, more difficult than for a grownup to become a child or for someone intelligent to act the fool, for someone educated to believe in miracles. The art of Cubism raises the question of consciousness's rejection of itself, of humanity's return to the world of things.

This is why Cubism means the end of art in the proper sense of the word, the refusal to depict life. The pictures of this school can only be understood as visualised theses of a modern idealism long-since unaccustomed to stringent thinking and saturated with mythmaking. It is hard to find an effort stranger than the attempt to present not a depiction of an object on canvas, but the object itself. This is highly reminiscent of Baron Munchhausen's fox who jumped out of its own skin. For the mystics of the twentieth century, however, such fantasies are child's play.

There is nothing more widespread in contemporary bourgeois philosophy than the myth of the destruction of the border between the subjective and the objective thanks to the discoveries of new physics and the development of the newest, non-pictorial art. Cockamamie confabulations are repeated a thousand fold, as if the difference between an object and its reflection in subjective perception had ceased to exist. Cubism and the ensuing tendencies of bourgeois art were all completely based on an imaginary identity of a picture and its object in self-sufficient 'pure' painting, *peinture pure*. The new aesthetic either takes a stand against outer reality, declaring it to be the artist's subjective illusion, or against the subject, demanding that art should not reflect life but leave the bounds of human consciousness to make pieces of life itself.

---

63   Hess 1956, p. 54.

That is the second thesis of Cubism's aesthetic. Developed to an extreme, subjectivity now turns against itself. The declarative disqualification of the outer world as non-existent turns into a struggle against the subject itself as the opponent's last redoubt. A simple rejection of excess intelligence in favour of the active life of the subject bathing in its most immediate sensations, this exit from the crisis of tired decadence opened by the Fauves did not satisfy the Cubists. They were right to note that the cult of sensation and savage volition are an even more refined kind of intellectual weakness than the Hamletism of the nineteenth century. So what yesterday looked like the last word of the 'new spirit' – a victorious dance of life, free from all the rules regulating a crowd of slaves – now seems backward. What Matisse and his friends rejected so energetically – knowledge, pure knowledge – now comes to the fore in the role of an ideal against deceptive, banal appearances.

Here, there is a full analogy between the complex entanglements of modernist reflection in art and the development of modernism in bourgeois philosophy, because philosophy, expounded *ex cathedra*, philosophy in its own repertoire also turns against psychological subjectivity as if it were the last ancient scrap of Adam in us. In the first years of our century, new schools of bourgeois philosophy announced their departure beyond sensation into a neutral world of 'events' or 'acts', they pride themselves on their false 'objectivity', and turn to the field of pure 'description', hallucinating in logical forms and mathematics.

It would be naïve to take these words at face value. Aside from the element of mystification inherent to even the most scientific systems, however, there is no doubt that the idealist fashion of recent decades has fostered not only an extreme subjectivism, but also a no less extreme self-denial of subjectivity up to and including the ideal of the Cubists, that is, to the surprising formula 'you yourself need to become a thing'. It seems that modern bourgeois thought is so attracted to these philosophical positions precisely because they are extreme.

The old idealism was distinct in its desires to raise the spirit above the dirt of matter. The new idealism wants to draw a mystical accord from spiritless materiality, devoid of any relation to the human world.[64] This shows that all

---

64   When Matisse was turning away from Fauvism to further transformation of visible reality,
      Ardengo Soffici already wrote: 'Can't one cast a glance at nature with new, as if non-human
      eyes? To somehow pierce the veil of the practical relation between subject and object?' (cf.
      Lunacharsky 1941).

the ideal motifs of the previous civilisation have exhausted themselves – it is time to solve life's question on the grounds of life itself, in its irresistibly real historical conditions. Yet if the outer side of old clothes are all worn out, there is always still the seamy side.

In the sphere of bourgeois ideology on the whole, the magnetic needle tends away from positive values to negative ones, while the old morality looks for support not in convincing arguments, but in irrational affirmations of power. Much in the same way, contemporary idealism plays at the complete negation of the spirit in the name of things. It often seems like a more decisive opponent of empty ideals, a more sober appreciator of facts, a more outspoken voice of modern science and technology than even the adherents of materialism themselves. To defend the ideals of classical art, 'the tradition of the Renaissance' in our age of atomic physics and parapsychology – how unmodern!

Admirers of the revolt against the 'traditions of the Renaissance' will be angry at us, of course. There is little they can offer up against the accuracy of the facts above, but they will try to push them aside as an attempt to 'humiliate' famous people that they are in the habit of worshipping. So let us say once again that this is not our intention. Those who took this fateful turn in the history of art are victims of a blind craze, emerging from the conditions of the twentieth century, rather than evil geniuses corrupting the world.

As for the accusation of wanting to humiliate anyone, we should remember an old rule. People eagerly turn to moral indignation when they have run out of weightier arguments. Of course, one could say that immediate feeling is more important than logic. Yet if you understand with some sixth sense that Cubism is a great turn in art, why even intellectualise at all? All the while, the proponents of the 'completely new art' do not simply intellectualise about its merits, but often themselves say that it is painting based on knowledge, on thought, and not on feeling. 'I understood', Picasso says, 'that painting has a self-sufficient value, independent of any real depiction of its object. I asked myself wouldn't it be better to depict things as they are known rather than as they are seen'. Braque expresses himself in no less definite terms: 'The senses deform, the mind forms. There is no certainty except in what the mind conceives'.[65]

If this is so, Cubism is open to an analysis from the vantage of rational thinking. Then again, in truth, all talk of the 'rationality' of such art is based on an ambiguous use of the term. Cubism's ideal is hardly knowledge, but rather ignorance and the forgetting of all the actual knowledge gained in the course of

---

65   Braque 1992, p. 210.

history, forgetting with the goal of returning to the dark abstractions from the time of Egyptian soothsayers or the scholastics of the early Middle Ages. Here, the 'rational' means the irrational, but in the shape of dead order, blind dogma, and the destruction of knowledge – including the knowledge of perspective, anatomy, and chiaroscuro developed by world culture from the Renaissance to the nineteenth century.

The Evolution of Cubism

So, what was it that emerged in painting on the basis of an aesthetic hostile to the eye? By raising volume to a function of plasticity, Cubism falsely excludes subjective vision; the 'new spirit's' second step is a negation of the first. We are told that this is, in fact, the famous 'realisation' of the subject that Cézanne wanted so passionately but couldn't attain.

You cannot exclude vision, however, if you want to see anything at all, just as you cannot jump out of your own skin. Thus, the Cubists had to invent different magical means to reach this crazy goal. Cubes or prisms depicted on canvas are not real volumetric figures, after all. They only seem as such to us thanks to perspective and chiaroscuro, which the artist uses to force their surfaces to recede into the painting's depths. That means that there is no real liberation from visual illusion. This is why Picasso and Braque begin to look for other means as early as 1908–9.

One of the former Cubists, André Lhote, describes the point of departure for their evolution as follows:

> The paintings are composed of simple planes and broad facets, like those of crystals, and what's more, the peaks and bases of these facets fade out unexpectedly. These subtle refractions of geometrical forms, passages, are Cubism's first and most important discovery. They already existed in Cézanne, who already contains everything in the drawing-together of value and local light in the finest erasure of contours. But it was only Cubism that gave this confluence its particular and primary meaning. The 'passage' is the free and musical expression of atmospheric light that dissolves objects in those places and turns the painting in an integral formation of parts inseparably fused to one another: a closed figure made up of open figures.

In 1909 the number of planes and refractions grows.

> Even the roundest and smoothest forms like for example a vase or a
> hand are subject to the caprice of lighting and fall apart into previously
> unfamiliar facets; surfaces overcome with the agitation of some silky
> vibration.[66]

This is the peak of so-called analytical Cubism, depicted in the most flattering
terms, as the reader can see. But we should not be surprised when we look at
what these eloquent phrases describe and compare them to the original. André
Lhote's generous eloquence presents us with yet another example of verbal
hypnosis. Is his enthusiasm sincere? No, nobody could be so naïve. Is it simply
a ruse? No, that isn't it either. It's a matter of principle, an honest mystification,
doublethink – a special kind of modern consciousness when legends are made
on purpose and in the heat of conviction. In a word, 'that's how it has to be'.*

Still, let us forge ahead. Analytical Cubism is followed by 'the Cubism of
representations'. By 1910, a house pictured on canvas no longer resembles the
image of a specific house, 'seen by the eyes of an ordinary person in frontal
projection'. The house is first 'analysed'; then it is spread out into different
aspects at the same time, in different 'forms of representation'.

What follows is another portion of verbal hypnosis:

> The ordinary structure of perspective has been toppled. We see part of
> one and the same object, for example a vase with fruit, from below,
> another part in profile, a third from yet another side. All of this fuses
> as surfaces that collide with a crash on the picture-plane, falling next to
> another, blocking or penetrating one another.

In Lhote's opinion, Cézanne's still lifes already anticipated this revolution,
but in the Cubists, it takes on a more decisive character. 'Since the days of
Impressionism, painting has in the best case been one arrangement that could
already be turned into something different. The Cubist painting is an irresolv-
able blending and interpenetration of objects between one another and with
the surface of the painting'.[67]

If we discard the floridity of its eloquence, the inner meaning of this mysterious procedure turns out to lie in the following. The artist's goal, we should

---

66   Lhote 1956, pp. 128–30.

*   This colloquial saying refers to the insincere obedience so widespread during Stalin's
      dictatorship.

67   Hess 1956, p. 59.

not forget, is to transform the image into an independent thing, thus overcoming his own weakness and the ulcer of consciousness, becoming a thing himself. Signs of volume are not enough for this purpose. Having only just been born on canvas, they now cede their place to other hieroglyphs. To do away with the semblance of real volumes, these remainders of visual illusion, the false mediator between us and the mysterious realm of essences, it is necessary to strip the real body of its characteristic trait of contiguity. Hence, these 'refractions'. One of Cubism's captains, Robert Delaunay, says: 'Refraction, as the term itself shows, destroys contiguity'.[68]

The negation of the contiguity of independent bodies through the fragmentation of their real images turns the painting into a hash of chunks, and consequently removes it from vision, bringing it closer to independent objectivity, much like a *macédoine* or a mixture of vegetables cut into small pieces is more of an object than the sum of those vegetables lying separately and only unified by our eye. In other words, refraction is a tool for 'integral realisation'. A similar role falls to the 'passages' through which different bodies blend into one mass on the canvas.

The painting's materiality grows before our eyes, through a consistent subtraction of characteristics necessary to recognise real things. Here, the technique of painting, transformed into a dense, opaque environment, is no longer capable of serving as a glass letting through visual illusions. The element of semblance, reflection, that is, consciousness recedes; as a consequence, the element of genuine materiality grows, which is what painting wanted to prove in the first place.

By 1910, Cubism finally breaks with perspective. In place of an object, pictured from a certain angle, the artist strives to transfer its traces onto the canvas as a geometrical placement of points, a flat imprint, and that, moreover, from different sides at once. In this way, the picture turns into a collection of different aspects of form, cut up into little pieces. This leads to the emergence of so-called Simultaneism or the simultaneous depictions of the object's different sides that we cannot see at one and the same time.

This provided an occasion for the utterance of so many loud and empty phrases on the fourth dimension, that is, time. The crux of the matter, however, is that Cubism leads a struggle against visual perception, which, in its view, is a false obstacle between the artist and the thing-in-itself. 'Simultaneism' was an

---

68   Hess 1956, p. 67.

attempt to reach this mysterious essence, the thing-in-itself, through the help of a multitude of aspects, since one single point of view only yields a deceptive semblance.

The Cubists ask that one not mistake their voyage into the field of time with the 'street noise' of Futurism in the spirit of Carrà and Boccioni, who would pile up chaotic mixtures of houses, people, buses, and cars motivated by the dynamic life and the need to introduce a 'fourth dimension'. Cubism's task does not run down to provoking elation or fear at the big city's roar. It deems such experiments too pictorial and psychological. It is fully absorbed with its own dark task, one that follows logically from the development of previous systems, and that is the 'integral realisation' of painting and human consciousness at large. Back to unthinking matter! – that is the final goal of its strategy, which it also pursues in its incursions into the realm of time.

Strictly speaking, movement itself is something beyond the limits of pure materiality. This is why dynamism is not always good for Cubism. It is only a means for destroying the contiguity of real objects. In itself, the real movement or displacement of bodies in space is impermissible, as are other signs of visible reality. It is no surprise that the Cubists' 'plastical dynamism' ultimately gave rise to total immobility. 'A picture is a silent, immobile revelation', write Gleizes. He makes a distinction between simple changes in position, assuming the passivity of the observing eye, objective contemplation, set into motion by agitation, and movement in the higher sense of the word, movement without movements, movement as a thing, whose shape can be found in Delaunay's 'monotonous colour circles'.[69]

'Time-form', writes Gleizes the Catholic mystic, takes the place of 'space-form'. The latter is connected to the tradition of the Renaissance, its object-ive, scientific ideal. As for 'time-form', it returns us to the early Middle Ages when the artist did not yet reckon with the outer world as something existing independently of consciousness, boldly intruding into it at will and bringing together events of different times in one and the same space.

It must be said that for the entire Cubist literature, the Renaissance is the chief enemy. After all, it is in this time that people grew accustomed to consciously making a distinction between objective reality and phantasms, drawing a strict line between thought and its object. Yet from the vantage of the new aesthetics, precisely such a differentiation comprises humanity's original sin, from which the world and Adam's descendants now must be rescued.

---

69   Gleizes 1924, pp. 39–40.

Cubism's holy scriptures proclaim that freedom was already attained in the so-called 'abstract Cubism' of Delaunay. He constructs his pictures from nearly non-objective elements, thus generating a new reality, some third space beyond the limits of spirit and matter – in short, his works are products of fully emancipated creation. In his 'Simultaneous Windows' and 'Circular Rhythms' he finds the object as such, devoid of problems or doubts. Here, we immerse ourselves in pure materiality and at the same time we are in the realm of the spirit. 'Painting new ensembles through elements taken not from visible reality but completely generated by the artist, who endows them with a powerful reality', 'this is pure painting'.[70]

With a characteristic knack for thinking up attractive names for the inventions of his friends, Guillaume Apollinaire dubbed these half-abstract symbols nearly devoid of any pictorial content 'Orphism', after the legendary Orpheus whose song was endowed with material strength, capable of lifting rocks and mortifying wild animals. In another terminology, it is here that Cubism finally conquers its passion for analysis, becoming constructive or 'synthetic'.

The reader will hardly require any refutation of this twentieth-century mythology, as it invokes the new Middle Ages and heralds the resolution of all of modern culture's contradictions in a mystical third kingdom or empire. Such reactionary theories have brought humanity too much suffering. Their memory is too vivid to warrant any return. What deserves a brief refutation is another thought. One might say that the speculative fantasies of Apollinaire, Gleizes, Delaunay, or André Lhotes do not deserve so much attention. The Cubists are not thinkers but artists, and one cannot demand anything more from them in the field of theory; it makes sense, rather, to detach their art from philosophy.

This theme already appeared in the literature ten years after 'Cubism's revolution'. One can find it in Picasso's own interviews and in the deliberations of the 'completely new art's' sympathetic devotees, including those in our country. Yet sadly this reasoning does not apply to Cubism. It can be applied, to a degree, to an art depicting the endlessly various world of history and of nature. One cannot pass judgement on an old Florentine or Dutchman for his Catholic or Protestant ideas. The life reflected in this painting overcomes the narrow frame of its time and raises it to the level of a higher intellectual programme, accessible to later centuries. Often we do not even notice the religious content of the Italian quattrocento's madonnas and martyrs, because we are dealing with something more meaningful.

---

70   Gleizes 1924, p. 31.

Another thing entirely is an art that has turned its back on the depiction of life. It is fully hostage to its own declarations and programmes. Despite all the cunning gambits to detach painting from the philosophy upon which it was based, this painting itself is philosophy, and not of the better sort. Even Picasso's famous formula – the poet sings like a bird and that song cannot be explained – is a certain philosophy, well-known in our time. The only thing that has no content comprehensible to thought is what does not exist. Since art exists, however, it either has a real content outside of itself, or it is its own content, its own negation of any outer content, in other words, its theory.

Art that has its content not in the outer world but in the artist's state of mind is possible indeed, since this state of mind is also an object for more speculative figurations. Indeed, such art is quite possible, but that is what one should say then, without all these military ruses and verbal hypnosis. Cubist painting is an attempt to prove on canvas that an artist inspired by the spirit of Orphism, Lyricism, or pure poetry is capable of creating a world from nothing through an irrational, non-pictorial act. Engrossed in art's inner matters, lacking any real subject to sing about, the new type of artist only sings his own theory. It is the only content of his song.

Of course, here too, there is still a difference between more and less talented singers. Some supposedly reactionary thinkers are people of considerable literary talent. Some founders of religious sects can also be gifted, especially at exerting a great hypnotic influence over the feeble and the perplexed. You cannot say that these people have no talent; but you can say that their talent is misdirected and thus deserves condemnation.

Painting in the Other World

In the more abstract variety of Cubism represented by Delaunay, one can already clearly see the entire movement's principle vector, its departure beyond the boundaries of art as the depiction of life and its path to what is called abstract art in our own time. It is known that one of those to be influenced by abstract Cubism was Theo van Doesburg, a Dutchman who joined with Piet Mondrian to found the group De Stijl in 1917. Van Doesburg and Mondrian – both apostles of contemporary abstraction – would further develop the polemic against real forms as illusions and the search for the absolute that would dissolve the border between things and their reflection in consciousness.

Abstract painting is predominantly flat because even the beginning of three-dimensionality, according to Mondrian, is a deception of sorts, a stumbling block for human weakness. Plato's ideas as the eternal idea-matter preceding all creation are flat ideas, according to Mondrian's theory, known as the theory of neo-plasticism, presumably because it rejects all plasticity. Yet we can already see the victory of flatness in Cubism proper, in the principle tendency represented by Picasso and Braque.

In 1911–12, we already see the complete dissolution of the object into a real kaleidoscope of separate parts. All elements run down to 'one common denominator of mass', to use Gleizes's expression. After all, the depiction of separate bodies in space would be a concession to vision on the account of a unified, solid being, that absolute of pure form to which the unhappy consciousness of the artist wants to return. The dissolution of the object is the natural result of these efforts. To Cubism, the whole is an illusion, at least when we see it in front of us in the surrounding world. It can only be depicted as a semblance conveyed through linear perspective, chiaroscuro, etc. Instead, part of the object can be transferred to the canvas in the form of a projection or traced the way children do. From then on, the paintings of Picasso and Braque are flat. Or rather, they consist of several planes, superimposed above another, depicting partial imprints of real objects (see, for an example, *Musical Instruments*, 1912).

The curse of representation is not so easy to elude, however. This is why Picasso turns to nearly abstract constructions of straight lines, geometrical boundaries, all kinds of points and spirals (as in *The Blue Shop, Poet, Memories of Le Havre*, etc., 1912). There are still some distinct pieces of reality swimming in this sea of despair; they have to serve as a guiding thread for the viewer, and thus are still indispensable.

Thus, the escapade to volume ended with a return to flatness. But this is no longer the flatness of the Fauves with its traditional connection to conventional representation. The new turn of the artist's will turns flatness into a symbol of the total agony of visible images. It is a two-dimensional surface, and nothing more. The presence of any spatial aspects intruding into its depths would be a concession to despicable illusion. Only the flat is valid.

'Painting', writes Gleizes, 'is the art of bringing a flat surface to life. A flat surface is a two-dimensional world. Thanks to these two dimensions, it is "truth." To enrich it with a third dimension means to change the very nature of its being: the result will only be the imitation of our three-dimensional material reality through the means of deception in perspective and various tricks of the light'.[71] So, the flat surface is a stage of 'integral realisation', and on it, there are only signs of representation.

---

71 Gleizes 1924, p. 39.

There is not enough space here to describe the fate of other pictorial elements from the laboratory of Cubism. Suffice it to note that neither volume, nor surface, nor line, nor colour, nor the negation of any of these elements or all of them at once truly expresses what is actually going on. Everything is subject to destruction, and everything is revived, but in a very special sense.

It is from this point of view that we should view even the later turn to Ingres and the fake restoration of classicism during Cubism's denouement. There is a magical formula switching reality to a 'different higher plan'. Everything is an enemy to Cubism if it continues to depict the real world outside of us, and everything can be taken as a means of expressing the 'completely new art's' chief idea. We already know what it is: to abolish the difference between painting and its object, to free consciousness from the duty of being a mirror of the world, 'to oneself become a thing'.

In this strange system of imaginative thinking – a person can only become a thing in his imagination, and it is only for the sake of a system that one can torture one's own aesthetic senses with such consistency – there is a general scheme made of two principle themes. Chaos, deformation, destruction, the irrational flow of lyrical creativity, impossible to explain and inducing hypnotic, 'suggestive' effects in other people, that is one side, but there is another side as well.

The reader is already familiar with the new painting's connection to the great principle of Karl Schmidt. The Cubists themselves, and especially their apologists among the writers, heralded the approach of a new organised, rational era. In place of the whirling mess of sensuous experience in Monet or Renoir, Cubism promises humanity something durable, based not upon illusion or semblance, but upon knowledge. Apollinaire already considered the artist a genuine dictator, endowing the world with a certain organisation, the creator of systems bringing order to the chaos of sensation.

It would be impossible here to make a step-by-step description of Cubism's typical folklore. It expressed not only a sense for the dissolution of earlier forms of life, but also a mystical striving toward a life of stability, the search for a rigorous organisational system, yielding the desired quantity of calm at any price, independently of life's actual content. In its historical sympathies, Cubism vacillates from glorifying the irrational vitality of primitive tribes, from 'negritude' and 'Peruanism', to the apology for ancient Egypt and the Middle Ages with their rigid hierarchies and rigorous orders.

Such is the anatomy of the modern myths created by the 'completely new art'. One could say a great deal to compare this pattern with the political and philosophical ideologies of bourgeois parties in the modern epoch. Yet these comparisons are hardly flattering to Cubism, and ours should be an aspect of tranquillity; after all, we are talking about the errors of honest people, about a malaise of the spirit that enthrals artists with its deceptive daydreams. There is one thing we should not forget, however. The worldview of Matisse and his friends was dominated by a variety of vitalist philosophy, of life unfettered and free to the point of 'wildness', while Cubism appears in a gloomier light from its very beginning. It is a utopia from the kingdom of the dead.

There is much bitterness in the explorations of Western art at the turn of the century. Truth is a convention of tradition, beauty a hypocritical pose, it wants to say. Picasso goes further than others; his search for a way out is more incisive, more dramatic. He asks himself: aren't the beginnings of these general vicissitudes to be found in life itself? Already at the end of the 'Rose' period, his melancholia turns into a special condition of the soul that medical science calls *tedium vitae*, a loathing of life.

Cubism makes a theory of this sentiment. The entire evolution of previous art leads it to draw extreme, breathtaking conclusions: mistrust toward all organic forms, toward their inconstancy, incomprehensibility, and their vital warmth! Only dead abstractions are something solid and unconditional, free of posing and hypocrisy. Everything living is deceptive from the vantage of the new geometrical mysticism. Isn't life itself an illness of form? This is the lesson the Cubists learned from Cézanne. The hermit of Aix had already discovered the special dark poetry of petrified forms, working to place everything living into its geometrical case.

With the growing tendency to simplification already evident in Impressionism and its closest successors, the line gradually becomes too general and abstract. Van Gogh dreamed of a painting like the circle that Giotto once drew to prove his artistic ability to the Pope. Many works by the early Picasso are already clearly geometrical. But it is only after 1906 that one sees a real orgy of straight lines, corners, figures cubic and flat. Geometry distorts the human body, subjecting it to humiliating torture, finally displacing any remainder of organic form from the artist's field of view.

The detested Renaissance is already present as an embryo in the emergence of life itself. The only genuine paradise is the fully inorganic, especially prominent in manmade mechanical things, the peak of the new style's negative value. Ortega y Gasset would later clearly derive his theory of the 'dehumanisation of art' from this Cubist experience. Cubism's predilection for the cold, the dead, and the inhuman is the other side of a world of beauty and life, a response to the all-too-obvious corruption of that world, and an attempt to freeze our consciousness to kill any harmful microbes it might contain. Apollinaire wrote about 'the traits of inhumanity' in the new art. 'Wishing to attain the proportions of the ideal, to be no longer limited to the human, the young painters offer us works which are more cerebral than sensual'. These works express 'metaphysical forms'.[72]

So what does painting encounter in the other world? As the literature of Cubism assures us, it finds genuine reality, Reality writ large. All previous art, write Gleizes and Metzinger, strove to depict the world of appearances, perceived by the human eye as something real. The practices of the Impressionists supposedly proved that visual illusions are only illusions, that is, subject impressions. But if the world of appearances is no more, then what is left of that Impressionism? It lacks reality.

The real world is a world of pure geometrical forms. It is to be grasped with the mind and not perceived with the eye, since what we see diverges from pure form as something blurry, bendable, watered down, illusory, blemished by life. The goal of art, the theoreticians of Cubism tell us, lies in reaching the essence of things, bypassing sensuous visibility. This is why, in painting, 'conceptions' must prevail over optics, mathematical intuition must win out over the superficially obvious. The mathematician Maurice Princet took part in the Cubists' philosophical debates.

There are many words in the world, but even more different senses in which they are used. Words make up legends. For example, there is a rather widespread legend saying that it was with Cubism that painting began to move toward genuine realism. This mystification, banal though not yet exhausted, as the many facts of its repetition show, fully bases itself on the ambiguity of the term realism itself.

The aesthetic of the 'completely new art' fully rejects the realism that arose in the late Middle Ages, passed through the period of the Renaissance, and continued to develop, though not without deep contradictions, over the following centuries up until our time. It goes without saying that such a realism existed long before the Renaissance, in the more distant epochs, beginning with the cave paintings of Altamira and Lascaux. Yet this entire lineage of depicting reality in its visible forms, and especially in forms of life as the basis of the beautiful, is unacceptable to those who worship the kingdom of the dead. They stand for a realism in a different sense of the word, in the sense of a late Medieval neo-Platonic scholasticism. The thinkers of Medieval realism really did believe metaphysical abstractions to be as real as or even realer than living bodies: *universalia sunt realia.*

---

72   Apollinaire 1968, p. 224.

And still, despite the reference to Plato, only natural in this case, we need to detach the ancient thinker and even his Medieval admirers from the astonishing operation that they are subjected to by modern irrationalists. Plato never denied the presence of a similarity between a thing's 'idea' and its outer appearance, while the Cubists, much like some other modern followers of Plato, disaffirm the existence of any such resemblance. This is why they do not say that their paintings are the sum of depictions or semblances of actual reality, which, according to this theory, are hidden by our ordinary world. The question of truth is cast aside entirely. 'We all know', said Picasso himself, 'that Art is not truth'. Cubism consciously creates unprecedented combinations of form without guaranteeing that they will resemble anything at all in our ordinary, sinful world or even in the otherworldly realm of pure form. 'Art is a lie'. 'Those lies are necessary for our mental selves, [...] as it is through them that we form our aesthetic point of view of life'.[73]

To depict life as we see it around us is not good, because vision only yields illusions and deceives us, while inventing obvious, conscious lies, on the other hand, is good and useful 'for our mental selves'. Plato never dreamed of such a philosophy!

There is yet another difference between the doctrines of the Cubists and the philosophy of Plato. The old idealism saw ugliness as a symbol of the imperfection of a transitory, relative material life, while beauty was absolute and eternal.

The Cubists, on the contrary, consider formal beauty as something like a corruption or a blemish, while the new world they create in the name of suprasensuous reality is endlessly ugly. Cubism has its own Absolute, but it basks in the mystical light not of Truth and Beauty but of Lies and Ugliness. Admittedly, the sophists of our time will have no trouble saying that the highest ugliness is in fact real beauty, but such verbal hypnosis changes nothing at the heart of the matter.

This course of thinking is rather incoherent, but at the same time typical of modern mysticism. There really is a certain analogy to the demonic, negative quests of the philosophical schools and religious tendencies from the epoch of the crisis of the ancient world, which exhibited the first symptoms of suffocation as early as the fifth century BCE. It goes without saying that today's sophists, Carpocratians and Cainites do their service to the lord of the world, the

---

73   Picasso 1968, p. 264.

devil, under different historical conditions. The broad social movements and the science of our time have opened the doors to the future. This adds a new nuance to the various modernists' demonic grimaces and in fact turns them into pursuits less serious than the naïve experiments of the mystics and anarchists of bygone days. However, on the other hand, the reactionary tendency of such phenomena in our time is greater.

The reason is that the old class society has exhausted itself. Liberal rhetoric of humanity, parliamentary eloquence, superficial culture, bourgeois morality, in short, all the things that capitalism customarily uses to adorn its cannibalistic feats, its 'social anthropophagy', to use Herzen's expression, this whole ideal cover has been worn down and lost any credibility. Thousands of books and articles have been written on this subject. Now, bourgeois ideology and thinking that poisons the brain in which it lives has one last resort: to turn its natural feelings of disappointment into a certain moral and aesthetic vacuum, into the feeling of a gaping void.

If the dream of the old world has withered, it needs to be turned inside out. If the 'eternal truths' of class society are hypocritical, all there is left is the right to lies. If, finally, the appearance of the surrounding world induces disgust and boredom with its colourless, senseless movement of forms, with its marketplace attractions and its cheap imitations of beauty, doesn't it then make sense to put an end to painting? That is the crux of Cubism's entire 'Copernican turn', and the point of departure for all ensuing histories of the 'completely new art', including its abstract variety.

One might ask: is there really nothing valuable in Cubism at all? Artists should be judged by their achievements, and not by their limitations. Every historical phenomenon contains plenty of weakness, limitation, and falsehood. And Cubism, by the way, is already history.

Yes, there is such a rule, it is justified, and it won't deceive us. However, its implications can differ. One and the same force shoots the shell far ahead and pushes back the butt of the rifle in the opposite direction.

While art is on the rise, what seems most important is the artist's achievements over those of his predecessors. But when art is in a state of 'regressive metamorphosis', as the biologists put it, every next step works against the artist. In such cases, any consideration from a favourable point of view will have to take note of what remains in his work in spite of the work of destruction undertaken by the movement he has joined. From this perspective, the best thing about Cubism is that it has not yet reached the point of full abstraction, that it has not yet fully broken with pictorial art.

'Abstract art', said Picasso in conversation with Christian Zervos, 'is only painting. And drama? There is no abstract art. One must always begin with something. Afterwards one can remove all semblance of reality; there is no longer any danger as the idea of the object has left an indelible imprint'.[74]

It is not hard to understand that these words are an attempt to stave off that terrifying force brought to life by Cubism's own logic. In an interview printed in the magazine *Arts* (September 1953), Braque also attempted to distance himself from his immediate heirs: 'Abstract art may be an otherworldly art, but its prices are quite concrete'. The abstract painters answered that Braque never refused to sell his own paintings to the same audience, and for handsome sums at that.

The protagonists of non-pictorial art will find the position of Picasso and Braque to be half-measured and backward, deserving little respect. If the essence of a painting is a sum of destructions, it goes without saying that the fullest nothingness will be the most consistent position, and blessed be he who can start from there.

Yet if the essence of art lies in the depiction of the real world, and not in the discovery of some unimaginable 'metaphysical forms', Picasso's relative moderation speaks in favour of his art. From amongst the fragments of reality, gathered in his still lifes, the different 'collages' and 'counter-reliefs' from the time of the First World War, from amongst human figures cut up and rehashed, multiplied and dismembered into various parts, from within this modern version of Dante's inferno, pictorial symbols sometimes float to the surface, capable *pars pro toto* of evoking the sadness of the city, memories of chance encounters, the despair of unneeded things, maybe, and other more or less real feelings, bereft of that disgusting, cold, 'dehumanising' otherworldliness that poisons Cubism on the whole.

What speaks in favour of Cubism is the criticism it faces from representatives of later, even wilder tendencies. 'By now' we can read in a book by the theoretician of 'abstraction', Michel Ragon,

> the whole world finally knows about abstract art. In any case, no one can ignore it any longer. Nevertheless, Lionello Venturi wrote in 1950: 'Today, when we speak of abstract art, we mean Cubism and its heirs.' Forty years after the discovery of non-figurative art, M. Lionello Venturi devotes no more than two lines to this new aesthetic and, probably out of contempt, mixes it up with Cubism, which in fact is antagonistic to abstract art. To grasp the senselessness of this often-made alignment, it is enough to remember that the Cubists immersed themselves in a real inventory and dissection of objects, while abstract artists strive to move beyond

---

74   Picasso 1968, p. 270.

the object. Even more, Cubism is subject to the limitations of its time. Abstract art, born in the same moment, has been growing, changing, and becoming richer ever since. Cubism was only one of those schools, while abstract art is a far broader movement, and the only comparable aesthetic revolution in the past is the one known as the Renaissance.[75]

Thus, the defenders of pure abstraction lose sleep over Cubism's laurels, as they argue over who has the honour of burying the old art, and who really undiscovered the America discovered by the Renaissance. Michel Ragnon finds that Cubism is too particular a phenomenon on the path of the full negation of painting depicting the real world. In the early 1950s, he made a series of personal attacks on Picasso, whom he was so bold as to compare to the inventor of the dustbin, Eugene Poubelle, long since forgotten, although every garbage receptacle of any kind is called a *poubelle*. In that sense, the uneducated philistine calls everything Picasso, though Picasso himself, at least to his successors, is only a myth. Picasso is outdated. 'The time for vivisections is over. Modern artists construct a new world'.[76]

Really, Cubism leaves a narrow gap between the artist's consciousness and the unthinking world of things. Abstract art wants to plug this gap through a creativity both irrational and senseless, and factually real. The contemporary French artist Dubuffet said, 'I like painting when it almost isn't painting anymore'. In Cubism, this 'almost' has not yet vanished entirely, and such backwardness, such a lack of modernity speaks in Cubism's favour. Sadly, you won't get far with your time machine in reverse.

---

75   Ragon 1956, pp. 21–2.
76   Ragon 1956, pp. 67–71.

The Phenomenology of the Soup Can: The Quirks of Taste

Could a simple soup can become the centrepiece of twentieth-century culture?

- If an art gallery sells it, rather than a shop, if it has been signed by a famous artist, and if its price is 2,000 dollars and not 20 cents.
- If it makes enough of a ruckus in the world's press and if it is reproduced by the latest typographic technologies in the most expensive art magazines, whose writers afford equal attention to a porcelain vase from the Ming Dynasty, Giotto's frescos, and the Pop Art* of today ...
- If this soup can is the last word in a long chain of art's ultra-modern trends, and if disparaging it means putting yourself in a tricky position. After all, you should remember, philistines failed to understand the Impressionists! In 20 years, this soup can might grace the collection of the Louvre.
- If ... – It would take too long to list all the conditions, including the more substantial economic, social, and political ones. This way or that, such nonsense will rise from the depths of culture under certain conditions. Everything Flaubert described in *The Temptation of Saint Anthony* pales in comparison to this trade fair of absurdities.

Not only in our own country, but all over the world people are making light of these wonders of popular taste. The famous French newspaper *Le Figaro* has been laughing too, for example. Let us take the first random note in a series of taunts, in their own way necessary in the larger complex economy of contemporary bourgeois ideology. It talks about an old pair of trousers exhibited as the new reality by the artist Koliannis:

> In the photograph on the left, the pair of trousers, the work's main material, have not yet been positioned in the picture. Thus, they do not yet express the artist's creative intent; they have not yet been laid out with

---

* In the Russian original, Lifshitz writes 'pop art' small and in quotation marks, reflecting the novelty of the term in the Soviet Union. The present translation reflects the familiarity and academic solidity of the term, capitalising it as a proper noun like Cubism.

the necessary folds. The use of metal wire (see the other photograph) imparts the work with a new significance. There is nothing left but to add a few sticks covered in plaster, dirt, and paper to bring the author's creative powers to their highest limit and to free the artwork from conventional conceptions.*

Funny, isn't it?

Somewhere mid-century, the boundaries of art once again have undergone a massive shift. The recently deceased Yves Klein, often considered a near-genius, turned heads by ingeniously burning blotches onto pasteboard with a gas torch. Another twentieth-century fire worshipper ignited rows of matchboxes on aluminium plates. The Argentinian artist Marta Minujín dragged a pile of old mattresses from her studio. Lending artistic expression to her personality with this material, she then held a public auto-da-fe in the presence of journalists from the newspaper *Combat*. This was already a so-called 'happening', a work of art as something in progress, a living picture of sorts.

During one of these happenings, the Korean Nam Jun Paik threw peas at the audience, covered his face with soap suds, jumped into water, swung on a chin bar, all to 'trance music' that he himself had composed. If one is to believe the newspapers, this music consisted of pistol shots, breaking glass, whistling, grating sounds, scratching, bursting balloons, etc. In the end, Paik crossed the stage with his pants down and sat on a high bench with his naked bottom pointing at the audience. His partner Charlotte Moorman, covered with only a transparent plastic cape, accompanied him on a cello, jumping into a barrel of water from time to time. All of this transpired at the Gallery René Block in West Berlin in the summer of 1965.

If one wanted, one could make a huge list of no less astounding feats of creative energy, but whoever has read Montaigne knows that humanity should not be surprised by anything. The morbid desire to go beyond the boundaries of art now appears in yet another striking twist of sophistication from a decaying modernism: the production of all kinds of mechanised toys, combining sculpture, painting, movement, sound, and light effects. Machine-caricatures, manufactured with Swiss precision, have made the sculptor Jean Tinguely famous all over the world. His 'assembled mechanisms ... can be set into motion by the viewer', writes the Hamburg-based journal *Der Spiegel*. 'Tinkered together out of bent rods, doll's legs, broken bottles, cowbells, these grotesque mechanisms

---

* No footnote or citation in the original.

are set into motion by baby buggies, roller skates, or bicycle wheels. They wobble to daredevil rhythms; they clatter, hiss and whistle; they twitter like birds or wind up for massive drum beats; they swing red scraps of cloth through the air or wave around spirals of steel'.[1] Such amusements make light of the consumer's sedate lifestyle, opines the magazine. So what is the meaning of a simple can of soup?

Admittedly, the soup can has already been subject to no small amount of ridicule. One journalist went to the shop next door to ask how much a can of Campbell's soup would cost without the signature of the artist who gave it its second lease on life. The price difference to the original turned out to be staggering, even if the artist added exactly nothing. The Italian writer Dino Buzzati has said that there are some excellent examples of such art in his refrigerator at home. There has been much ribaldry in newspapers more and less reputable, in official media and in the yellow press. *Le Figaro*, the *Frankfurter Allgemeine*, and *Die Welt* all snigger at the worn-out imagination's unexpected twists ... Every day, you hear something ever more fantastic; all our own critics of Western 'degeneracy' have left to do is to tap this source for readymade material.

All the while, the soup can continues its victory march – it even gains something from such mockery. And how! We'll see what happens tomorrow. Today, even the most diehard defenders of antiquities no longer scoff at earlier modernist movements; on the contrary, they doff their caps in respect. Who today would dare claim that there was anything funny about the megalomania of the former customs official Henri Rousseau? When the Salon de Independents held a survey exhibition of its former participants, including Rousseau, it proved impossible to show any canvases by this oddball with a near-genius confidence in himself; even insuring them for exhibition would have amounted to bankruptcy. You can't laugh at something that costs millions. People are still laughing at soup cans, but not without trepidation.

Will the soup can enter the Louvre or not? That is the question. The famous American architect Philip Johnson is sure that it will. He only buys works of such art, now known as Pop. Another patron of Pop, the New York taxi park owner Robert Skull is betting on prices to rise. His wife, Mrs. Ethel Skull, tells the readers of a glossy French magazine that 'even the most ordinary objects can become real objects of artistic creation beyond their usual context'.[2] In one

---

1 *Der Spiegel* 1964, p. 64.
2 Bernier 1963, p. 15.

of her favourite showrooms, there is a whole rack of Campbell's soup can labels. The defenders of abstract painting, on the other hand, condemn the soup can as if it were the devil's spawn. And that debate is ridiculous indeed.

Five years ago, abstract painting was still the height of innovation, trampling down the protests of the founders of earlier modernist tendencies, such as Braque, Picasso or Léger. In our country, not only the authors of *Sovietskaya Kul'tura* but even Ilya Ehrenburg* himself wrote against abstraction. In a word, it still had the air of desperate boldness on the edge between art and something unseen.

The cards were reshuffled when the soup can burst onto the scene. The roles were reversed. By now, there is something academic about even the most aggressive forms of abstraction, such as 'gestural painting' or 'action painting', that is, the formless drips, lines, and mysterious dots of Jackson Pollock, Willem De Kooning, or Georges Mathieu, while the leaders of abstract painting consider themselves to be the last classics. Their piteous laments remind the world of the death of art under the pressure of Pop from America.

Events unfolded as follows. In mid-1962, there was a massive drop in prices of abstract painting in New York and London. The French press immediately noted this change in the climate of trade. 'The price of paintings on the international market has fallen. Is it a crash or a return to normalcy', asked the reviewer of the weekly *Express* on 12 July of the same year. Some influential newspapers like *Le Monde* displayed a noticeable coldness toward the taste for abstraction, helping the panic to spread. The champions of abstraction, whose triumph in the 1950s was, in the opinion of many observers, a well-organised business enterprise, raised a ruckus over art's subordination to financial concerns. Thus, Geneviève Bonnefoi, writing in a special issue of the journal *Les lettres nouvelles* (February 1963) complained: 'After the cold shower of the New York crisis, bankers are now trying to withdraw their investments into works of abstract art in exchange for "more reliable" commodities. This is sending the petty dealers into a panic and leading them to conclude that abstract art is not worth a farthing'.

The 'New York crisis' of 1962 was the first jolt in a general decline in demand for painting by the masters of abstraction and it sowed real panic in their ranks.

---

* Ilya Ehrenburg (1891–1967) was one of the Soviet Union's most prolific writers. His novella *The Thaw* gave its name to the era of the liberalisation after the death of Stalin. Ehrenburg was known for his familiarity with cultural life in the West and his friendship with Picasso, whose art he famously brought to Moscow in one of the first modernist exhibitions of the postwar period in 1957. He did not support abstract expressionism or later movements, however.

'The prices for abstract paintings in France', reported Niels von Holst in the Munich magazine *Die Weltkunst* on 15 January 1963, 'have fallen by forty per-cent. French art dealers claim only German, Dutch, Swiss, or Swedish collectors are still buying abstract work: the French and the British have abandoned them'. Even more: 'The abstract form is no longer innovative in art'. The decline of abstraction continued for all of 1963. 'Works of non-objective painting are less successful this year', the same journal reports in September, 'interest in them has clearly declined'.

It was then that the soup can first appeared from across the sea. Like in ladies' fashion, where it is more or less natural, taste in so-called modern art moves in leaps and bounds from one extreme to another. For a whole decade, the dominant trend was a taste for anything at a remove from the real world, so an interest in objects had to and really did come in its place, just as long skirts replace short skirts and vice versa. 'Abstraction is going out of style', wrote *Die Presse* in Vienna in January 1963, going on to report that a movement 'back to the object' was underway all over the world. There had been similar cycles in the past, of course, but this time, the whole business was more extreme; the forms of the alliance between the creative work of the subject and the concrete world of things had already unravelled considerably, not to mention that this dissolution was deeply based in the entire history of culture. Thus, matters did not stop at a sham restoration of reality on canvas like the one in the early 1920s (with the New Objectivity movement). Instead, real objects now took the place of depicted ones. This is how a real soup can found its way into art after it was shown to the public in different forms and combinations by one of the most active artists of the new tendency, the super-popular Andy Warhol.

The term Pop Art was invented in 1956 by Lawrence Alloway, a curator of the Guggenheim Museum, and referred to the word pop as it appeared in the picture of one British artist. It's hard to say what it means exactly. In its ordinary usage, 'pop' means cheap mass production bearing the mark of stereotypes and vulgarity. In that sense, the term 'Pop Art' would be an abbreviation for 'popular art'. But there are no direct references in this regard, so it might be that the little word 'pop' means nothing more than a senseless sound made by infants, like the dada of Dadaism, itself by now famous and crowned with academic laurels, and really, the movement called Pop Art is little more than a repetition of Dadaism from the time of the First World War.

The father of Dadaism, Richard Huelsenbeck, has long since left behind such artistic antics, going on to become a famous psychiatrist in New York. However, in the general uproar around the new movement, this veteran of modern iconoclasm came to the attention of the press. In a series of articles written for the *Frankfurter Allgemeine*, Huelsenbeck defines Pop Art as 'the last cry of those hoarse from wailing aesthetic dirges'. Here are a few sentences from his description of an exhibition of the new direction in New York: 'Everyone wanted to stay abreast of this novelty and stood in line. The matter in question was an exhibition of the vulgar, the absurd, the anti-artistic – giant sandwiches, old cooking pots, scraps of advertising posters. This is called neo-Dadaism or factualism, the art of life, the art of the street, the art of the simple man. They want to leave behind the last ideals and already curse the spread of symbolism to every nook and cranny; they bring the atmosphere of the cafeteria into the artistic salon' (6 August 1963).

We will continue explaining Pop Art's programme a little later; for now, a few words on its fate. Even more than the career of abstract painting, Pop's success is linked to the influence of real economic and political forces. The fact of the matter is that New York has long since been sharpening its teeth to take over the leading position until now inhabited by Paris as both a stock market of art and an academy of sorts for hyper-modern tendencies. Until then, America's participation in the chemical processes creating different sorts of surrogate art was largely passive. Paris fashions still ruled Yankee taste, even though the entire industry's financial nerve had long since moved across the ocean. But, as Huelsenbeck and other competent witnesses admit, wherever matters run down to the organisation of business, economic forces inevitably strive to reach full hegemony; the creation of false artistic value has undergone such a simplification and come so far from any organic tradition or loving relation to art, long periods of study, and immediate transfer of skills from one generation to another that the production of new articles of this type can be relocated to any place on the globe. It is hardly surprising that the more militantly entrepreneurial group among the American patrons of modernism would decide to take advantage of the falling price of abstract painting to relocate the centre of innovation from Paris to New York. The conductor's baton is all too noticeable in Pop Art's quick success, a new 'revolution in art', and this time, a purely American one.

The first to open the Pop Art campaign was the gallery owner Sidney Janis with an exhibition called *The New Realists*. New York's biggest museums followed suit, and Pop came to the Guggenheim and the Museum of Modern Art, which had largely shown abstract work for the last 30 years. The *New York Times* gave the new school the stamp of popular approval. 'Many culture insiders believe it may be a bigger craze than folk-singing before the summer is out'.[3]

---

3   Baker 1963, p. 26.

There were rumours of a real epidemic of Pop Art in America. The new wave immediately led to a dramatic rise in price for works such as a spade with a long handle fixed to a black canvas, a bag of oranges on a stool, trousers made of sailcloth hung on a clothes hanger, water faucets, metres, mannequins, Coca Cola bottles and in the best case 'object combines' consisting of more or less decoratively arranged everyday objects, combined with poster-type painting on canvas. 'Wesselman', writes the German magazine *Die Weltkunst*, 'sells his compositions for 2,500 dollars, James Rosenquist for 7,500'.

Last summer, the newspaper *Die Welt* made an even more encouraging report: 'In New York, Pop Art has created an unbelievable masterpiece. James Rosenquist recently finished a painting up to three meters high and twenty six meters long. Rosenquist has named his monstrous creation *F-111*, after one of America's bombers (the original is only 24 meters long). The painting was immediately bought by one New York businessman who declared that this was the most significant art work to be created in the last fifty years. The painting is priced at 60,000 dollars'.[4]

The entire campaign culminated in yet another international exhibition in Venice, the Biennale of 1964. Observers from the Paris school discovered the manoeuvres of the American contenders in advance and went to war in the press, which was all the more dramatic, since the Pop epidemic had reached Europe by that time. It turned out that there had been a fifth column of 'new realists' in France since 1960, headed by the critic Pierre Restany.[5]

The Venice Biennale of 1964 saw a stark clash between abstract painting and Pop Art, sparking an international competition that flared up into real chauvinism. Overwhelming force was introduced by the American side. Aside from its national pavilion, the US Embassy also gave its artists use of its former Consulate building. In advertising booklets and in his foreword to the catalogue, the commissar of the US pavilion announced that 'the world center of art has moved from Paris to New York'. This all was cause for extreme irritation among the abstract Europeans. But tempers flared to a blaze when the international exhibition awarded its main prize. The Paris school's contender was the abstractionist Roger Bissière, who died in 1965, while the American party rallied around the founder of Pop Art, Robert Rauschenberg, who showed a

---

4   To be fair, we should note that Rosenquist wanted to express his horror at militarism. According to the newspaper *Express*, he condemns the war in Vietnam. This does Rosenquist an honour without changing Pop Art's role in contemporary artistic life.

5   Cf. Restany's Manifeste de Nouveaux Réalistes (Ragon 1963, p. 136) and his articles in the journal *Art in America* in 1963.

wall-high 'object combine' including a scrap of a poster, a photo of the assassinated president Kennedy, an advertisement for an automatic lock, clippings from illustrated magazines, and brightly coloured postcards. All of this was arranged on one canvas, and according to the connoisseurs, not without elegance.

In the end, the prize went to Rauschenberg, to jeers of indignation and hate from the vanquished. 'They declared themselves to be the defenders of the old, good humanism against the barbarism of the New World', wrote Pierre Schneider in the more objective weekly *Express* on 2 July 1964, 'but sadly the good traditions under discussion in this case are those of abstract art, while barbarism is the return to figuration. Everything here is confused to the extreme'. The newspapers reported on the pressure exerted by the US ambassador in Italy, but even more obvious was the influence of fat chequebooks. 'In Venice, we saw', writes the same Schneider, 'billionaire collectors chasing after painters and sculptors, the stars of the season, waving their chequebooks like sharks following a passenger liner'.

In his interesting pamphlet *The Other Side of Painting*, Robert Lebel describes the situation as follows:

> Painting has entered a certain economic system not only recently, as is often wrongly claimed, but already in the mid-nineteenth century. Thus, it was completely inevitable that the Americans, better organised as they are to conquer international markets, would succeed in imposing their art just like they impose their other products using the more perfect means at their disposal. The French 'propaganda' in the cultural sphere was always pitiful to the point of ridicule. The only effort of any significance were those of the art dealers, sporadic at best, while the American government did not hesitate to place the full weight of its diplomatic machine behind its most controversial talents.[6]

With this machine's help, the new trend emerged victorious, and as is often the case, the victors mingled with the vanquished, forming intermediate sects. Abstract painting did not die, of course; it was still backed by the solvent taste of its larger holders unwilling to devalue their collections. The game of speculation continues. By now, the Paris school has even regained some of its former primacy; the leader of so-called optical art ('op-art'), Paul Vassarely, received the international prize at the Saõ Paulo Biennial. Still, its golden days

---

6   Lebel 1964, p. 93 ff.

have clearly passed; the aura of bold innovation has faded. Next in line are 'kinetic sculptures', mobile and self-destructing sculptures as well as painting based on chemical reactions, remote control, magnetic effects, or fusions with photography and film. Robert Rauschenberg already announced his desire to work with electronic painting. All kinds of 'happenings' with completely naked celebrities are now in style.

But all of that basically is Pop. On 25 April 1966, *Newsweek* rightly noted that Pop has become a lifestyle. In the five years of its existence since it emerged as an industrial aesthetic, it has turned into a 'mass psychosis', spreading to even the deepest backwater. If the antics of Dada in the First World War were limited to a small group of anarcho-decadents in neutral Switzerland, today's Pop reaches 30 million American viewers of the weekly TV programme *Batman*. It is an invincible comic book hero on the sidewalks of Broadway. It lives on in Andy Warhol's nightclubs, where several films are shown at once. Pop Art has its own popular beauties and starlets – Baby Jane, Edie Sedgwick, Nico, or the mysterious Ingrid. Newspaper reports make it clear that the style of Pop has its adepts in film and music, and the entertainment industry, too, has not gone untouched. Pop means airline stewardesses in extravagant plastic hoods; it means those strange dresses at the height of fashion that now grace the front pages of influential journals on the 'finest art of tailoring'. According to the director of a large New York confectioners,* Gwen Randolph, at present between 10 and 15 percent of all fashion products are Pop, while a style of intentional vulgarity dominates clothing for young people. Paul Young, Vice President of Puritan Fashions, opened a special shop to sell all kinds of Pop-style products with branches in other cities in America and Europe. He foresees a turnover of 50 million dollars for 1967. 'Pop is happiness', he says. 'It's todayness'. In a word, Pop is everything. 'It has captivated the Great Society', writes *Newsweek*, 'thrived on its prosperity and exploited its restlessness'.[7]

The Economy of Painting

The story of the soup can requires some clarification. In the modern Western world, the trade in paintings is if not the most important then at least a very

---

*   Here, Lifshitz is mistaken. Gwendolyn Randolph Franklin (1918–2015) was fashion editor at the magazine *Harper's Bazaar* for 25 years, which Lifshitz may be confusing for a department store. Randolph was also the wife of Gordon P. Franklin, a president of Saks Fifth Avenue and later Bergdorf Goodman. However, she never headed any of these companies herself.

7   Benchley 1966.

striking example of capital's dominance over all areas of human activity. The battle of talents and tendencies had already become a speculative game of sorts in the middle of the previous century, in the time of Durand Ruel and Vollard. This is a topic in its own right, rather interesting from a sociological point of view. The total value of a posthumous exhibition of Jackson Pollock held in 1963 was estimated at 5 million dollars; these paintings – paint splattered onto canvas – are essentially nothing but symbols of the artist's fame. It goes without saying that the value of such works is based on a rather ephemeral utility. It wholly depends upon the recognition of abstract painting as art by the organs of public opinion, especially the press. These, in turn, are subject to the interplay of real interests, and can thus be quite fickle. The capital invested into such artefacts thus hangs on a thread, while the dance of millions and the runaway speculation surrounding them is an example of the arbitrary nature inherent to material relations of a certain kind.

The moral death of machines familiar from political economy is nothing in comparison to the purely arbitrary life of the works of Yves Klein, who at one point in his unusual artistic career sold not paintings but empty space. The weekly *Art* (21–27 April 1965) writes of the 'pneumatic period' in Klein's work: 'Instead of paintings, he offered "immaterial painterly states", and agreed to sell them only in exchange for bars of gold. In 1958, he invited the audience to an exhibition opening of his immaterial works, and all they saw were empty walls'.

Such antics may seem wildly eccentric, but if you look at the turnover of the trade in painting and the fortunes collectors invest in various spectral artistic activities, you must admit that art's economic life – utterly virtual from the vantage of its qualitative, natural basis – presents an actual fact of modern history more astounding than any tales that travellers might tell of strange savage customs.

So, Koliannis's old pants and other wonders of the imagination run wild are not that funny. When capital subordinates intellectual creativity to the laws of material production, this economic order's unnatural quality and the hypertrophy characteristic of social forms detached from real content manifest in a feverish conventionality of staggering proportions. In the work of the modernist artist, the depiction of life as a source of value is increasingly displaced by the arbitrary side, so that it is an ideal object for speculation. When capital enters this sphere, it uses Pollock's drips or the receipts Yves Klein gave to his collectors instead of paintings as simple signs of value, and remains essentially indifferent to painting's aesthetic merits. The commodity's real content doesn't worry capital in the least.

The reader might find this argument strained, an all-too-direct reduction of art's caprice to economic reality. To calm his conscience, it will be enough to briefly hear the testimony of one of the authorities of today's 'avant-garde'. The renowned critic Michel Ragon says: 'As an end result, the notion of the artist has changed somewhat since the days of the destitute daubers of Montmartre or Montparnasse, caught up in the romance of poverty and booze, as has the notion of the art lover. Today's artist is more like a high-ranking bureaucrat or an industrialist, while the art lover often only buys paintings as a place to put his capital, since in his eyes, shares of Cézanne are more solid than shares in the Suez Canal'.[8] Snobbery and speculation on rising prices aside, it is also significant to the trade in painting that capital invested in artworks is tax exempt.

As for the arbitrary nature of this commodity, which sometimes reaches the point of utter absurdity, for example, in the work of Yves Klein, who only took a general tendency *ad finem*, what can one do if reality itself is so full of arbitrary things? By its very nature, capitalism subordinates the use value (or 'worth') of all goods to exchange value. It represses the qualitative side of labour in favour of its quantitative side, and turns the production of commodities from a means into an end. It makes no difference to capital whether it arises through the production of useful products or poisonous substances, whether its commodities are foodstuffs or deadly weapons. The latter are also useful, but in a special, purely formal sense. In that way, the notion of the commodity itself takes on an arbitrary quality, so fundamental and one could say massive that it sometimes reaches the point of paradox. It may have grown especially strong over the last decades, but it is inherent to all bourgeois civilisation.

There was a time when the difference between capitalism and other, more consumption-oriented modes of production expressed itself with greater clarity, as the production of the means of production developed at a quicker pace. Now, the magnetic needle of profit eagerly points in the other direction, and that has led to a certain change in the structure of the final product of industry. In search of as yet unexploited sources of life, capitalism has turned its attention back to objects of consumption (and it goes without saying that this includes cars, houses, and domestic appliances). For this reason, Western sociologists, for example the Harvard professor David Riesman, author of the famous book *The Lonely Crowd*, see ours as the era of consumption. Not that production is now defined by people's actual needs, determined from the vantage of social utility under given historical conditions. Nothing has changed in the capitalist order's chief principles. The paradox is that in reaching a new

---

8   Ragon 1963, p. 17.

level of technology in the sphere of consumption, where the natural, qualitative side plays a more important role, capital remains just as indifferent to the content of the matter and is just as enthralled with the spirit of the boundless growth of value as before. Even when it is realised with the best possible quality, a given product's utility can have a wholly fictitious or even negative magnitude; mass production defined by business will catch up to you, imposing itself in all situations of life.

It is in this connection that we see the emergence of a huge apparatus for distribution and sales, historically justified in part, and partially artificial. In the USA, employment in the retail sector grew 30 times faster than in production between 1952 and 1962. This has also allowed advertising to become such a tremendous force of its own. Its goal is to fully take possession of the consumer's consciousness, eliminating the difference between what is and what seems that worried Hamlet so. Everything could be bad or good depending on a given product's reputation, now fabricated by specialised opinion-makers. The goal is to make the consumer believe in the miraculous qualities of one of the 279 brands of washing powder on sale. Of course, the consumer isn't so stupid as to believe this good news with utter naïveté, but then again, he doesn't have to. Influenced by all the collateral conditions grinding up any remaining belief in objective truth, denizens of the 'era of consumption' have already reached a level of doublethink where the existence of anything good is taken as a matter of pure convention. Half a century ago, one fashionable philosophical system claimed that all truth runs down to useful functions and everything only exists *als ob*, as if it existed. In the frame of the social system described by David Riesman, the consumer does not actually live, he lives 'as if' – in an arbitrary world of nominal, imposed qualities that do not actually exist. And this is even the case if he is in fact fed up with all the benefits of production and service.

Irrepressible self-disgust is one of modern bourgeois society's distinctive features. It expresses itself not only in films about the 'sweet life', but in the scientific critique of civilisation, whose most recent wave now addresses an 'industrial' or 'technological' society. It often tends to reconcile itself with the life it describes, yet despite its weaknesses and the often tendentious character of its generalisations, this literature rings true in many ways.

In the opinion of the incisive scholar of contemporary American society, Vance Packard, consumption itself has taken on a 'ritual' character, and this ritual serves as a surrogate for a real taste for life. The length of a car, an apartment in a particular neighbourhood, the different goods offered by industry, these all are 'status symbols'. Packard compares the arbitrary ideological role of consumption with the circuses of antiquity, which served as a vent for the social restlessness of the masses.

> Employees in big offices, as well as big plants, are finding their work roles fragmentised and impersonalised. There has been, perhaps unwittingly, a sealing-off of contact between big and little people on the job. And there has been a startling rise in the number of people who are bored with their work and feel no pride of initiative or creativity. They must find their satisfactions outside their work. Many do it by using their paycheques to consume flamboyantly, much as the restless Roman masses found diversion in circuses thoughtfully provided by the emperors.[9]

The Emperors knew that 'bread and circuses' are what the throng really needs. In contemporary imperialist states dominated by production for the sake of profit, there is no difference between these two elements. The capitalist's calculations already include the symbolism of consumption, which, on the other hand, also belongs to the field of social psychology, that is, to 'circuses'. People seek something new and essential in life to suppress the loneliness eating away at them. Meanwhile, industry turns disgruntlement with the existing order into a source of profit. Inflamed by the force of advertising, the thirst for consumption grows to the point of resembling a spiritual hunger, muting all other higher needs. It comes down to endlessly acquiring the newest things, consuming them quickly before they get old, and replacing them with even newer ones. Driven by its own inner logic and the fear of catastrophe, capital needs this mechanism to constantly grow, erasing the objective boundary between the spectral and the real. Novelty becomes the main measure of value, while the clash of a new standard of living with an antiquated one turns into a formal life pattern, just as it does in the world of 'completely modern art'. As is typical of capitalism, the dissolution of all concrete activity into abstract labour appears as an example of diabolical irony; consumption itself takes on ever more abstract traits and even sleep becomes a function of pharmaceutical sales.

Against this backdrop, it is easier to understand the twentieth-century consumer's trite wisdom, according to which everything is arbitrary and constructed. There are no objective values, there never were, and there never will be! Truth, beauty and the good are relative and transitory; they depend upon habit and outer influences. Information and commands replace the notion of thought.

---

9   Packard 1959, pp. 9, 10, 317.

'Why do you think a hill or a tree is more beautiful than a gas pump?', asks Roy Lichtenstein, one of the pioneers of Pop. 'It's because you're conditioned to think that way. I am calling attention to the abstract quality of banal images'.[10]

Similar deliberations justified the legitimacy of abstract painting, Cubism and so on, going further back. They all represented themselves as struggling against the outer determination of good and bad on the artist's creative will. Why do you think that the classics of Greek art or those of the Renaissance are better than a drawing on a fence? This is what you've been taught. There is no such thing as progress or regression in art, everything depends upon customs and conventions. Erasing any trace of objective content from aesthetic life, this pressure of commonplace relativism is one of the main forces of modern ideology, and it leads to the complete artificiality if not of individual then at least of mass judgements of taste. Just wait a little, we will teach you that a soup can is no worse than the Venus of Milo, you yourself will admit that it's true! All too obviously, Pop is a product of the ploys and bluffs of advertising and has a close inner link with the 'era of consumption', that is, with capital's latest way of working, as it finds a deep source of profit in the permanent forming and re-forming of consumer taste. This is what the Western critics of 'industrial society' describe in their writing, which, while approximate and inaccurate, is poignant enough.

According to *Newsweek*, David Riesman had no comment on Pop Art, while Marshall McLuhan from Toronto University lectures in all too optimistic a tone. But here is a fragment from an article by Matthew Baigell in *Studio International* (January 1966, p. 15):

> If we once read Sartre to break into the universe of abstract expression, we now need to consult other authors. One can understand Pop Art by including it, so to speak, in John Kenneth Galbraith's *Affluent Society*, since Galbraith finds that America's main problem is not production but slavery to things. Be it the weight of production or the weight of things, both one and the other give rise to dark thoughts, of course, if we look at them as a part of those societies studied by Jacques Ellul in *The Technological Society* and Herbert Marcuse in his *One-Dimensional Man*. Both point to the subordination of man to the technologies of his own creation, technologies that enter all sides of his life and to a large extent determine our reactions to different stimuli (we know that in our day, even leisure time is subject to planning or programming.)

---

10   Benchley 1966.

In Pop Art, a fractured industrial civilisation reaches its apotheosis, in the author's opinion.

All of this presents a delicate situation. If you consider a soup can or a water faucet an artwork because the artist set these objects apart from their 'usual context', thus endowing them with new meaning, it should be completely clear that the proportion of convention in such works is far greater than in any other object ever known as painting or sculpture. After all, the crux of the matter is the act of separation, which must be recognised by the initiated. Neither the soup can's substance nor its outer appearance have changed in the least. In other words, it is the 'context', subject to negation and thus raised to exponential powers, that now plays a decisive role. The conspirators have to be in the know, because beyond this psychological convention, a soup can exhibited by an artist is indistinguishable from one on the shop shelf. 'Yet as time goes by', notes the *Express* art critic Pierre Schneider (2 July 1964), 'this disappearance of context renders the work indecipherable, since it contains no meaning of its own'.

Such is the movement into the realm of conventionality, often created out of nothing, from refuse, as in the works of the German artist Karl Mann. The newspapers say they consist of old junk gathered from garbage dumps with a certificate indicating the date and place at which it was found.[11]

Advertising and inflated reputations become ever more important as the distance to the realist tradition in the wider sense grows and the gulf widens between a painting's price, dependent upon the managed but still spontaneous fits and 'booms' of the market, and this strange commodity's actual aesthetic worth.

Not everything can be organised even with modern methods of trade and social pressure – there are limits to the power of convention. Hence, the singular nervousness of the art market for as long as it is ruled by a business that fabricates 'waves' of success.

A huge apparatus has upheld this artificial and unhealthy world like an inflated soap bubble for at least half a century, yet despite its size, the owners of its ostensible values will be left with nothing in hand but what the grandfather had at the end of Nikolai Gogol's story 'The Enchanted Place': '... rubbish,

---

11   'These objects have something in common with art because I selected and mounted them as an artist'. 'In his opinion', the *New York Herald Tribune* added to Mann's manifesto, 'the squashed lids of mustard glasses, banged-up coffee pots ... scrubbers and rusty bed springs are as beautiful and significant as the fragments found in Roman temples' (*Der Spiegel* 1965, p. 82).

sweepings ... it's shameful to say what it is'. This forces the 'completely new art's' owners to pursue the strategy of renewing their fictitious capital once they have grown rich on its rising price.

It is time to leave behind this mix of financial speculation, advertising, and coercion characteristic of everyday life in the epoch of imperialism. Let us now move on to the more spiritual sides of the matter, if one can speak of the spirit at all in this almost automatic life of art 'in the formidable realm of forces', as the expression of the old German poet Friedrich Schiller has it. Let us hear what the soup can's soul has to say.

Reflection's Malaise

To understand the soup can's strange speech, we first and foremost need to abandon the old habit of seeing such artistic antics as mere 'pranks', 'trickery', or 'madness', though they may in fact be worthy of Doctor Krupov's sanatorium.*

First of all, an exhibition of old junk or soup cans is no crazier than deposing a president with a rapid fire rifle or waging war as path to economic prosperity. There are all kinds of social madness in our day!

Second of all, 'pranks' on a scale like the one described on the pages above are not just simple stupidities. Instead, they are an objective phenomenon, a force to be reckoned with, just as we must deal with the fact that the influenza virus exists, though it is hardly a positive phenomenon.

Making light of such 'pranks' is only a step away from naïve or diplomatic reconciliation. Modern man is often influenced by fashion and a sense of protest at the readymade conclusions foisted upon him. Prohibitions and public ridicule excite pity. To retain an independence of thought from all derivative or negative reflexes, to firmly dismiss the influence of false ideas, they need to be understood and possibly more deeply than the bearers of such ideas themselves would understand them from the inside. To the uninitiated, for the Sunday visitor of the Tretyakov Gallery, this isn't easy. What is the source of fantasies like abstract painting or Pop Art? Why do the papers write about them

---

*   Dr Krupov was a literary alter ego of Russian writer Alexander Herzen (1812–70) who first appears in his novel *Who is to Blame?* and then in the separate, highly successful work *From the Works of Dr. Krupov. About the Mentally Ill Generally and the Epidemic Numbers of Such in Particular*, both published in 1847. Here, Herzen ironically claims that the insane are no less intelligent and no more damaged than the sane, only perhaps somewhat closer to genius.

so much, not only abroad, but in our country as well? And why do these phenomena arise on such a scale that even the Pope or the leaders of great nations mention them from time to time?

Of course, it would be a mistake to think that the phenomenon of social pathology more or less widely known under the name of modernism was only the making of art dealers and rich collectors. That isn't so. Modernism has its roots in the very development of human consciousness. A certain state of mind presents both the economic and the political interests of the propertied classes with a broad field to manipulate, but it is based on something more substantial – a malaise of the spirit that reflects the deep contradictions of the historical life of peoples in the period of the previous civilisation's decline and the transition to new, as of yet unseen forms of social organisation.

If our soup can could speak, like in Anderson's fairytale, it might say:

> I am a simple soup can, and I am speaking to whoever might hear! I am telling you that you have abandoned true happiness ever since you left the state of elementary, lifeless matter. But your chief crime and your greatest misfortune is that you think at all. To be done with this hell on earth, with all these ideas and all this responsibility – that is the ideal of modern man. Be as simple and irresponsible as the stupid piece of tin from which the machine made me. Verily I say unto you, come to me, all you afflicted and all you burdened with so many sorrows, and I shall soothe your woes!

Of course, that isn't all the work of Pop Art whispers into the spectator's ear, but the words above are accurate in any case. They correspond to the opinion of the soup can artist himself – Andy Warhol. When asked about the meaning of his outlandish creations, he answered 'Machines have less problems [...] I'd like to be a machine, wouldn't you?'[12] In his attempt to solve humanity's woes, Andy Warhol's solution is simpler than the Egg of Columbus – he puts a soup can on display, thus unburdening himself and others of all their problems.

Generally speaking, this is nothing new. For an entire century, if not more, the practitioners of creative and intellectual professions have grown more and more conscious of an excess in consciousness, the surplus weight of historically accumulated forms, an inner weakness of sorts that comes when everything is predictable – the beauty of a sunset, the words of love whispered before physical intimacy, the iambic tetrameter, the one-point-perspective, the art of chiaroscuro.

---

12   *Time Magazine* 1963.

When Meyrink's centipede stopped to think about what its 35th leg was doing, it could no longer walk. They tell us that much to its bane, mankind has lost touch with life's crude spontaneous forces, with simple unmitigated being. An overdeveloped intellect is what kills any vital principle. Reason, consciousness, ideology – these are the true enemies consuming us from within. Man's position in a world of things is fatal because he is actually free of the immediate dictates of his physical nature. This ambiguous being differentiates itself from itself, and acknowledges its own existence as a problem. Placing his hands on a stone parapet, the hero of one recent existentialist novel had an unexpectedly powerful sense that the stone might be better than us, because it doesn't suffer under such ambiguities.

To recount the biography of this idea, it would be necessary to outline the entire history of philosophy, beginning with Schopenhauer at least, and on through the entire history of painting from the first 'revolutions in art' to the Pop Art of today. There are countless nuances here, subtle systems of ideas, expounded with undeniable talent in print and on canvas, and there is a historical path from the refined to the vulgar, with the soup can on the horizon. And, in the end, there is the most frightening thing of all – when the artificial primitivism of educated people joins forces with our century's real primitivity, that is, with the outright lack of consciousness in huge masses of people affected and at the same time robbed by bourgeois civilisation. That special type of pseudo-folksiness or social demagogy has already brought much calamity in recent times.

Reactionary mythmaking was born from the depths of decadent philosophy, and made ample use of its most dangerous conclusion – the utopia of a happy new barbarism. Regardless of their often quite liberal packaging, such ideas are, in the end, very useful for stirring up the darkest hatred toward the intelligentsia. At the same time, the introduction of a schism between the educated and the people is a useful means of strengthening the nation. Those who have mastered it include not only the plebiscitary fathers of the fatherland, the gorillas of the Black Hundreds, like Hitler, but also the more liberal leaders of the propertied classes. Thus, the inner conflict of an afflicted spirit becomes a practical rule of reactionary politics: 'divide and conquer'. This is the real meaning of that contradiction inflated to the point of banality, the contradiction between thinking and the blind irrational will, between the development of the intellect and vital activity.

However, it would be all too easy to think that the centipede's dilemma – where a burdensome excess of consciousness robs the centipede of its ability to walk – bore no relation to the real characteristics of the modern world, that it is merely an invention of reactionary philosophy. The prevalence of such opinions already points to the existence of objective causes, which again and again give rise to obsessive illusions.

There is no absolute surplus of conscious life. Most of humanity has hardly had its fill, and fortunately for society, it never will. Another thing entirely is the relative surplus of intellectual development; it comes with a sense that all intellectual forms created by history are worn out; these forms themselves become transparent through and through, mechanical, and unneeded, 'nothing but endings', to use Alexander Herzen's expression. That happens, just as there can be a relative glut of goods inaccessible to the hungry consumer.

Complaints at excessive intellectual refinement have been known since the days of Plato and Euhemerus; many educated Romans of Cicero's time preferred crude forms of figuration to the more subtle manner of virtuosic art. The entire history of social thought, aesthetics, and artistic literature constantly acquaints us with manifold variations on this theme. 'Woe from wit' is its name.

Of course, Hamlet, Prince of Denmark, or the inwardly weak, reflexively corroded heroes of nineteenth-century literature, beginning with Adolphe (from Benjamin Constant's famous novel) would be at a loss if faced with a phenomenon like the soup can. Then again, an entire epoch of capitalist development lies between them and Pop's orgy of stupidity.

Everything is relative. There was a time when sowing machines were considered a hazard to the nerves. The famous freedom of initiative characteristic of small-scale commodity production and the early capitalist order now appears as a spectre of the golden age. Freedom has long since turned into monopoly, and its venom poisons society from head to toe, subsuming any human self-activity to material relations that hollow it out to the point of sowing a terrifying emptiness at the heart of even the sweetest lives. Funeral services, art, and extra-marital affairs all become subject to 'business activity', which draws in its wake the tragicomic effect of completely formalising all human relations. The entire world is overshadowed by a tremendous new development of bureaucracy in all fields of life and the fusion of the machine of the economy with that of the state.

This surplus of ready forms, a kind of deadly boredom in the face of the most ebullient motion, is contemporary capitalism's dangerous legacy for the society to come. Its 'reorganisation', as it is called today in the West, makes man's personal involvement in his own functions spectral and conventional. The individual becomes a marionette of his own social status. Hasn't the human being finally become obsolete? Isn't it time for humanity to hand over its duties to giant machines of its own creation? This is how the question is often posed.

An awareness of powerlessness in the face of the pre-packaged, conventional forms of life will paralyse the vital energies of any conscious being. Such consciousness, indeed, would be superfluous. The work of a mind unable to influence reality at any key juncture verges on empty reflection. And here, it is not hard to imagine that life is so hard because conscious thought prevails over spontaneous action. Meanwhile, the habit of passivity and a natural selection of sorts that entrenches it in large groups of people, especially among the intelligentsia, confirms that there is an antagonism between thinking and free life activity. Wouldn't it thus be better for the world to remain mysterious and obscure? Wouldn't it be better for the humanity that lives in such a world to act blindly and to create without any conscious control, if the analysis of our situation keeps us from moving like Meyrink's centipede?

Hence, the fatal desire to kill or at least to weaken the intellect, replacing it with spontaneous activity at least for a moment, if possible. Hence, the various forms of artificial savagery ranging from simple hooliganism as a Sunday outlet for downtrodden creatures to the philosophical cult of the will, 'the will to power' or 'the artistic will' (*Kunstwollen*), all the way to automatic, consciously thoughtless painting and other paradoxes of a civilisation voluntarily taking a regressive view. Hence, as the last word in this self-denial of human thought, the desire to be a machine and the sacred dance of Pop Art's admirers around an ordinary soup can. 'Intellectuals hate pop', says the new Zarathustra Andy Warhol, 'but average people like it'.

Of course, Pop Art's originality is relative. Read the 'Technical Manifesto of Futurist Literature' of 1912. In principle, it already contains all of the Pop artists' disavowals of the spirit in favour of things, taken *brutto*, so to speak, in their crude, vulgar materiality. And the manifestos of Futurism's second wave in the 1920s? What about Prampolini's 'machine aesthetic', his ideal of man's transformation into a mechanism?

It makes perfect sense to draw an analogy between Pop Art and the Dadaism of the First World War. Marcel Duchamp already exhibited a bicycle wheel and a bottle-dryer with his signature. In 1917, he amazed the world with an ordinary urinal, shown in New York under the title 'Fountain' (there is an extensive literature on this historic event). Recently, an ageing but sprightly Duchamp gave an interview to a reporter from *Express*. He explained his prank through the desire to carry out an experiment on public taste. 'I choose the object least likely to be liked'. But since art is a mirage, 'the audience can be forced to believe in whatever'. This is why Pop Art's experiments have Duchamp's approval. 'It is quite fascinating to see works that introduce pictures from comics in great art's holy of holies. And to force the audience to swallow it all – that delights me'. What the audience swallows is not important; what is important is that there is 'an intellectual position' behind it, says Duchamp.

What is the 'intellectual position' that expresses itself in the vulgar, anti-poetic aesthetic of prefabricated objects or readymades discovered by Duchamp and other Dadaists? Why did Otto Van Rees, Francis Picabia, Kurt Schwitters and others who have gone down in art history (whether we like it or not) make all kinds of collages and counter-reliefs of real objects of everyday use, rags, machine parts, playing cards, tins, and old newspapers? What is the meaning of the 'lyricism' they found in sanitary fixtures, object of personal hygiene, machines, and electric fittings? As strange as it might be for the uninitiated reader to hear about such artistic phenomena, we should get used to the fact that they exist and have even come into common use among the 'cultivated people' of our own day.

Montaigne was right. Man is truly a strange creature! The spiritual position of Dada or Pop Art is a suicide of the spirit, or to use more scientific terms, an attempt to save oneself from an excess of feedback by fleeing to the opposite extreme – complete disengagement. Dada and Pop Art are extreme stages of a process akin to the sickly feeling of 'the powerlessness of the spirit' in the face of the spontaneous course of things, turning it into a kind of readymade subject to the laws of material production and administration.

On the basis of this 'materialised thinking', as it is sometimes called, consciousness flees from itself, giving rise to a special type of perverse pleasure in spoiling matters of the mind and turning them upside down. The cheapest, most vulgar, shameful things are now the most refined. This is how slaves act out against their slavery, thus reinforcing its bonds. If you cannot reach the desired degree of freedom, you have to kill the need for consciousness and debase the mirror reflecting such an abominable world, putting an end to any difference between consciousness and its object. Hence, the strange idea of replacing objects pictured on canvas with real objects and the most senseless ones at that. Figuration is cancelled as unneeded and secondary.

Still, the harder excessive consciousness tries to fall back onto unthinking matter, the more important the artist's 'spiritual position', and the more the life of his mind is shaped by tension, detachment from real content, and entanglement in self-reflection. Needless to say, this is a consciousness limited and satisfied by the conditions of the bourgeois order, limitations it tries to reinforce. Its main goal lies in the search for dumb self-confidence, a goal arising from the very practices of capitalism in its latest formation. Of course, contemporary bourgeois consciousness does not just live in the minds of millionaires, and no longer strives to be as transparent as glass, as it did in Descartes' day. On the contrary, it now seeks to attain opacity – that is its holiest goal. You need to force yourself into childish naïveté, to 'join the idiots', as one of Gorky's heroes famously put it. On the whole, Pop, that new lifestyle, is a form of nostalgia for a traditional, thick Americanism described with horror by writers of a more critical inclination.

Through Pop Art's deafening campaign, certain specifically American patterns of so-called mass culture have been reborn on a new level. There has been a revival of superheroes from detective films like the invincible secret agent James Bond; he is a familiar character, a healthy optimist who knows no doubt, for whom everything is conventional to the point of absurdity. In the opinion of Ivan Karp, the director of a private gallery that deals with Andy Warhol's work, the superman of Pop is the complete antithesis to the critically thinking individual; he is an optimiser who raises the audience's level of activity by lowering intellectual expectations. 'This is a stylised personality. It has no flaws, no self-observation, no self-analysis'.

It is not hard to see that the creators of this 'stylised personality' – the artist and his manager – reserve a place for themselves in the highest floor of consciousness. It is from here that they must regulate themselves and others, arousing the social psyche in the spirit of self-satisfied optimism. Thus, a characteristic form of doublethink emerges – the point of the game is to classify your true consciousness as top secret while banging it into your head that you are as simple and impervious as a machine.

Having passed through an extreme negation of philistine taste – long since the hallmark of a properly modern person – the so-called avant-garde now thirsts for peace in the embrace of the philistinism it once ridiculed. The modernist imaginary has seen such twists before – Maurice Barrès and Charles Maurras in France are example enough. The conscious revival of philistine primitivity is a phenomenon known to all modern nations, but it would lead us too far afield to discuss the political aspects of that phenomenon here. Let us simply note that this 'ambivalence' is a quality typical of contemporary bourgeois consciousness, returning to itself, to its own banality, after breaking with its surroundings in excessively 'leftist', anarcho-decadent forms. Of course, such philistinism raised to a new power presents something more than just a laboratory experiment of a new tendency. This chemical formula contains too clear a possibility for a transition from a refined pose to social demagogy on the scale of public squares and military parades, or at the very least, to a latter-day rendition of the Roman policy of 'bread and circuses'.

This is where we see the dangerous side and the darker shades of Pop Art's sham realism. We are dealing with the conscious imposition of a fashion for all kinds of trivia, for banal ideas, plots, forms, 'for American objects that speak for themselves because they are based on patterns you already learned as a schoolchild'. Pop is an aesthetic of patterns, of the vulgar taste of the crowd. Once snobbery has been rejected, overly subtle aesthetic sensibilities appear as a source of suffering, insufficiency, and even as a danger to society. It is much better to be born thick and stupid or to return to the first floor of consciousness through self-limitation, even at the price of losing the more complicated forms of spiritual life.

Is it possible to move in reverse like that? In part, yes, but ... The twentieth century's artificial primitivism – from the mimicry of African masks to replicas from the era of Ford the First – presuppose a complete absence of real naïveté. There can be little doubt that Pop Art is the worst kind of snobbery; it comes from a superficial, idle consciousness capable of shining through any naïve thought like an X-ray. Not only a simple relation to the world but overt sophistication are still too naïve for its liking. In a word, this subtle modern appeal to the psychology of the 'man in the street' presupposes a complex meta-structure of the spirit.

The taxicab company owner can rejoice; an enthusiasm for the vulgar atmosphere of business is the last word for the avant-garde. But for the new style's creator, vulgarity has become three times more sophisticated. (It is no coincidence that along with a wider Pop there also exists a 'min-pop', for the initiated, for the elite).* In that sense, the dissolution into mass culture has failed. Art loses many real values after so many speculative twists, but it has never succeeded in freeing itself from the idle reflection that persecutes it and drives it to oblivion. Despite all their thirst for thoughtless simplicity, there are two sides to these people. They often suffer under their own duplicity but even more make it into a life's vocation and a solid source of income.

Conclusion

It would be easy to show that this duplicity resembles the more tangible traits of bourgeois consciousness in political economy, sociology, and politics, not to mention the philosophical irrationalism of our time familiar from the Marxist literature. But one should hardly think that no one in the West or outside our own ecumene is capable of lucid thinking and that nobody is trying to find a solution to the great problems of modern life as conscientiously as possible. Even the contrivances of Rauschenberg or Warhol should not be seen as merely conforming to reactionary class interests. The apotheosis of vulgar commercial

---

*   This line is spurious and was omitted from the authorised German translation of the text, published in 1972.

taste can be an honest attempt to retain a special 'intellectual position' in a world of standardised subtlety and all-too-attainable cultivation.

What is at stake here is only the hopelessness of that position as it lures artists with promises of a return to ruddy-cheeked health. Of course, if you have enough surplus reflection in store, you can 'join the idiots' and make idiots out of others. But you won't be able to free yourself from your own odious intellectuality. The thirst for irrational forces free of thought and superfluous problems makes the artist's 'intellectual position' even more contemplative and passive.

Michelangelo, who imitated nature in his creations, made them by the sweat of his brow. Andy Warhol only bought a readymade soup can. The greatest work of Pop Art of all, said that modern master recently, is our planet Earth. That is a pithy statement. However, the planet Earth already exists, and there is no reason to create it anew. It is enough to separate this funny object from its 'customary context' or to look at it from the height of a detached 'intellectual position'. Under this transformative condition, it gains a second meaning and already becomes a work of art. Thus, art's great secret is to lead the simple life of a philistine, repressing its own indignation against such a life with the aid of special techniques of superconsciousness.

Pop Art did not invent this technique but only brought it to the point of total clarity. This is why it is only ridiculous when the defenders of abstract art complain about artistic life's infestation by soup cans, refrigerators, plastic products bought in the shop next door at standard prices, or old pots and pans. This is not the right material to foster the emergence of true beauty, explains Geneviève Bonnefoi in *Les lettres nouvelles*.* However, a few pages earlier, she enthuses over the work of the famous masters of the postwar Paris School, Jean Dubuffet and Jean Faurtrier. Let us now look at the substance of the excellent achievements of their art.

> Never before has anyone treated traditional painting and its very technologies so carelessly ... The tender palette of the Italian masters and the transparent, weightless, smooth-flowing oil painting – all of this has gone to the dogs, as if the Brothers Van Eyck had never walked the earth. Instead, painting now admits and recognises crude materials: tar, bitumen, plaster of paris, and sometimes just stucco, gravel, sand, white lead paint, or wet cement. The canvas is no longer able to bear this heavy burden and also disappears – it is replaced by wood or cardboard and sometime by imitation-marble stucco.

---

*   Footnote omitted in Russian original.

The academic critics did not like these bold innovations, writes Geneviève Bonnefoi mockingly. Why does she change her tune when faced with soup can paintings or a piece of junk taken from a trash pile? How is that any worse than dirt mixed with white lead paint? The most recent abstract painting yearns so for a confluence with crude matter and the spontaneous forces of nature that create optical effects without human help; it has come so far beyond the limits of figuration to the purely objective world that pioneers of the 'new reality' like Warhol have nothing left but to step across an almost non-existent boundary. You rejoice that the tender palette of the Italians or the transparent oil painting of the Brothers Van Eyck has gone to the dogs – then you shouldn't snivel if your mixture of sand and tar goes even further, into the desert of eternal nothingness where absolute zero reigns supreme.

Another opponent of Pop Art, the venerable Herbert Read, starts an octave lower than Geneviève Bonnefoi. The author of many works written in the spirit of earlier forms of modernism, which he always defended and justified, Read still considers them as the last word of innovation. In his view, this last word should remain the last. He thinks that modern art threatens to become incoherent, soulless, crude, and individualistic. Read still understands the beginning of abstract painting, but he is no longer convinced by the epileptic gestures of Jackson Pollock and other action painters. As for Pop Art, it is 'anti-art that completely lacks style'. There is nothing to speak about here. 'Crude scrawling and heaps of rubbish – what connection can they create between artist and viewer?' Moreover, 'this anti-art has no roots in the history of culture of the nations, it only serves tradesters as advertising for commodities', 'Pop Art is a product of capitalist competition', 'we have come within a hair's breadth of the problem of civilisational decline', etc.

Interestingly, these are the words of a rather authoritative representative of the new taste. Sir Herbert Read does not think much of American taste, as one can easily see in his article. That aside, he would like to see the triumph of modernism without its inevitable but utterly barbarous consequences. In a word, his position is the *via media*, the middle way, customarily considered a British virtue.

'Must the movement begun by Cézanne inevitably lead to decline? Of course not. Art must be revolutionary because it is an expression of the struggle against intellectual decline. But the social conditions of modernity have given rise to anti-art. And if art dies off, the human soul will become powerless, and barbarism will take over the world'.*

---

*   Footnote omitted in Russian original.

Rousing words! Sadly, having voluntarily conceded territory to the advance of barbarism, Herbert Read is powerless to avert his Dunkirk, to hold onto that narrow strip of bare earth. For decades, he himself bowed to the aesthetic of the aggressive artistic will (*Kunstwollen*), capable of imposing any command on the other's consciousness. Herbert Read's classical world is that of Cubism and its offspring. Where on this frontier can one defend art from 'crude scrawling'? It is amusing to see yesterday's barbarians defend their canons with a philistine umbrella.

'Must the movement begun by Cézanne inevitably lead to decline?', asks Herbert Read. Of course, there is no such fatal inevitability if the modern artist is still capable of returning to the objective truth of content and its realistic depiction. For Read, however, the main distinction between art and anti-art is not realism in a higher sense, but style, something akin to 'structure'. If an artist is capable of creating an organised, coherent form, even if it is partially formless and even crude, his work still remains within the boundaries of art.

However, this criterion of the new academism does not hold up to the facts. If the matter runs down to a form's submission to the unity of style, then Pop Art with its 'stylised personality' fits the bill quite well. Here, people really are trying to give back art some of its air-tight integrity. The deep flaw of tendencies like Pop Art is that the artist has no interest in the real content of matters. It doesn't matter in what name – what matters is to command elemental strength and the integrity of healthy being. And if this requires that one sacrifice one's aversion to vulgarity, then away with it! These people do not believe in truth, goodness, and beauty; they only believe in the formal organisation of the psyche through aggressive methods developed by modern advertising.

People's minds can be swayed, and the audience can be forced to swallow anything, as long as it is backed by a solid 'intellectual position'. The objective truth and its real images have been replaced by the hypnotic artistic will. Precisely therein lies the essence of modernism, as it negates the objective truth of any images we might see. This system of opinions has the aesthetics of suggestion, 'suggestivity' at its base. Anything else is just a stop or a way station. The path leading from Cubism to abstraction and from there to the art of refuse and readymades is not narrow and winding; instead, it is a broad superhighway, straight as an arrow.

It is not unintentional when Herbert Read overlooks the fact that the first experiments with the inclusion of real objects in painting date to the epoch of Cubism. It is enough to remember the so-called collages of Picasso and Braque from 1912–13, that is, the pasting-on of wallpaper, rags, newspapers or paper imitations of wood as well as the integration of readymade objects into painting and other miracles.

Jean Cocteau remembers that time:

> Picasso tried himself on whatever came to hand. A newspaper, a glass, a
> bottle of Anis del Mono, oil cloth, wallpaper, a pipe, a pack of tobacco,
> playing cards, a guitar, the cover of the romance Ma Paloma. Together
> with Braque, his fellow worker of miracles, he would hold veritable orgies
> of modest things. Why ever leave the studio? In Montmartre, one could
> find models to serve as a source for their harmony: these were ready-
> mades, for example, neckties bought in haberdasheries, fake marble and
> fake wood made of zinc, adverts for absinthe and other drinks, soot and
> scattered paper in place of dilapidated buildings, chalk drawings left over
> from hopscotch, the shop sign of a smoke store with two naïvely daubed
> pipes suspended on a band of sky blue coloring.[13]

Robert Rauschenberg and his friends have not invented anything new compared with this programme 40 years after the fact – nothing or almost nothing.
Just add a little to Cocteau's description; displays of standardised products and
collections of old rubbish, the so-called *Merzbau*, were already known to artists
from the age of Dada. Anti-art started long before Pop; it has already existed
for no less than half a century. If you will, its godfather was the poet Guillaume
Apollinaire, the Cubists' friend. Defending the right of the artist to make paintings from anything at all, he said: 'Mosaicists paint with marble or coloured
wood. There is mention of an Italian artist who painted with excrement; during the French revolution, blood served somebody as paint. You may paint with
whatever material you please, with pipes, postage stamps, postcards or playing
cards, candelabra, pieces of oil cloth, collars ...'.[14]

So, one can paint with paint – why can't one paint with collars? This is a
bold idea. One can pull a bad tooth – why not cut off the whole head to get rid
of a headache? Any idea taken to the point of limitless breadth will turn into
nonsense. Titian sometimes used his finger to paint; does that mean we can
dispense with brushes altogether? Why not then paint with your beard or your
hair, why not just daub the model in paint so that she might leave her trace
on the canvas herself (this is now called a 'living brush')? Even better is not
to paint at all, to let the forces of nature do their work on canvas. In the end,
the best thing of all is to turn one's back on art as such. Essentially, Apollinaire

---

13   *Cahiers D'art* 1932.

14   Apollinaire 1968, p. 232.

solves the problem of painting by abolishing painting and its difference from the reality it depicts. At this limit of abstraction, the artwork is identical with the real object and there is nothing left to separate them but the artist's purely notional 'intellectual position'.

Thus, Herbert Read could have noticed the beginning of art's withering away, a process that began when artists turned away from figuration. Hence, the search for materials incapable of depicting anything but themselves. Sawdust or sand take the place of paint. David Burlyuk threw his paintings into the dirt, anticipating Yves Klein and his 'cosmic art' by half a century. The next step is sculptural painting, consisting of spatial objects, sculpted or readymade, affixed to the canvas. The picture becomes a symbolic compilation of fragments from real life – old wheels and electric fixtures. More abstract constructions of metal, wood, glass and other technical materials follow suit. All that is left is to say farewell to visual art altogether and to declare that the highest sort of painting is to be found in simple life depicting nothing at all. In the words of one of the heroes of the novel *The Extraordinary Adventures of Julio Jurenito*, pork chops with peas are preferable to art.

This was the situation in the years of Herbert Read's youth, which is when anti-art first appeared along with the threat of voluntary barbarism. In Read's own books, we encounter the strange idea that it is time for art to leave behind depictions of life, since its goal is not to hold up a mirror to the world, but to become an independent reality. Beginning with Cubism, all modernist tendencies have prided themselves on discovering that pictures are special objects; they are independent of nature and do not repeat it. Much like the idealist philosophy of the twentieth century, painting wants to go beyond the accursed difference between subject and object. Its ideal is now the tortured spirit's happy identity with thoughtless matter. While Herbert Read writes of the intellectual powerlessness threatening the world, such powerlessness has long since been evident in the phenomena of ultra-modern art. Thought hates itself and attempts to use dark painterly techniques overflowing with crude matter to blind itself to the real appearance of the world – that has long since been the secret of that false, impotent philosophy habitually still called painting.

Why are you drying your tears, ladies and gentlemen? You didn't like the nasty faces made at your art by its naughty child, Pop? You wanted this yourselves, you taught it all kinds of bad behaviour, you broke the foundations of a normal upbringing created by centuries of noble work like useless trash impeding the creative will. So, now, don't complain; having lost your head, you shouldn't cry over losing your hair.

Art arose in a time out of mind as the depiction of real objects outside ourselves. At a certain level of artistic development, this figuration gave rise to the opposite tendency from its own depths. Depictions of the real receded until they became a negative value, an 'intellectual position' without a filling. The history of the soup can began on the day the modern artist thought of transforming his painting into an independent object bereft of any reflexive quality. The principle was discovered; all that was left was to find a technical solution. Take only one more step, and we will once again be facing the object with which the development of art began. The soup can is a soup can. Absolute identity has been attained.

CHAPTER 3

Why am I Not a Modernist?

Having written this heading in the style of Bertrand Russell, my answer should be a formula just as concise. It won't hurt to be sharp to the point of paradox. You have to obey the laws of the genre.

So, why am I not a modernist? Why does the slightest hint of such ideas in art and philosophy provoke my innermost protest?

Because in my eyes modernism is linked to the darkest psychological facts of our time. Among them are a cult of power, a joy at destruction, a love for brutality, a thirst for a thoughtless life and blind obedience.

Maybe I've forgotten something substantial in this list of the twentieth century's mortal sins. Already my answer is longer than the question. To me, modernism is the greatest possible treachery of those who serve the department of spiritual affairs – *la traison des clercs*, as the famous expression of one French writer has it. The conventional collaborationism of academics and writers with the reactionary policies of imperialist states is nothing compared to the gospel of new barbarity implicit to even the most heartfelt and innocent modernist pursuits. The former is like an official church, based on the observance of traditional rites. The latter is a social movement of voluntary obscurantism and modern mysticism. There can be no two opinions as to which of the two poses a greater public danger.

If an author dares write on this subject so directly, he must ready himself for the harshest of rejoinders.

– How could it be? You've painted a portrait of a German storm trooper or an Italian blackshirt, and now you want to convince us of his immediate kinship to the sultry Matisse, the gentle Modigliani or the sullen Picasso?

Of course not. I wasn't planning any attack on the moral reputation of these individuals. But still, let's not deprive ourselves of the capacity for judging historical phenomena independently of how we judge this or that individual protagonist. Bakunin was a man famous for his revolutionary largesse of heart, but anarchism is the bourgeois character turned inside out, as Lenin put it.

Still, wasn't it Hitler who persecuted the so-called modern artists, declaring them to be degenerates and pests? Didn't you know that the bearers of the Western avant-garde's refined aesthetic culture had to flee from the Nazis?

Of course, I know. But let me soothe your disquiet with a little story taken from life. In 1932, the National Socialist government of the state of Anhalt closed the Bauhaus in Dessau, a famous hotbed of the 'new spirit' in art, presenting quite a vivid symptom of the Third Reich's future cultural policy. The Parisian journal *Cahiers D'art*, published by Christian Zervos, an influential supporter of Cubism and later tendencies, answered this sad news from Germany with the following note (Nos. 6–7): 'For reasons we cannot comprehend, the National Socialist party displays a decisive hostility to genuine modern art. This position seems all the more paradoxical since this party foremost wants to attract the youth. Is it acceptable to absorb all these youthful elements, so full of enthusiasm, vital force, and creative potential, only to once again return them to the lap of outmoded tradition?'

Ah, you still don't get it, scumbag? Heinz, Fritz, come on, explain it to him! And explain they did.

That is the actual picture of manners in Europe on the eve of Hitler's Walpurgis night. How much grovelling is there in the note above, and how accurately it depicts the admiration for the false youth of barbarians that led to the cultural Munich of the 1930s. In the depths of their souls, the advocates of 'genuinely modern art' were infected with the same cult of vitality and spontaneous energy. It was the same wind that took them so far from the shores of the 'liberal-Marxist nineteenth century'.

I understand that the editors of the Parisian journal are educated, refined people at a great remove from the demagogy of street-criers offering lessons in amateurish *Heimatkunst*. This was hardly what they had imagined as a world rejuvenated, freed of canons and norms. And of course they were hardly expecting the petty demons of literary bohemia and the boulevard writers to actually rise to power as they expounded the myth of the twentieth century in the language of Nietzsche and Spengler, diluted with the slavering of a rabid dog.

Nietzsche himself cultivated a deep disgust for the plebeian tastelessness of beerhall politicians, and no doubt he would have disowned his spiritual heirs. Spengler managed in his lifetime to forswear them from the position of a more respectable bourgeois Caesarism ... The logic of things, however, acts on its own. There is such a thing as retribution, and it is terrible. Speaking in a Hegelian spirit, Marx and Engels called it the irony of history.

You wanted vitality? You were fed up with civilization? You fled from reason to the dark world of instinct, you scorned the masses in their aspirations to the basics of culture, you demanded that the majority offer blind obedience to the irrational call of the superman? So, here you are, you're welcome to all of what you have coming to you.

Here's another strange story. In 1940, an elderly Henri Bergson set out in the company of his nurse to register with the German occupation authorities in Paris. They say it was the last time he went outside – the world-famous thinker died before he could reach Auschwitz. Who can say that this man wasn't talented and honest somehow? There is enough proof in that he wanted to share the fate of his people, even though he had long since broken with Judaism.

Still, one fact remains incontestable. Henri Bergson was the leader of a new direction in philosophy that accomplished a far-reaching re-evaluation of values in the early twentieth century. He was one of the first to checkmate the king, to raise the question of reason's disavowal of its inherited rights. Since then, everything changed in the realm of ideas. The barons of vital power and the active life took centre stage. The price of suffering declined, and brutality became a token of noble character. The countless followers of Bergson and William James were ready to embrace the ideals of violence well before the First World War, with very different figures already visible on the horizon. The hero of Henry de Montherlant's novel *Le Songe* (1922) is out to 'negate the mind and the heart' when he shoots the first surrendering German soldier he sees in the face.

It goes without saying that the French were not alone in making such discoveries. On the contrary, an even darker evolution was underway on the other side of the Rhein. No one suspected that the weak 'will to power' of decadent thinkers would realise itself in the race laws of the Third Reich. What devilry was afoot to upset the game? It's none of our business; it's enough that it happened.

One could come up with quite a few more examples, but the one that best fits our historical subject is the fate of the German thinker Theodore Lessing, murdered by the Nazis in August 1933. It goes without saying that he had nothing to do with Nazism in his convictions, and he couldn't have. Still, Lessing's philosophy of history was one of a meaningless flow of facts and forces, set up to combat the 'spirituality' of modern culture and to polemicise against objective truth while calling for open mythmaking. All of these things entered the prehistory of Hitler's Germany in one way or another. But that's what you wanted, hapless Georges Dandin!

You might say that there is no direct connection between the teachings of Theodore Lessing and the murderer's bullet. Of course there isn't. Now nobody believes in the wisdom of providence leading us to our higher goal with rewards and punishments. Those are children's fairytales. In the world of facts, everything follows the laws of scientific necessity. Yet still, the religious imagination has real causes at its root and presents a poor copy of actual relations. There is no such thing as providence. There is, however, the natural interconnectedness of things, from which a moral meaning is not entirely absent. And when this moral meaning appears unexpectedly in the fate of persons or entire peoples, we witness it as the birth of a tragedy, or, more often, a tragicomedy.

You will tell me that there is a big difference between the subtle, partially justified polemic of a thinker in his study against the boundless power of intellection, and the famous phrase from the Nazi writer Hanns Johst's drama *Schlageter*: 'Whenever I hear [the word] "culture" ... I remove the safety from my Browning!' Of course, the difference is huge. Everything is very complicated in this most complicated of worlds. Among the creators of the *espirit nouveau* in art and philosophy, some really did sympathise with fascism in its different guises: we know their names, beginning with Marinetti. Others felt fascism's heavy hand, as fate would have it. We also know that the national upsurge of a people often goes together with the *Sturm und Drang* of new tendencies in art. Such obvious facts are impossible to deny. Among the modernists, there are individuals of an impeccable inner purity, martyrs, and even heroes. In a word, there are good modernists, but there is no such thing as good modernism.

Matters here are the same as in the field of religion. The Catholic monks of the Basque country fought on the side of the Republic against Franco, and when Mussolini's regime fell in Italy, some priests rang the Internationale from their steeples. These are our brothers; they are closer to our Marxist creed than all those political windbags who repeat Marxist phrases to further their careers. Many believers deserve respect. However, there is no such thing as good religion, since religion is always invisibly tied to centuries of slavery.

So don't be in such a rush to liquidate the legacy of the Renaissance or that of the free-thinking nineteenth century. Don't join the crowd of modern philistines in chanting that these are not will-o'-the-wisps in the dark night of the millennium, but flashes of distant lightning illuminating the path into the future. Don't cast your gaze back to the new Middle Ages like the prophets of regressions. And if you do, don't complain if they force you to believe in the absurd and tell you where exactly to find beauty, under blows or worse. That, after all, is the reality of spiritual primitivism.

You might say that my examples only concern the masters of theoretical invention, gentlemen who today enjoy less respect than people of the arts. Alright then, let's turn to the artists themselves.

Picasso was unhappy that the revolutionary governments place such an importance on museums and the general enlightenment of the broader masses in the spirit of the classical legacy. In 1935, he told Christian Zervos:

> The museums are so many lies, the people who occupy themselves with art are for the most part imposters. I don't understand why there should be more prejudices about in the revolutionary countries than in the backward ones! We have imposed upon the pictures in the museums all our stupidities, our errors, the pretenses of our spirit. We have made poor

ridiculous things of them. We cling to myths instead of sensing the inner life of the men who painted them. There ought to be an absolute dictatorship ... a dictatorship of painters ... the dictatorship of a painter ... to suppress all who have deceived us, to suppress the trickster, to suppress the matter of deception, to suppress habits, to suppress charm, to suppress history, to suppress a lot of other things. But good sense will always carry the day. One ought above all to make a revolution against good sense! The true dictator will always be vanquished by the dictatorship of good sense ... Perhaps not![1]

It is sad to read these lines, especially if one remembers that in 1935, there was already a totalitarian artist-dictator, or a failed artist, no matter. I mean Hitler, of course, whose biography we know. For some reason all dictators since Nero have imagined themselves to be very strong in the arts.

You tell me that this is not what Picasso wanted. Who would think otherwise? You can be sure that I appreciate Picasso's political views and the nobility of his intentions. As for his worldview, he is careless in his thinking to say the least.

There is great danger in such invocations of forces capable of driving the mindless masses into a new realm of beauty by force. There is no such thing as enlightened despotism. Despotism is always unenlightened. Moreover, the stick always has two ends, and this is something we should never forget. If Picasso meant the Soviet Union with his 'the revolutionary countries', our society rejected the dream of a 'total dictatorship' in the field of the arts, thank god. While such phenomena are familiar from the past, they bear no relation to the principles of the socialist order. They are abuses of power, just like any other iniquity.

In the years of my youth, the modernists were very strong in revolutionary Russia, and they often resorted to violence without ever suspecting that they would have to bear the consequences themselves one day. It was only with great difficulty that People's Commissar of Enlightenment Anatoly Lunacharsky could stem the tide of the ultra-left on orders from Lenin, who later reprimanded the former for being too lax. Once there was some sort of disagreement between Ilya Ehrenburg and the famous left-wing theatre director Vsevolod Meyerhold, who headed the theatrical section of the People's Commissariat of Enlightenment in the early days of the revolution. Unhappy with

---

1 Zervos and Picasso 1968, p. 53.

Ehrenburg's aesthetic views, Meyerhold didn't hesitate to call the commander of the guard to demand his interlocutor's immediate arrest. The commander had no right to make arrests and refused. Ilya Ehrenburg remembers this in his memoirs as a pleasant joke, steeped in the foggy past, but it sends chills down my spine. I remember Meyerhold from later on, when the sword was already hanging over his neck, and I feel deeply and honestly sorry for the artist and the man. So many tragedies, and all of them full of bitter meaning! 'We learn through suffering', chants the chorus in Aeschylus' *Oresteia*.

Ehrenburg presents the cult of power and destruction inherent to all modernism in the person of Julio Jurenito, who dreams of a bare humanity on the bare earth, and sees war and revolution as little more than steps to this long-cherished goal; the worse, the better. 'The great provocateur' of the writer's imagination may have been unhappy with the moderation of the Russian communists, especially in matters of culture, but Lenin liked Ehrenburg's novel. The figure of Julio Jurenito and his whole milieu reflected a force that he understood very well, deeming it the greatest enemy of communism, even if it played a certain role in the destruction of the old Russia. This force is petit-bourgeois spontaneity, capable of destroying and even razing the fundament of cultures like an act of nature, the breath of the desert, full of a great Nothingness.

This power is ever-changing and has many faces. Julio Jurenito killed himself, disappointed with Lenin's desire to save the legacy of the past to further develop its positive values. But what if the 'great provocateur' had lived to a later time? Who knows, he might have turned out to be the right-hand-man of Yezhov or Beria. I could also imagine him as a patron of the arts, supporting pompous pseudo-realistic painting with pictures of banquets, receptions and other celebrations. Why not? Doesn't the whole world now value such amateurish daubery as 'modern primitivism'? Didn't Henri Rousseau already drag up all the dredges of the petit-bourgeois soul? Isn't he a modernist classic? Don't the surrealists trace out the details of their works with a meticulousness that any academic painter would envy? There are possibilities for an as yet unheard-of modernism on the basis of the Victorian style, retaining all the features of nineteenth-century genre painting.

When you say that Hitler was a proponent of realistic pictorial forms, allow me to answer that this is untrue. First, there was plenty of ordinary modernist posturing in the Third Reich's official art. Its fake restoration of realistic forms is often reminiscent of the New Objectivity movement of Munich in its inflated pathos and its striving to monumentality, soaked through and through with arbitrary artifice. This is even more obvious in Italy, where Marinetti's futurism took up a position as official art along with the artificial neoclassicism that emerged from the same decline.

Second, the social demagogy of reactionary forces always appropriates some of its mortal enemies' outer traits. This is necessary to draw crowds and to attract 'the man in the street'. It's enough just to remember the name of Hitler's party. There are many 'socialisms' that have nothing in common with the real content of this notion. Does it really follow that we should renounce socialism? An old legend says that Christ and the Anti-Christ look alike. And really, such optical illusions are no rarity in fateful moments of history. Woe to those who cannot tell the living from the dead! We first need to reject the outer analogies so readily used by the enemies of socialism when they confuse the illnesses of a new society with the purulent ulcers of the old world.

Third, the future is born in agony. 'We learn through suffering'. Art must rise up out of the deep hole in which it now finds itself (as many authoritative witnesses of various directions recognise), and anyone who thinks there is any other way is simply a very nervous gentleman. The field of literature has been luckier than painting, if only because its strongest time is not so far from our own. The tradition of classical realism is still alive in literature, for which there is also some evidence in the works of contemporary Western writers popular in the Soviet Union (often more than at home).

Still, let's get back to Picasso. To prove our loyalty, let's compare him to Balzac. In one of his novels, the great French writer drew up a utopia of social Bonapartism that came true as a terrible caricature just in the moment after he died and Napoleon III came to power. The real course of history doesn't follow orders; it will take a path of its own, and the only conclusion you might draw is that the initial idea needs a more concrete development, allowing one to draw a maximum use from history's unexpected twists. As for ideas like that of the total artist-dictator who liquidates history to forcibly impose Cubism, abstract art, or some other modernist balderdash, it's better not to have such ideas at all.

Picasso's conversation with Zervos appeared in Nos. 7–10 of the *Cahiers D'art* in 1935. When Zervos wanted to show the artist his notes, the latter answered: 'You need not show them to me. The essential, in these times of moral misery, is to create enthusiasm. How many people have read Homer? Nevertheless everyone speaks of him. Thus the Homeric myth has been created. A myth of this kind creates a precious excitation. It is enthusiasm of which we have the most need, we and the young'.[2]

I have no desire to accuse Picasso of anything. All the more since he must have had occasion to hear much strong abuse from his fellow modernists. What

---

2 Zervos and Picasso 1968, p. 48.

is important to me is to mark the main features of the worldview we are offered as the lodestar of the future art – the renunciation of realistic pictures, which Picasso sees as an empty illusion, that is, deception, and the affirmation of a wilful fiction, designed to spark enthusiasm, that is, the conscious deception of mythmaking. For the lack of space we will leave aside the social causes that give rise to these strange, contradictory phantasms as they appear in the tide of forms created by 'genuine modern art'.

Let's just say that the main inner goal of such art lies in suppressing the consciousness of the conscious mind. A flight into superstition is the very minimum. Even better is a flight into an unimaginable world. Hence, the constant effort to shatter the mirror of life or at least to make it muddy and unseeing. Any image must now be given qualities of 'unlikeness'. In the way, pictoriality recedes, eventually becoming something free of any association with real life.

The founder of surrealism André Breton once complained that the demon of real imagination is strong. Once it was enough to present a few geometrical figures on the canvas to avoid any associations. Now this is too little. The self-defences of consciousness are so refined that even abstract forms are reminiscent of something real. That requires an even greater degree of detachment. Hence, there appears anti-art, Pop Art, which largely consists of the demonstration of real things, enclosed in an invisible frame. In a sense, this is the end of a long evolution from real depictions to the reality of bare facts.

It might seem we've already achieved that goal: the life of the spirit has ended, the worm of consciousness has been crushed. Still, that is an empty illusion. The ailing spirit's attempts to jump out of its own skin are senseless and hopeless. When reflection revolves around itself endlessly, it only gives rise to 'boring infinity' and an insatiable thirst for the other. If any phenomenon needs to be taken on its own terms, then 'modern art' is only comprehensible to a mind that has been initiated into this mystery. All else is either a naïvely pedestrian adjustment to the last fashion, or the unconscionable phraseology of interested parties wishing to smuggle their wares under a false flag.

Yes, 'modern art' is more philosophy than art. It is a philosophy expressing the dominance of power and facts on lucid thinking and poetic contemplation of the world. The brutal demolition of real forms stands for an outburst of blind embittered volition. It is the slave's revenge, his make-believe liberation from the yoke of necessity, a simple pressure valve. If it were only a pressure valve! There is a fatal connection between the slavish form of protest and oppression itself. According to all the newest aesthetic theories, art's effect is hypnotic: it traumatises or on the contrary blunts or calms a consciousness that no longer has any life of its own. In short, it is the art of a suggestible crowd at the ready to run after the emperor's chariot. In the face of such a programme, my vote goes to the most mediocre, derivative academicism, since that is the lesser evil. But it goes without saying that my ideal lies elsewhere, as the reader can guess.

People who delight at the revelations of the kind conveyed through Zervos have no right to find fault with the theory of the 'big lie' in politics, the mythologies created through film, radio, and press, the 'manipulation' of human consciousness by the powers that be, and so on. The modernists never opposed such methods. On the contrary, their idea is mass hypnosis, 'suggestive persuasion', raising a rather dark enthusiasm, and not reasonable thinking and a light sense of truth. Modernism is a modern superstition, slightly insincere, much like the one in late antiquity that gave rise to the belief in the miracles worked by philosopher Apollonius of Tyana.

However, such superstitions are now asserted with the most modern means. One recalls Lev Tolstoy's words on 'epidemic suggestions', spread through the printing press.

> With the development of the press, it has now come to pass that so soon as any event, owing to casual circumstances, receives an especially prominent significance, immediately the organs of the press announce this significance. As soon as the press has brought forward the significance of the event, the public devotes more and more attention to it. The attention of the public prompts the press to examine the event with greater attention and in greater detail. The interest of the public further increases, and the organs of the press, competing with one another, satisfy the public demand. The public is still more interested; the press attributes yet more significance to the event. So that the importance of the event, continually growing, like a lump of snow, receives an appreciation utterly inappropriate to its real significance, and this appreciation, often exaggerated to insanity, is retained so long as the conception of life of the leaders of the press and of the public remains the same. There are innumerable examples of such an inappropriate estimation which, in our time, owing to the mutual influence of press and public on one another, is attached to the most insignificant subjects.[3]

We must factor in the coefficient of 'epidemic suggestion' whenever we talk about the miracles of modernism. Whatever Tolstoy might have seen has long

---

3 Tolstoy 1906, pp. 98–9.

since been eclipsed by modern advertising. In the old art, it was important to depict the real world as lovingly and conscientiously as possible. The artist's personality more or less stepped into the background with regard to its output and thus rose above its own level. In the newest art, exactly the opposite is true: the artist's work is merely a sign, a token of his personality. 'Everything I spit out is art', said the famous German Dadaist Kurt Schwitters, 'because I am an artist'. In a word, it doesn't matter what you make. What's important is the artist's gesture, his pose, his reputation, his signature, his sacerdotal dance for the camera, his wondrous acts, proclaimed for the world to hear. He can heal by the laying-on of hands, they say.

This new mythology has little in common with the one from whose depths art was born. The art of real primitives is far superior. Everything in it has the charm of awakening minds and hearts, everything promises to flourish as desired. There is much to learn from the Old Masters of our old Europe, from the Africans, or from the artists of the pre-Colombian Americas. But what will you learn? That is the main question. Goethe said that there is no returning to your mother's womb.* As charming as childhood is, so savage is the adult's desire to lay down the burden of thought and return to infancy. If you don't see the onset of night as a fatal feature of the modern world, you must be against an art that draws from the Middle Ages, Egypt, or Mexico dark primordial abstractions, the happy absence of personal thought, 'conciliarity', as the Russian decadents of the early twentieth century put it, that paradise of educated souls, fed up with their own intellectuality, their own odious freedom.

The language of forms is the language of the spirit. It's the same philosophy, if you please. For example, you see the bowed heads, humble eyes, and hieratic gestures of people dressed up in worker's overalls or peasant jackets, you know exactly what the artist wants to say. He is seducing you with the dissolution of individual self-consciousness in the blind collective will, the absence of inner turmoil, mindless bliss – in a word, a utopia far closer to the one Orwell draws up in his caricature of communism than to the ideal of Marx, Engels, and Lenin. I feel sorry for this artist. Blessed innocence! Pray to your god that your higher mathematics never find their real model in the actual world. Then again, I can already see your dismay when the man in the peasant jacket finally awakens from his century of slumber and, one would hope, decides he no longer wants

---

*   There is no such direct quote attributed to Goethe. The reference here is possibly to one of Goethe's proverbs: 'In mother's lap, in comfort's glow, / The child his life would make; / Yet if to man he e'er shall grow, / The child must stir and wake.'

to pose in the role of an Egyptian slave subject to monumental rhythms and the laws of frontality. By the way, for the majority of people, museums are not 'so many lies' (as Picasso put it), since these people hardly suffer under a glut of culture. They want to be individuals.

Caesar fawns over the consecrated crowd, but the communist has no need of a crowd blinded by myths. He needs a people composed of conscious individuals. 'The free development of each is the condition for the free development of all', it says in the *Communist Manifesto*. This is why I am against the so-called new aesthetic, whose outer shell of novelty hides a mass of old, brutal ideas.

May Lenin's teachings always be our banner. Their subject is the historical self-activity of the popular masses, and all Caesarism along with the attendant atmosphere of miracles and superstition is hostile to our idea. We stand for the combination of living popular enthusiasm with the clear light of science and an understanding of the actual reality accessible to any literate person, with all the elements of an artistically developed culture attained by humanity ever since the individual emerged from blind obedience to inherited ways of life.

So let them tell us tall tales of the happy land of Archaia and of the new primitivism of the twentieth century. Modern primitivism, to speak with Hobbes, is 'a robust but malicious boy', somebody you don't want to argue with in dark alleyways. May Kafka – an intelligent but ailing artist – rise from the grave to write a bold allegory on the modern worshippers of darkness, including his own, like that of Capek's tale of the newt who rejects conventions and tradition. As for me, I've had my fill of the twentieth century's primitivism.

This is why I am not a modernist.

References

Agamben, Giorgio 2009, 'What is the Contemporary', in *What is an Apparatus*, Stanford: Stanford University Press.

Apollinaire, Guillaume 1968 [1913], 'The Cubist Painters', in *Theories of Modern Art: A Sourcebook*, edited by Peter Selz and Herschel Chip Browning, Berkeley, CA: University of California Press.

Baker, Russell 1963, 'Art Goes Popular', *New York Times*, vol. 112, no. 38.

Benchley, Peter 1966, 'The Story of Pop! What It Is and How It Came to Be', *Newsweek*, vol. 67, no. 17, 56–70.

Berdyaev, Nikolay 1982 [1914], 'Picassos in the Shchukin collection', in *A Picasso Anthology. Documents, Criticism, Reminiscences*, edited by Marilyn McCully, Princeton, NJ: Princeton University Press.

Berger, John 1965, *The Success and Failure of Picasso*, Harmondsworth: Penguin.

Berne-Jouffroy, André 1962, 'L'art et la critique' [Art and Criticism], *Preuves*, no. 138.

Bernier, Rosamond 1963, 'Robert et Ethel Scull', *L'Oeil, Revue d'Art Mensuelle*, no. 106.

Braque, Georges 1992 [1912], 'Thoughts on Painting', in *Art in Theory 1900–1990: An Anthology of Changing Ideas*, edited by Charles Harrison and Paul Wood, Oxford: Blackwell.

Cahiers D'art 1932, nos. 3–5, special issue devoted to the Picasso exhibition at Galerie Georges Petit, Paris.

Chastel, André 1955, 'Le jeu et le sacré dans l'art moderne' [Game and the Sacred in Modern Art], *Critique*, no. 97.

Chukhrov, Keti 2013, 'Classical Art and Human Resignation in Soviet Marxism', in *Sweet Sixties: Specters and Spirits of a Parallel Avant-garde*, Berlin: Sternberg Press.

Ehrenburg, Ilya 1930, *The Extraordinary Adventures of Julio Jurenito and His Disciples*, trans. Usik Vanzler, New York: Covici-Friede.

Everdell, William R. 1997, *The First Moderns: Profiles in the Origins of Twentieth-Century Thought*, Chicago: University of Chicago Press.

Feher, Ferenc 1979, 'Lukacs in Weimar', in *Telos*, 39: 113–36.

Fridlender, Georgy 2008, 'Myshi kota khronili' [The Mice Buried the Cat], 'Conspectus of public discussion of The Crisis of Ugliness in Leningrad', in *Pochemu ya ne modernist* [Why Am I Not a Modernist], Moscow: Iskusstvo – XXI Vek.

Ganteführer-Trier, Anne 2004, *Cubism*, New York: Taschen.

Garaudy, Roger 1963, *D'un Réalisme sans rivages: Picasso, Saint-John, Perse, Kafka* [Realism without Borders: Picasso, Saint-John, Perse, Kafka], Paris: Plon.

Garaudy, Roger 1964, 'Reflexions sur le Realisme et sur ses Rivages' [Reflection on Realism and its Frontiers], *Les Lettres Francaises*, no. 1014.

Garaudy, Roger 1965, 'O realizme i ego beregakh' [On Realism and its Frontiers], *Inostrannaya Literatura*, no. 4.

Gehlen, Arnold 1965, *Zeit-Bilder: zur Soziologie und Ästhetik der modernen Malerei*, Frankfurt a.M.: Athenäum Verlag.

Gerovich, Slava 2002, *From Newspeak to Cyberspeak: A History of Soviet Cybernetics*, Cambridge, MA: MIT Press.

Gleizes, Albert 1920, *Du cubisme et des moyens de le comprendre*, Paris.

Gleizes, Albert 1924, *La peinture et ses lois*, Paris.

Gleizes, Albert and Jean Metzinger 1968 [1923], 'From Cubism, 1912', in *Theories of Modern Art: A Sourcebook*, edited by Peter Selz and Herschel Chip Browning, Berkeley, CA: University of California Press.

Gleizes, Albert 1992 [1912], 'Cubism', in *Art in Theory 1900–1990: An Anthology of Changing Ideas*, edited by Charles Harrison and Paul Wood, Oxford: Blackwell.

Golding, John 1959, *Cubism: A History and an Analysis, 1907–1914*, London: Faber and Faber.

Golding, John 1988 [1959], *Cubism. A History and an Analysis 1907–1914*, Cambridge, MA: Belknap Press of Harvard University Press.

Gray, Christopher 1953, *Cubist Aesthetic Theories*, Baltimore, MD: Johns Hopkins Press.

Hess, Werner 1956, *Dokumente zum Verständnis der modernen Malerei*, Hamburg: Rowohlt.

Hoctin, Luce 1964, *L'Oeil, Revue d'Art Mensuelle*, no. 120.

Hourcade, Olivier 1912, 'Discussions. A M Vauxcelles', *Paris Journal*.

Illés, László 1993, 'The Struggle for "Reconciliation"?: György Lukács's Marxist Aesthetic in the 1930s', in *Hungarian Studies on György Lukács*, Budapest: Akadémiai Kiadó.

Jubara, Annett 2010, 'Universalism in cultural history and the meaning of the Russian Revolution: on some aspects of cultural theory in the work of Mikhail Lifšic', *Studies in East European Thought*, 62, 3/4.

Kahnweiler, Daniel 1946, *Juan Gris. Sa vie, son oeuvre, ses ecrits*, Paris.

Kasakow, Evgenij 2013, 'Die Fantasie von der Macht fernhalten. Michail Lifschitz. Ein Westmarxist im Osten', in *Ästhetik ohne Widerstand. Texte zu reaktionären Tendenzen in der Kunst*, Mainz: Ventil.

Klemperer, Victor 1957, *Moderne französische Lyrik*, Berlin: Deutscher Verlag der Wissenschaften.

Korallov, Marlen 2008, 'Kak poyavilos' esse' [How the Essay Appeared] in *Pochemu ya ne modernist* [Why Am I Not a Modernist], Moscow: Iskusstvo – XXI Vek.

Le Figaro litteraire 1963, 'Banalité sans rivages', no. 920.

Lebel, Robert 1964, *L'Envers de la peinture. Moeurs et coutumes des tableauistes*, Monaco: Editions du Rocher.

Lenin, Vladimir I. 1960 [1897], 'A Characterisation of Economic Romanticism (Sismondi and Our Native Sismondists)', in *Collected Works*, Volume 2, Moscow: Progress Publishers.

Lenin, Vladimir I. 1963, 'Marxism and Revisionism', in *Collected Works*, Volume 15, Moscow: International Progress Publishers.

Lenin, Vladimir I. 1964 [1902], 'Revolutionary Adventurism', in *Collected Works*, Volume 6, Moscow: Progress Publishers.

Lenin, Vladimir I. 1965 [1918], 'The Valuable Admissions of Pitirim Sorokin', in *Collected Works*, Volume 28, Moscow: Progress Publishers.

Lenin, Vladimir I. 1965 [1922], 'Notes of a Publicist', in *Collected Works*, Volume 33, Moscow: International Progress Publishers.

Lifshitz, Mikhail 1954, 'Dnevnik Marietty Shaginyan' [The Diary of Marietta Shaginian], *Novy Mir*, 2. Online at http://www.gutov.ru/lifshitz/texts/dnevnikm.htm

Lifshitz, Mikhail 1979, *Iskusstvo i sovremenniy mir*.

Lifshitz, Mikhail 1988, 'Iz avtobiografii ideiy. Besedy M.A. Lifshitsa' in Kontekst 1987. Literaturno-teoreticheskie issledovaniya', Moscow: Nauka, pp. 264–318. Online at http://www.gutov.ru/lifshitz/mesotes/avtobiograf.htm

Lifshitz, Mikhail 1990, 'Dva vzglyada na proizvedeni Solzhenitsyna: "Odin den' Ivana Denisovicha", "V kruge pervom"' [Two Views of Solzhenitsyn's Work: 'A Day in the Life of Ivan Denisovich,' 'In the First Circle'], in *Voprosy literatury* July 1990, 73–83.

Lifshitz, Mikhail 2007, 'Pro Domo Sua', *Novoe literaturnoe obozrenie*, 88. Online at http://magazines.russ.ru/nlo/2007/88/li4.html

Lifshitz, Mikhail 2009, 'Iz perepiski Mikh. Lifshitsa s G.M. Fridlenderom po povodu stat'i 'Pochemu ya ne modernist'', 1966–67, in *Pochemu ya ne modernist*, Moscow: Iskusstvo – XXI Vek.

Lhote, André 1956, *La peinture libérée*, Paris: Grasset.

Lunacharsky, Anatoly V. 1941a, 'Salon nezavisimykh' [The Salon de indépendants], in *Stat'i ob iskusstve* [Articles on Art], edited by Igor A. Sats, Moscow-Leningrad: Iskusstvo.

Lunacharsky, Anatoly V. 1941b, 'Vil'gel'm Gauzenshteyn' [Wilhelm Hausenstein], in *Stat'i ob iskusstve* [Articles on Art], edited by Igor A. Sats, Moscow-Leningrad: Iskusstvo.

Maritain, Jacques 1962, 'Frontiers of Poetry', in *Art and Scholasticism and the Frontiers of Poetry*, trans. Joseph W. Evans, New York: Charles Scribner's Sons, available at: https://maritain.nd.edu/jmc/etext/frontier.htm

Marx, Karl 1976 [1867], *Capital: A Critique of Political Economy*, Volume 1, trans. Ben Fowkes, London: Penguin.

Mauclair, Camille 1906, *Trois crises de l'art actuel* [The Three Crises of Modern Painting], Paris: E. Fasquelle.

Mitchell, Stanley 2006, 'Mikhail Lifshits: a Marxist Conservative', in *Marxism and the History of Art*, Ann Arbor MI: Pluto Press.

Novotny, Fritz 1932, 'Das Problem des Menschen Cézannes im Verhaltnis zu seiner Kunst', *Zeitschrift Fur Aesthetik and Allgemeine Kunstwissenschaft*, no. 26.

Oitinnen, Vesa and Andrey Maidansky 2016, 'Special issue on Mikhail Lifshits – An enigmatic Marxist', *Studies in East European Thought*, 68, 4.

Ozenfant, Amédée and Charles-Édouard Jeanneret 1925, *La peinture moderne* [Modern Painting], Paris: Editions G. Crès.

Packard, Vance 1959, *The Status Seekers: An Exploration of Class Behavior in America*, London: Pelican.

Picasso, Pablo 1926, 'Letter to the Journal Ogonek', *Ogonek*, 20.

Picasso, Pablo 1968 [1923], 'Conversation with Marius de Zayas', in *Theories of Modern Art: A Sourcebook*, edited by Peter Selz and Herschel Chip Browning, Berkeley, CA: University of California Press.

Plekhanov, Georgii V. 1956, *Unaddressed Letters. Art and Social Life*, Moscow: Foreign Languages Publishing House.

Time 1963, 'Pop Art – Cult of the Commonplace', vol. 81, no. 18.

Ragon, Michel 1956, *L'aventure de l'art abstrait*, Paris: Robert Laffont.

Ragon, Michel 1963, *Naissance d'un art nouveau* [The Birth of a New Art], Paris: Editions Albin Michel.

Rosenblum, Robert 1966, *Cubism and Twentieth-Century Art*, New York: Harry N. Abrams.

Sérrulaz, Maurice 1963, *Le Cubisme* [Cubism], Paris: Presses Universitaires de France.

Sochor, Zenovia A. 1998, *Revolution and Culture: The Bogdanov-Lenin Controversy*, Ithaca, NY: Cornell University Press.

Sziklai, László 1993, 'Lukács and the Age of Fascism (1930–1945)', in *Hungarian Studies on György Lukács*, Budapest: Akadémiai Kiadó.

Der Spiegel 1964, 'Tinguely. Meta 8', vol. 18, no. 32.

Tolstoy, Lev 1906, *Tolstoy on Shakespeare*, trans. V. Tchertkoff London: Funk & Wagnalls.

Zervos, Christian 1932, 'A propos de Manet' [On Manet], *Cahiers D'Art*, vol. 7.

Zervos, Christian and Pablo Picasso 1968 [1935], 'Conversation with Picasso', in *The Creative Process: A Symposium*, edited by Brewster Ghiselin, Berkeley, CA: University of California Press.

Index

Illustration Section

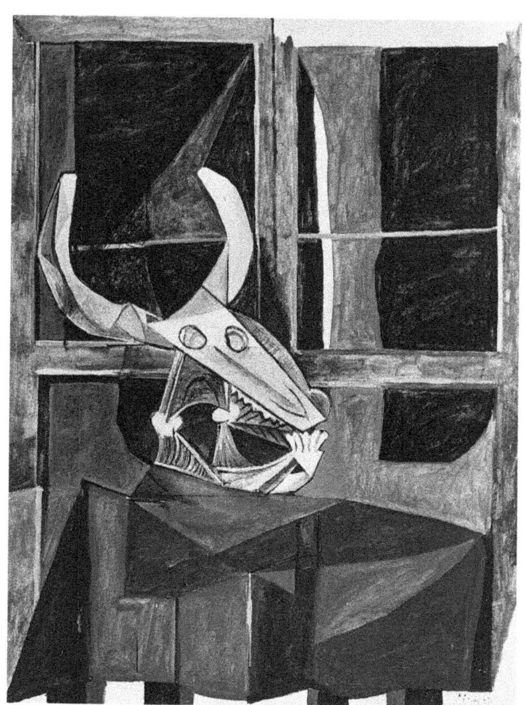

ILL. 1   *Pablo Picasso,* Still Life with Bull's Skull,
5th April 1942. Oil on canvas, 130 × 97 cm.
Kunstsammlung Nordrhein-Westfalen,
Dusseldorf, Germany.

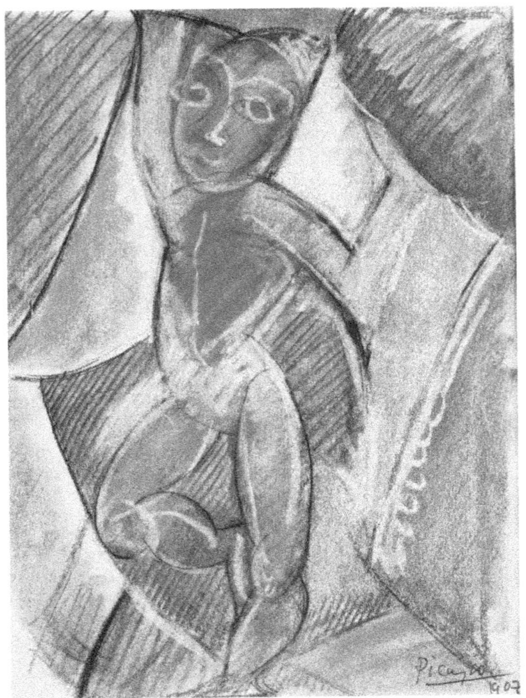

ILL. 2   *Pablo Picasso,* Nude with Raised Arms, *1907.*
Pastel and black chalk over pencil. Private
Collection.
© 2018 ESTATE OF PABLO PICASSO
/ PICTORIGHT, AMSTERDAM. ©IMAGE
PRIVATE COLLECTION / CHRISTIE'S
IMAGES, LONDON / BRIDGEMAN IMAGES,
LONDON

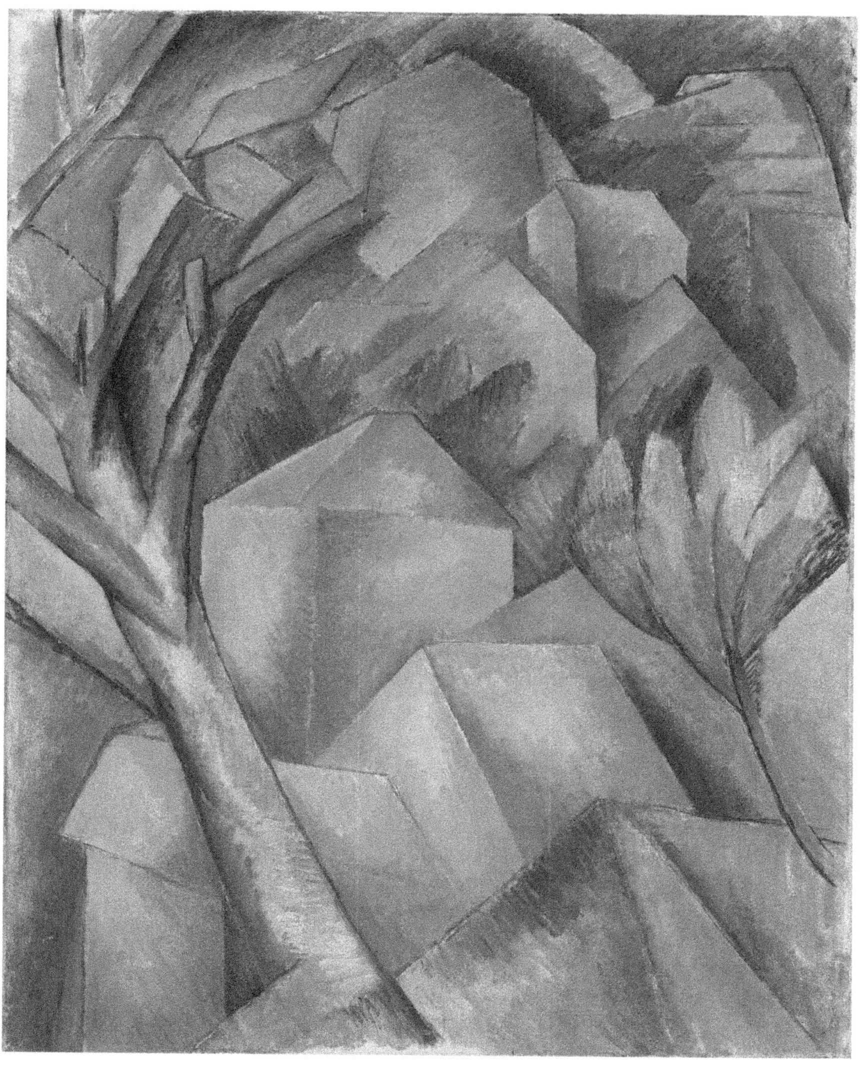

ILL. 3   *Georges Braque,* Houses at L'estaque, *1908. Oil on canvas, 73,0 × 59,5 cm. The Museum of Fine Arts Bern. Hermann und Margrit Rupf Foundation.*

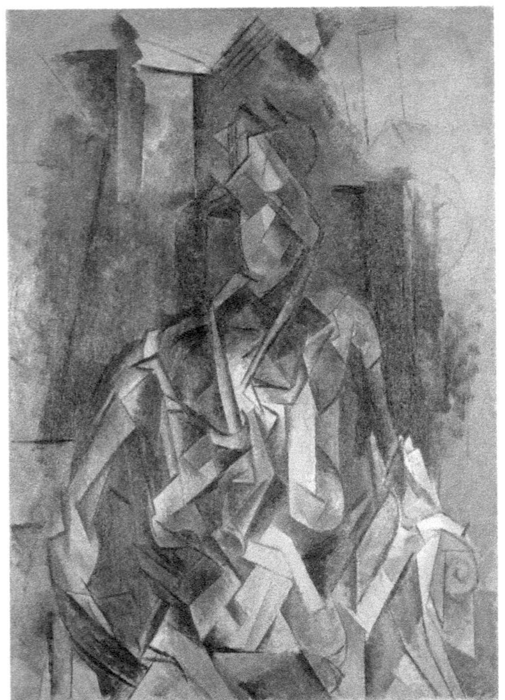

ILL. 4　*Pablo Picasso,* Seated Woman, *1909. Oil on card, 100 × 73 cm. National Museum of Modern Art, The Centre Pompidou, Paris, France.*

© 2018 ESTATE OF PABLO PICASSO / PICTORIGHT, AMSTERDAM. ©IMAGE NATIONAL MUSEUM OF MODERN ART, THE CENTRE POMPIDOU, PARIS / BRIDGEMAN IMAGES, LONDON

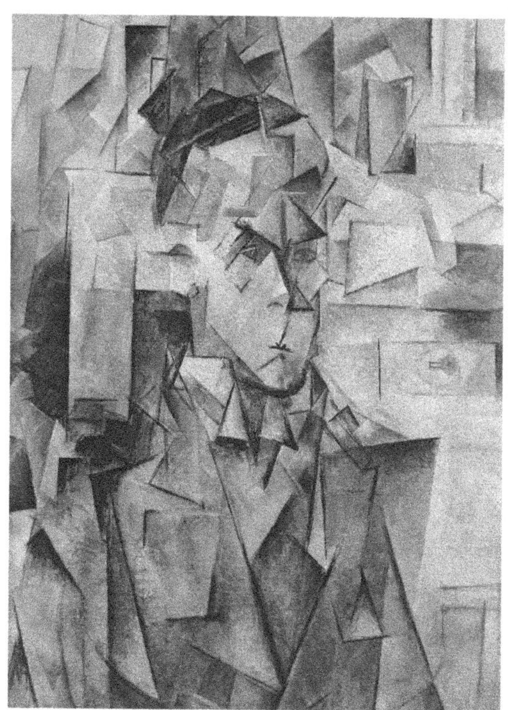

ILL. 5   *Pablo Picasso,* William Uhde (1874–1947), *1910. Oil on canvas, 81 × 60 cm. Private Collection.*
© 2018 ESTATE OF PABLO PICASSO / PICTORIGHT, AMSTERDAM. ©IMAGE PRIVATE COLLECTION / BRIDGEMAN IMAGES, LONDON

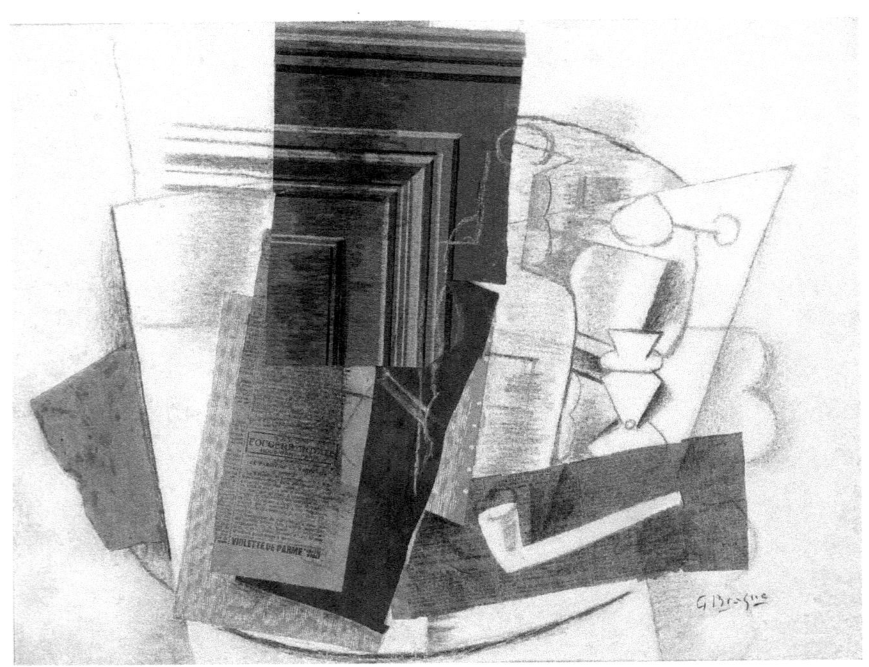

ILL. 6   *Georges Braque,* Bottle, Newspaper Pipe and Glass, *1913. Charcoal and collage on paper, 48×64 cm. Private Collection, New York.*

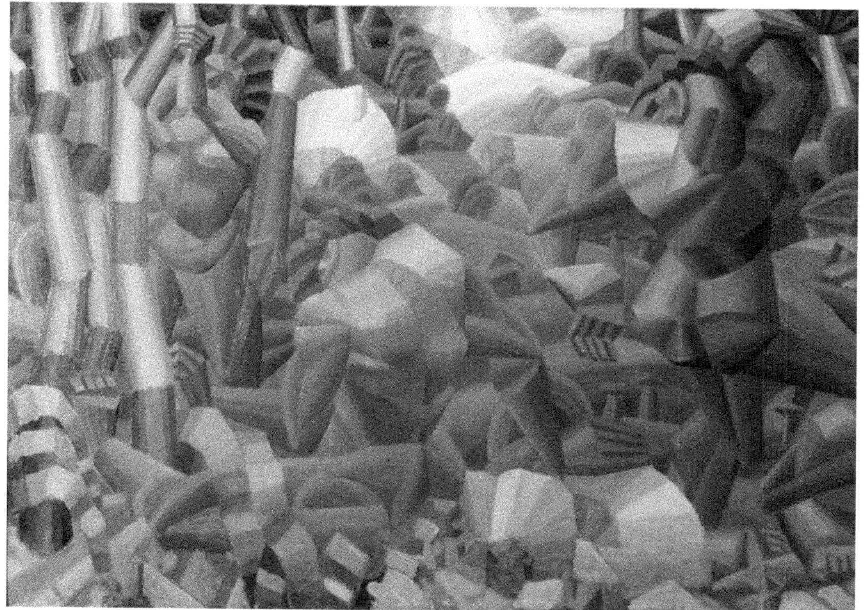

ILL. 7   *Fernand Léger,* Nude figures in a Wood, *1911. Oil on canvas, 120.5×170.5 cm. Kröller-Müller Museum, Otterlo, the Netherlands.*

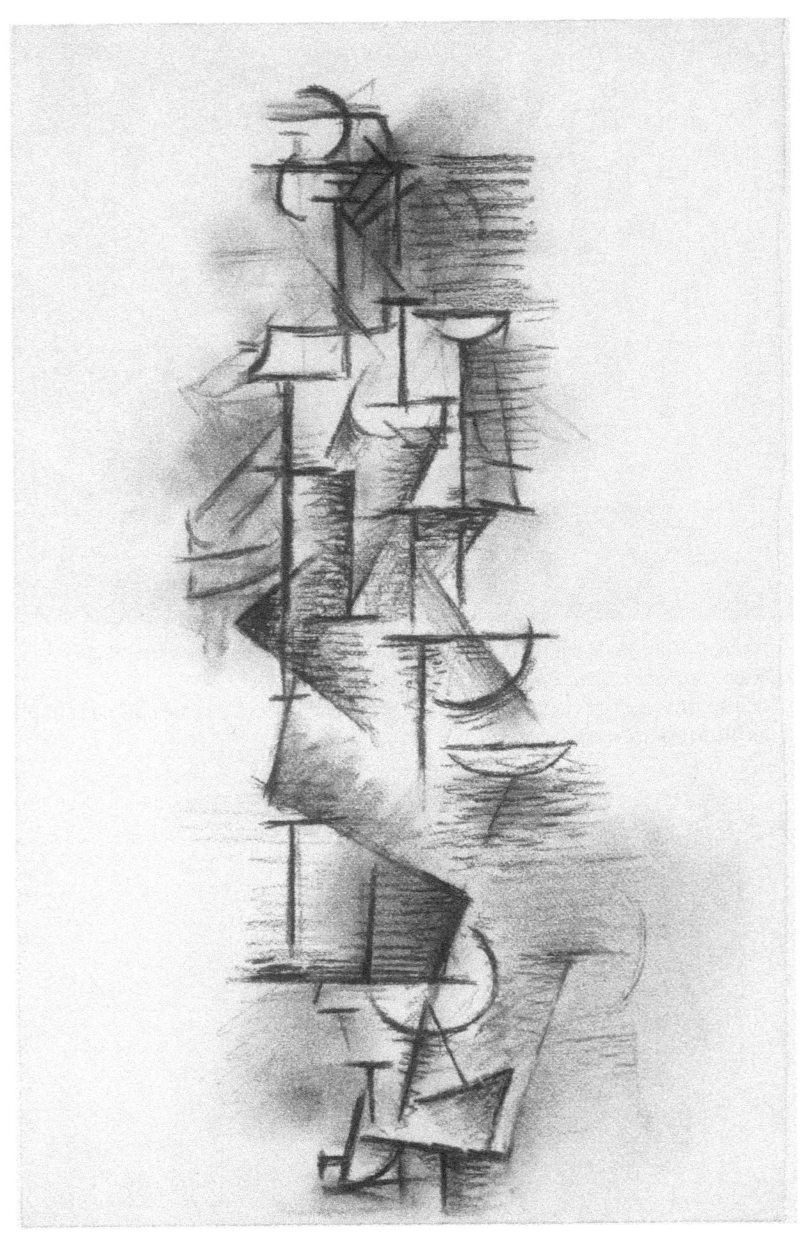

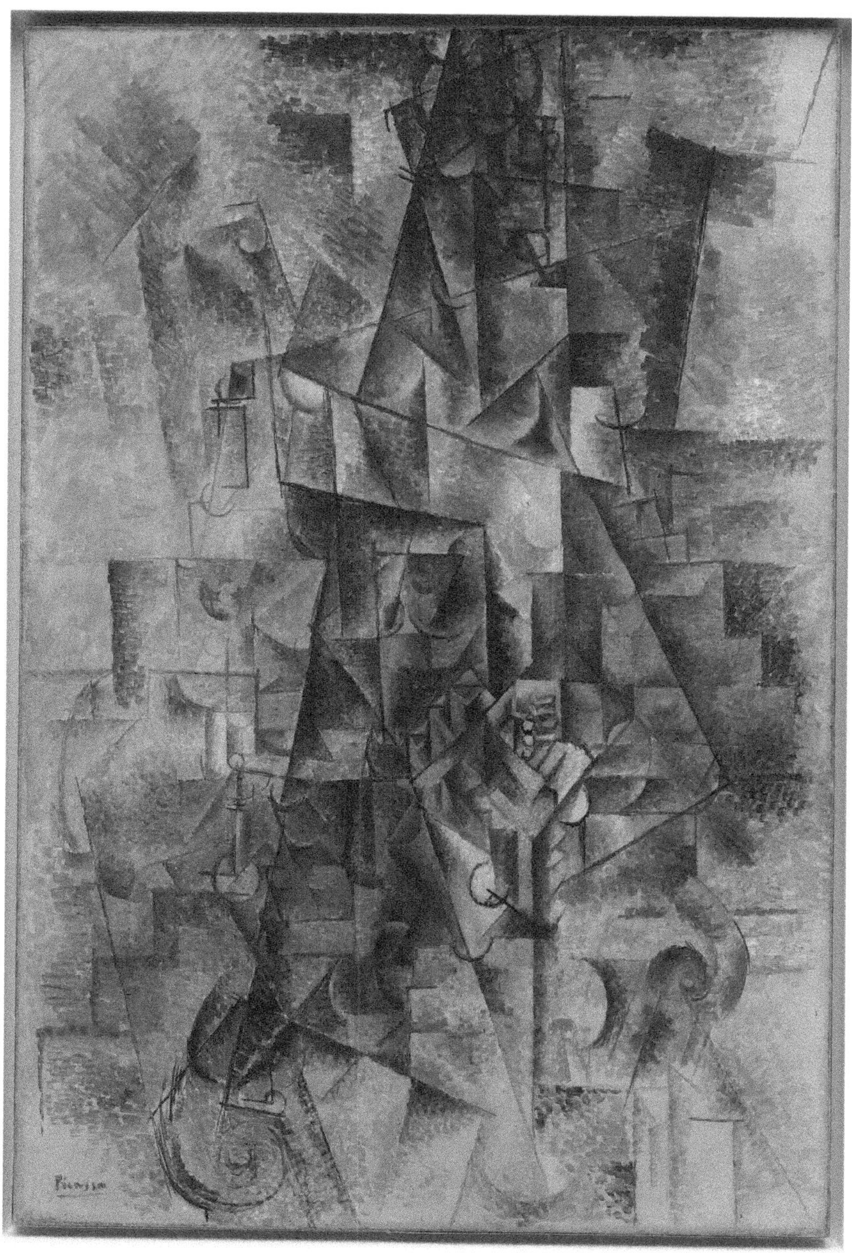

ILL. 9   *Pablo Picasso,* Accordionist, *Ceret, Summer 1911. Oil on canvas, 130.2 × 89.5 cm. Solomon R. Guggenheim Museum, New York, USA. Solomon R. Guggenheim Founding Collection, by gift.*
© 2018 ESTATE OF PABLO PICASSO / PICTORIGHT, AMSTERDAM. ©IMAGE 2018 SOLOMON R. GUGGENHEIM FOUNDING / ART RESOURCE / SCALA, FLORENCE

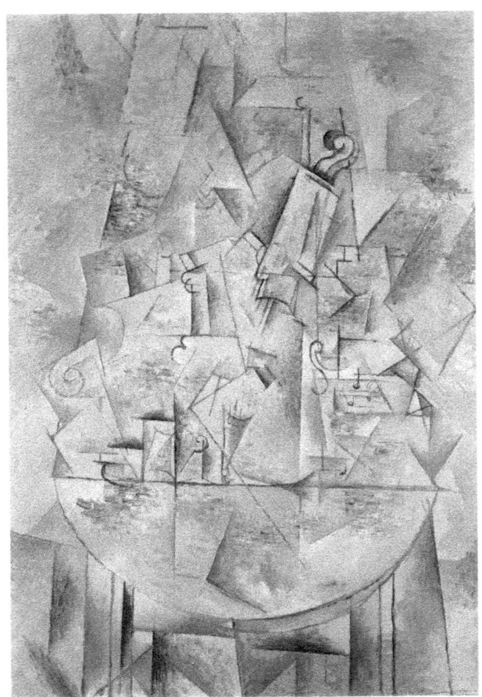

ILL. 10 *Georges Braque,* The Gueridon, *1911. Oil on canvas, 116.5 × 81.5 cm. National Museum of Modern Art, The Centre Pompidou, Paris, France.*

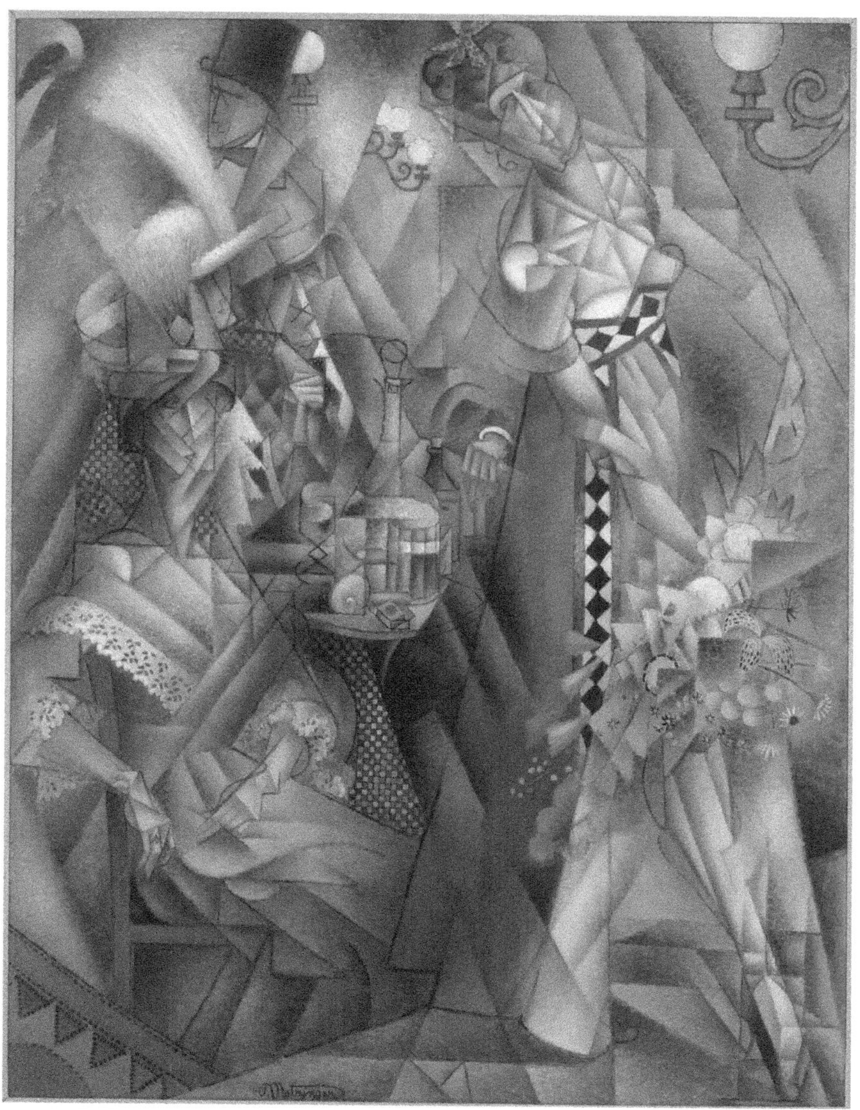

ILL. 11 *Jean Metzinger,* Dancer in a Café, *1912. Oil on canvas, 146.05 × 114.3 cm. Albright-Knox Art Gallery, Buffalo, New York, USA. General Purchase Funds, 1957.*
© ESTATE JEAN METZINGER / PICTORIGHT, AMSTERDAM. ©IMAGE 2018 ALBRIGHT-KNOX ART GALLERY / ART RESOURCE / SCALA, FLORENCE

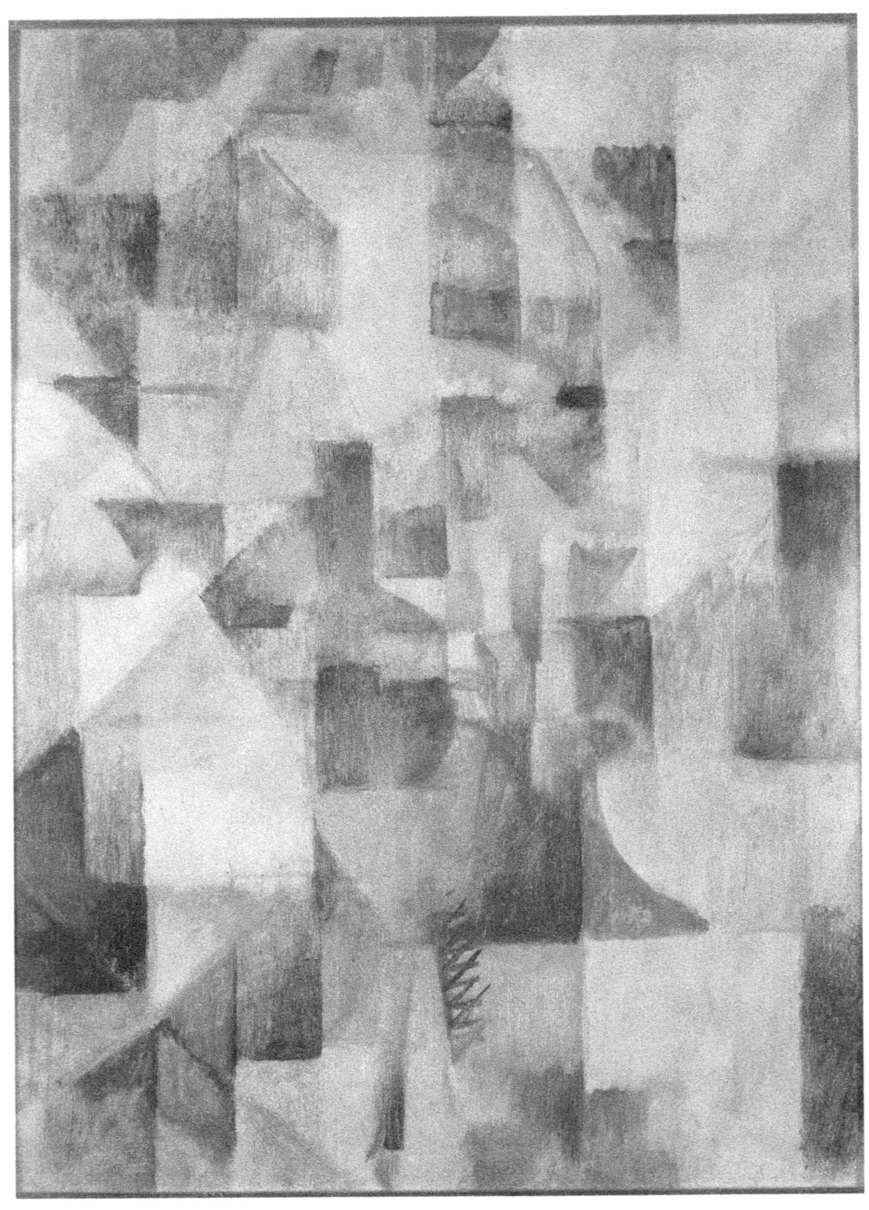

ILL. 12   *Robert Delaunay,* Window on the City No. 2, *1912. Private Collection, France.*
©IMAGE 2018 ALBUM / SCALA, FLORENCE

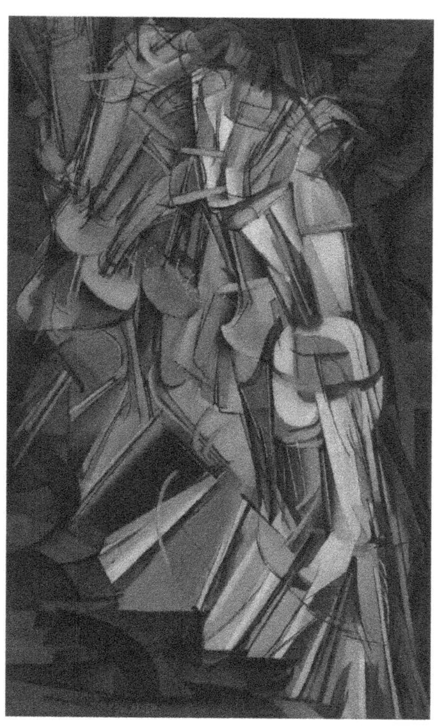

ILL. 13   *Marcel Duchamp,* Nude Descending a
Staircase, No. 2, *1912. Oil on canvas,
147 × 89.2 cm. Philadelphia Museum of
Art, Pennsylvania, PA, USA. The Louise
and Walter Arensberg Collection, 1950.*
© ESTATE OF MARCEL DUCHAMP /
PICTORIGHT, AMSTERDAM.
©IMAGE PHILADELPHIA MUSEUM
OF ART, PENNSYLVANIA /
BRIDGEMAN IMAGES, LONDON

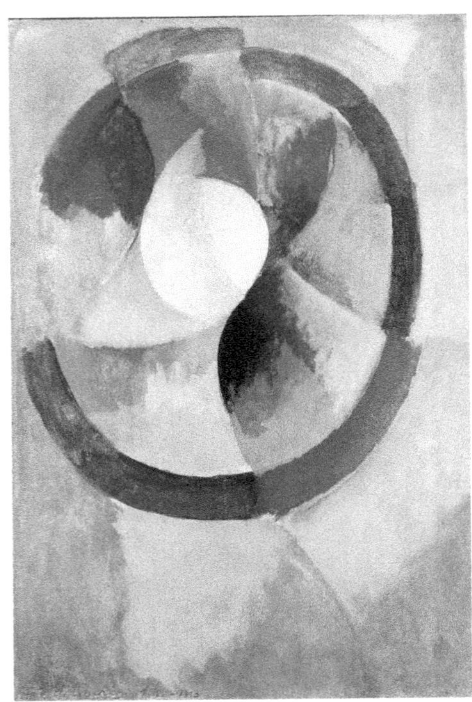

ILL. 14 *Robert Delaunay,* Circular shapes, Sun
No. 2, *1912–13. Tempera on canvas,*
100 × 68.5 cm. National Museum of Modern
Art, The Centre Pompidou, Paris, France.
©IMAGE NATIONAL MUSEUM
OF MODERN ART, THE CENTRE
POMPIDOU, PARIS / LUISA
RICCIARINI/LEEMAGE / BRIDGEMAN
IMAGES, LONDON

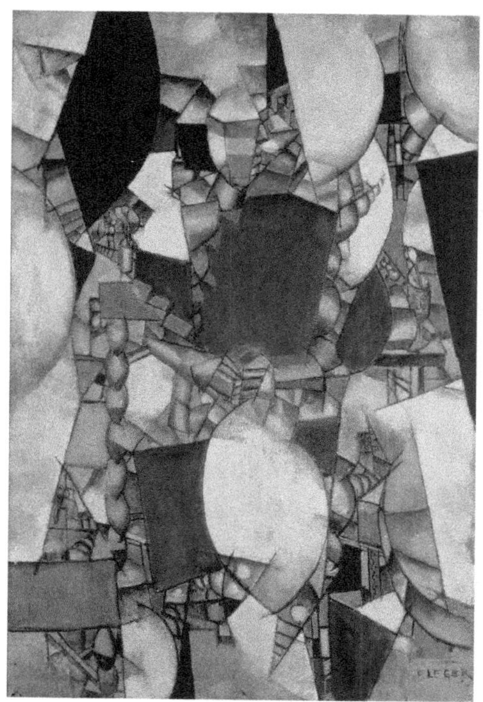

ILL. 15   *Fernand Léger,* Woman in Blue, *1912. Oil on canvas, 193×130 cm. Kunstmuseum, Basel, Switzerland. Gift of Dr. h.c. Raoul La Roche, 1952.*
© PICTORIGHT, AMSTERDAM. ©IMAGE KUNSTMUSEUM, BASEL / PETER WILLI / BRIDGEMAN IMAGES, LONDON

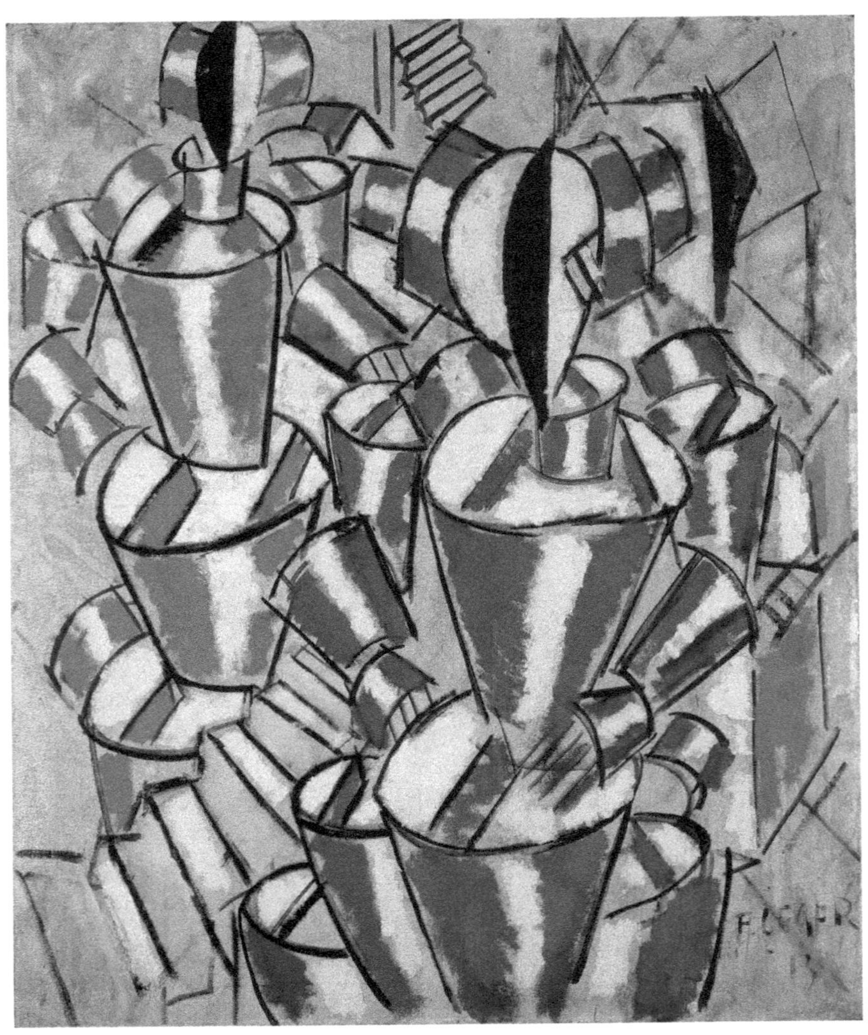

ILL. 16 *Fernand Léger,* The Staircase, *1913. Oil on canvas, 144×118 cm.*
© PICTORIGHT, AMSTERDAM. IMAGE REPRODUCED BY PERMISSION OF
KUNSTHAUS ZÜRICH

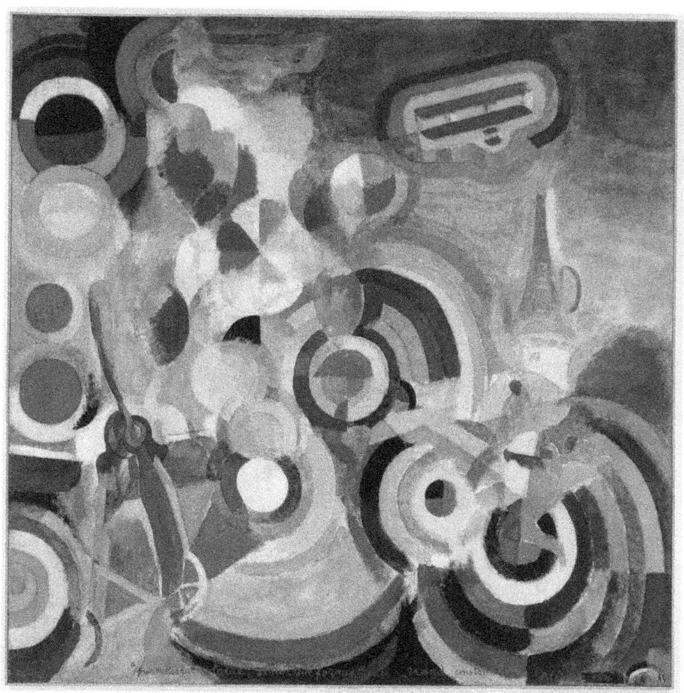

ILL. 17   *Robert Delaunay,* Homage to Bleriot, *1914. Tempera on canvas, 250 × 251 cm. Kunstmuseum, Basel, Switzerland.*

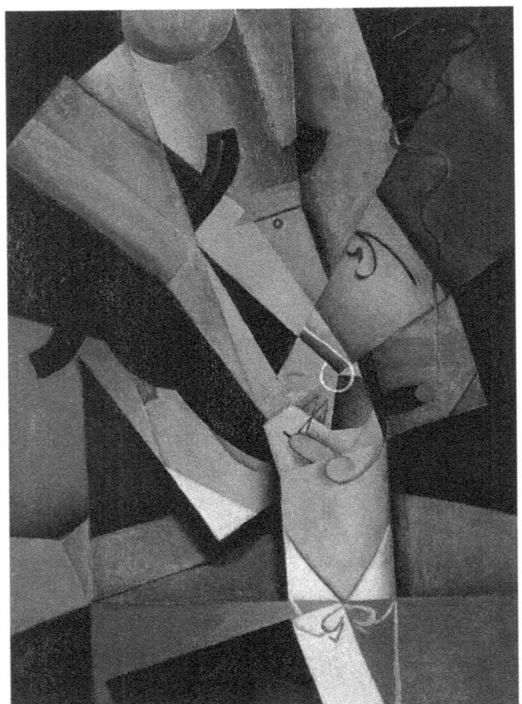

ILL. 18   *Juan Gris,* Smoker (Frank Haviland), *1913. Oil on canvas, 73 × 54 cm. The Thyssen-Bornemisza Museum, Madrid, Spain.*
©IMAGE DE AGOSTINI PICTURE LIBRARY / G. NIMATALLAH / BRIDGEMAN IMAGES, LONDON

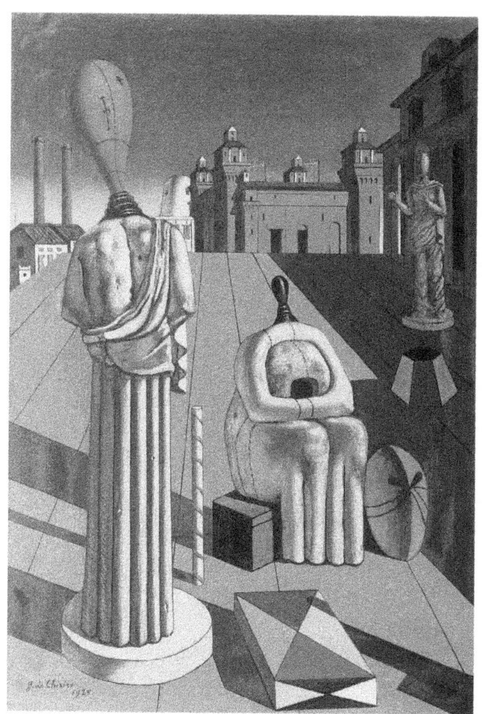

ILL. 19 *Giorgio De Chirico,* Disquieting Muses, *1925. Oil on canvas, 100 × 70 cm. Private Collection.*

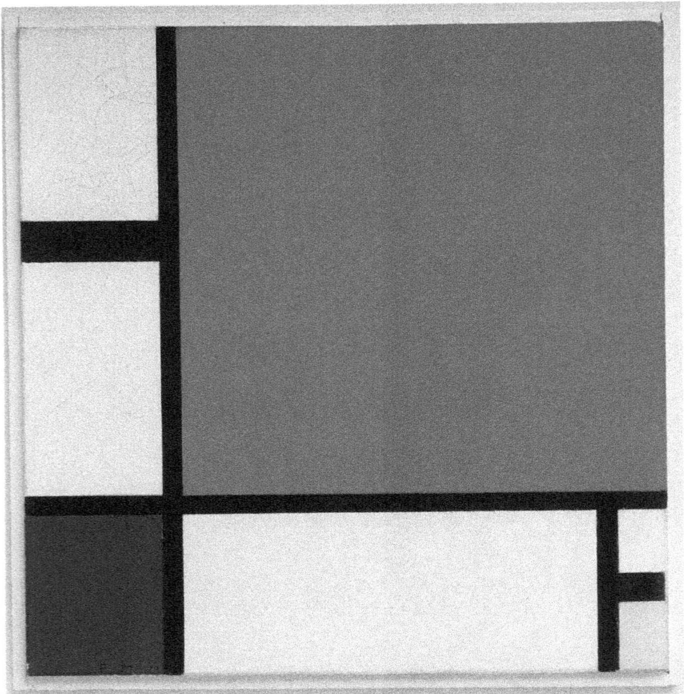

ILL. 20   *Piet Mondrian,* Composition with Red, Blue, and Yellow, *1930. Oil on canvas, 46×46 cm. Private Collection.*
© PICTORIGHT, AMSTERDAM. ©IMAGE PRIVATE COLLECTION / BRIDGEMAN IMAGES, LONDON

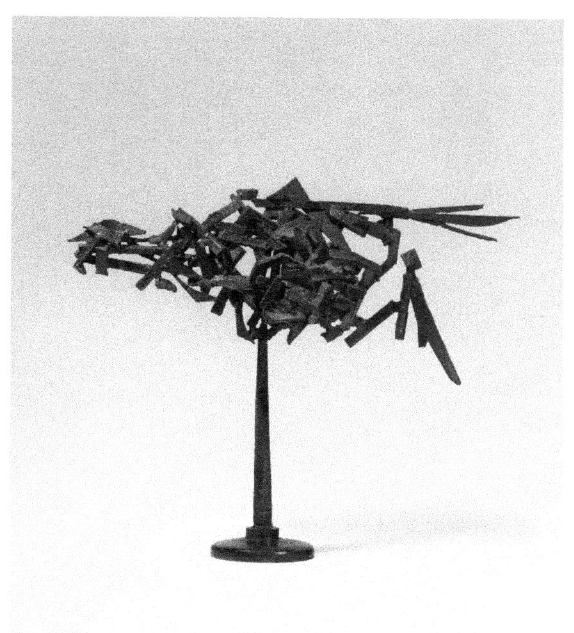

ILL. 21   *David Smith,* Raven II, *1955. Steel, painted black, 64.8×77.5×23.8cm. Executed in 1955. Private Collection.*
©IMAGE PRIVATE COLLECTION / CHRISTIE'S IMAGES, LONDON / BRIDGEMAN IMAGES, LONDON

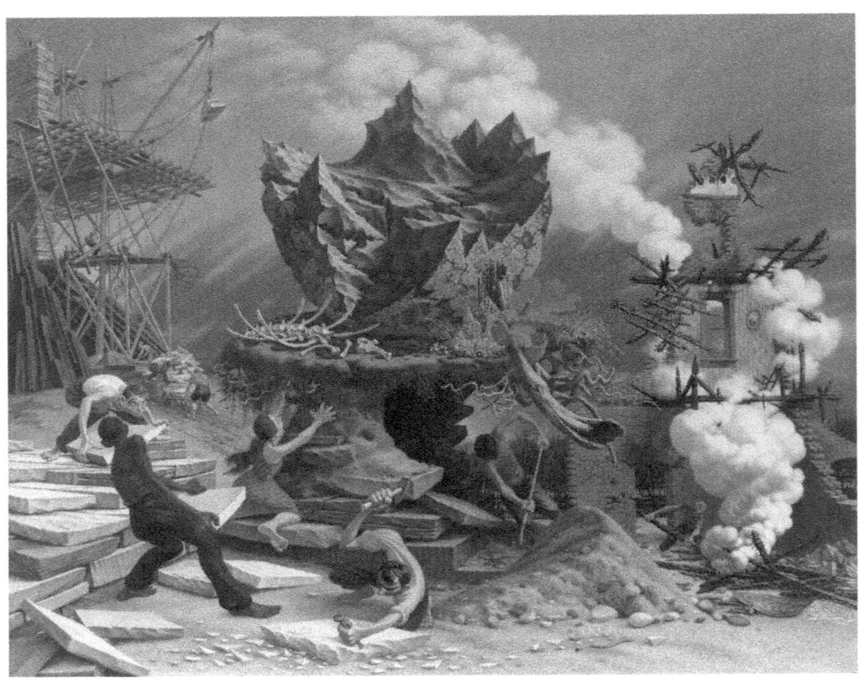

ILL. 22   *Peter Blume,* The Rock, *1944–48. Oil on canvas, 146.4 × 188.9 cm. The Art Institute of Chicago, IL, USA. Gift of Edgar Kaufmann, Jr.*

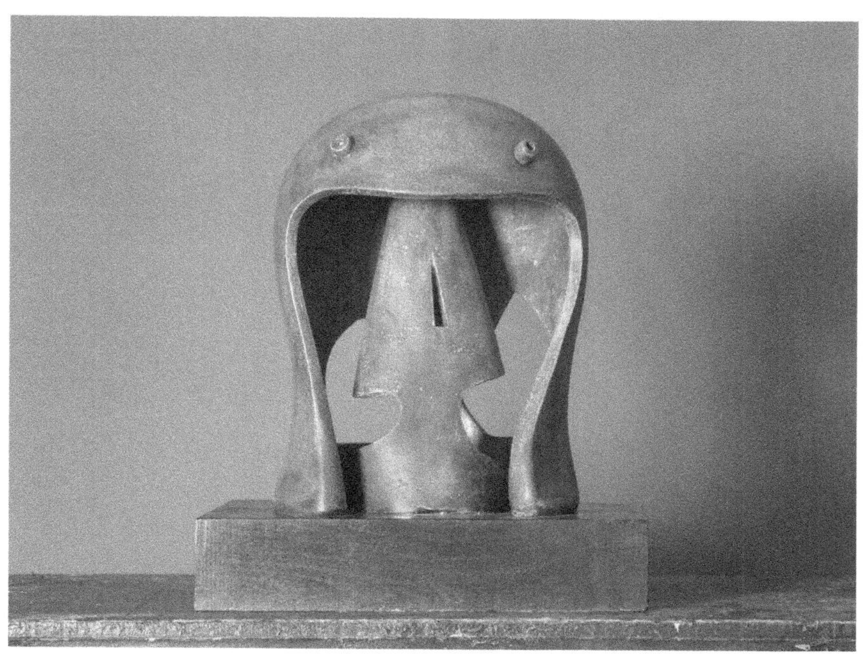

ILL. 23   *Henry Moore,* Helmet Head No.1, *1950. Bronze, 40×35.5×30 cm. Tate Gallery,* UK.

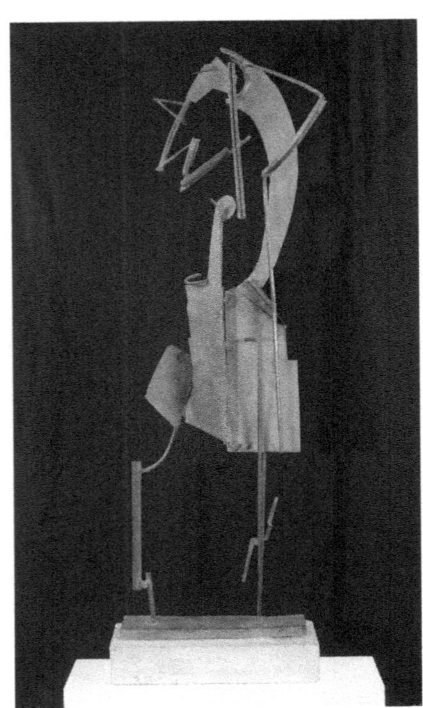

ILL. 24 *Julio González,* Woman Arranging her Hair, *1929–30. Metal, 168,5 × 54 × 27 cm. National Museum of Modern Art, The Centre Pompidou, Paris, France.*
©IMAGE NATIONAL MUSEUM OF MODERN ART, THE CENTRE POMPIDOU, PARIS / BRIDGEMAN IMAGES, LONDON

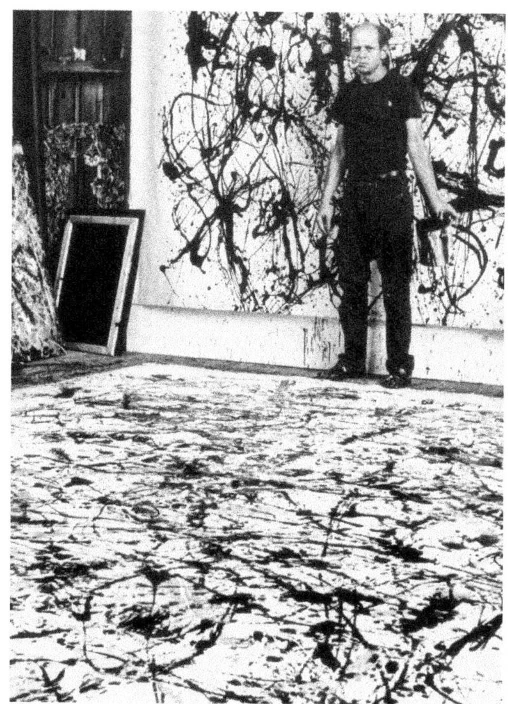

ILL. 25   *Hans Namuth* [*?*], Jackson Pollock in his studio, *1950. Black and white photograph.*
©IMAGE BRIDGEMAN IMAGES

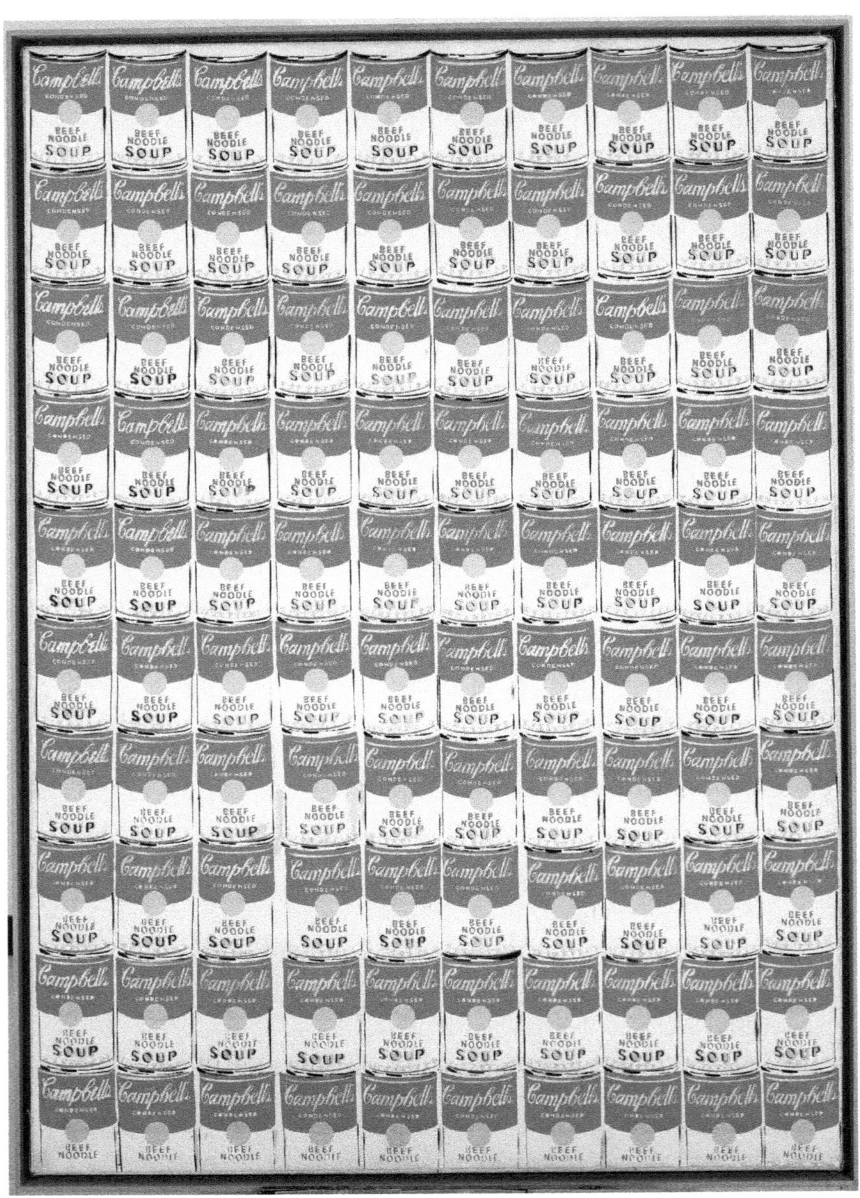

ILL. 26   *Andy Warhol, 100 Cans, 1962. Casein, spray paint and pencil on cotton, 182.88 × 132.08 cm; framed with plexi cap: 187.96 × 138.43 × 6.98 cm. Albright-Knox Art Gallery, Buffalo, New York, USA. Gift of Seymour H. Knox Jr., 1963.*

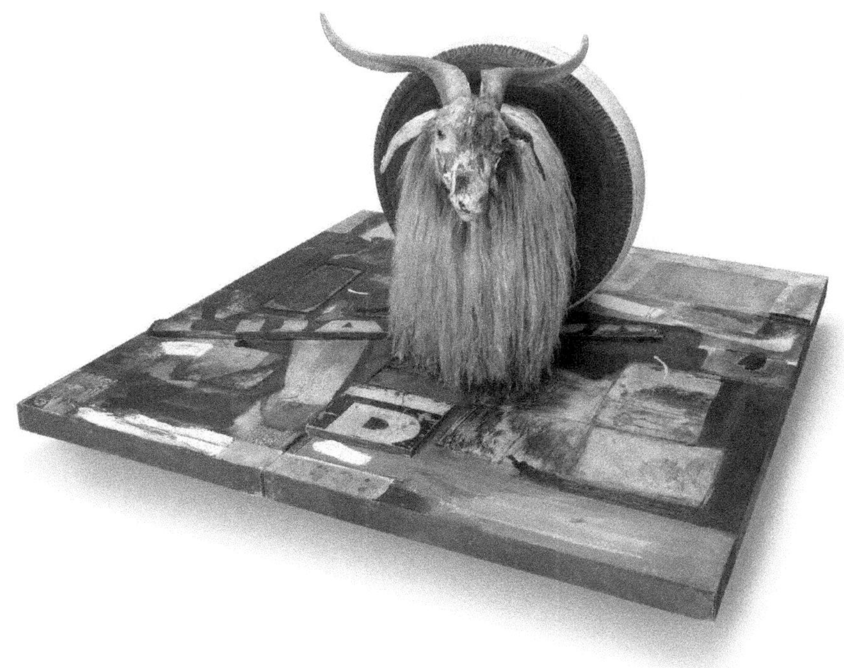

ILL. 27   *Robert Rauschenberg,* Monogram, *1955–59. Combine: oil, paper, fabric, printed paper,*
printer reproductions, metal, wood, rubber shoe heel and tennis ball on canvas with oil
and rubber tire on Angora goat on wood platform mounted on four casters,
106.7 × 160.7 × 163.8 cm. Moderna Museet, Stockholm. Purchased with contribution from
Moderna Museets Vänner/The Friends of Moderna Musee, 1965.
© PICTORIGHT, AMSTERDAM. IMAGE REPRODUCED BY PERMISSION OF
MODERNA MUSEET, STOCKHOLM

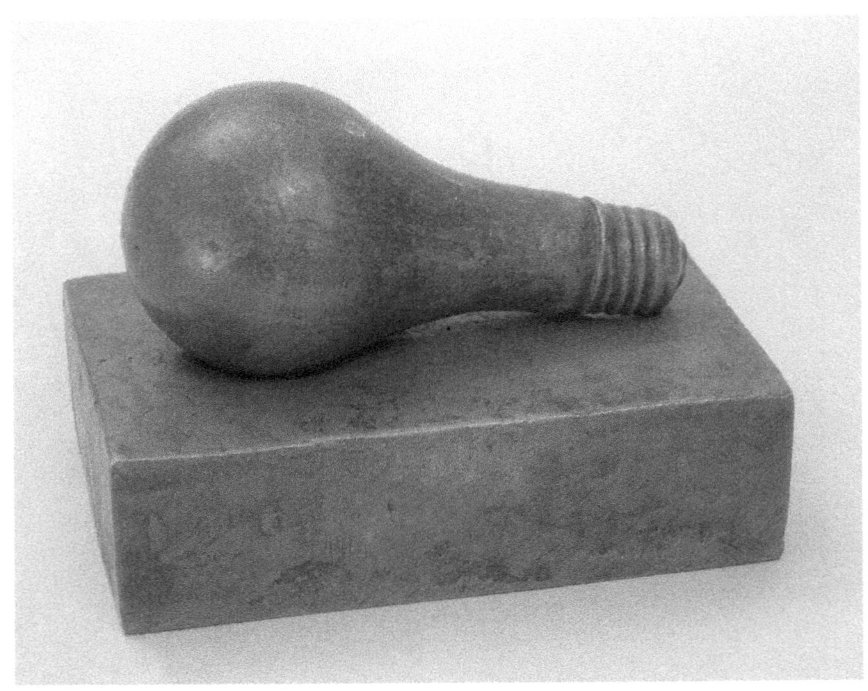

ILL. 28   *Jasper Johns*, Light Bulb, *1960. Bronze, 10.8×15.2×10.2 cm. Edition of 4. Private Collection.*
©IMAGE PRIVATE COLLECTION / BRIDGEMAN IMAGES, LONDON

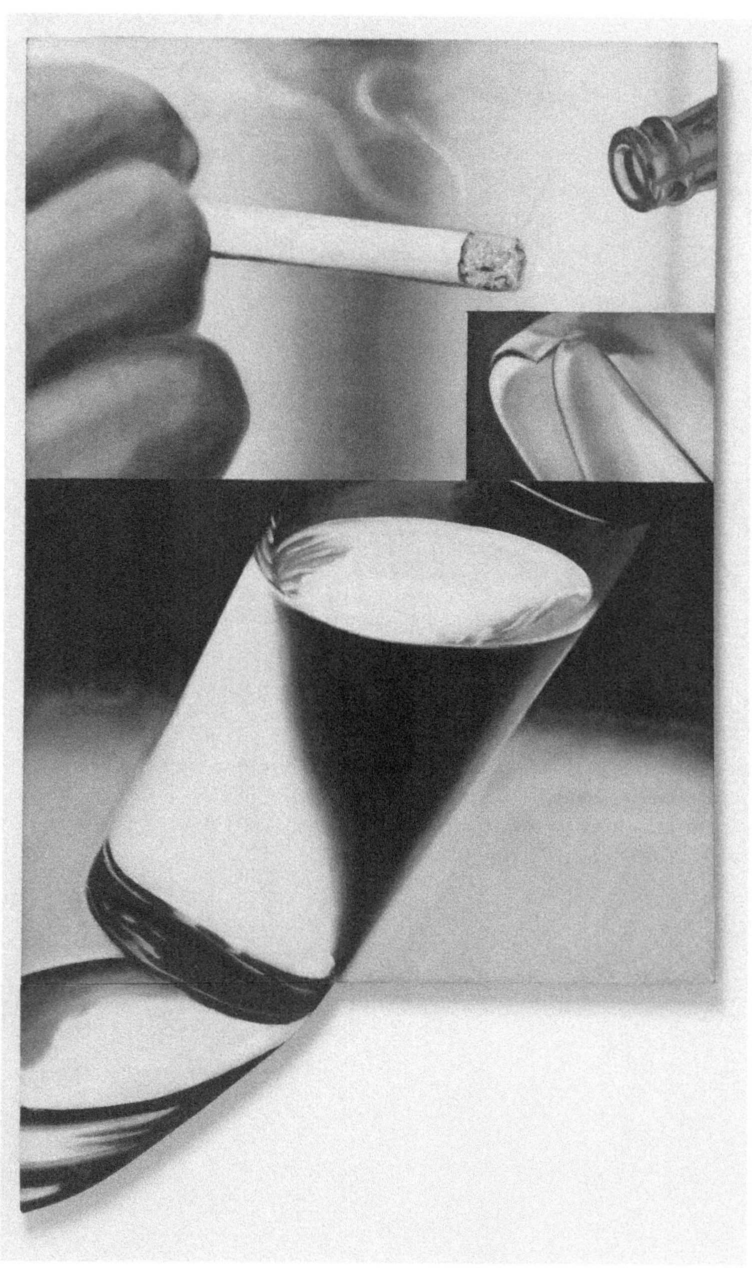

ILL. 29   *James Rosenquist,* White Cigarette, *1961. Oil on canvas,*
154.94 × 91.44 × 2.54 cm. The Museum of Contemporary Art, Los Angeles, USA.
The Panza Collection (Acc.n. 87.21).

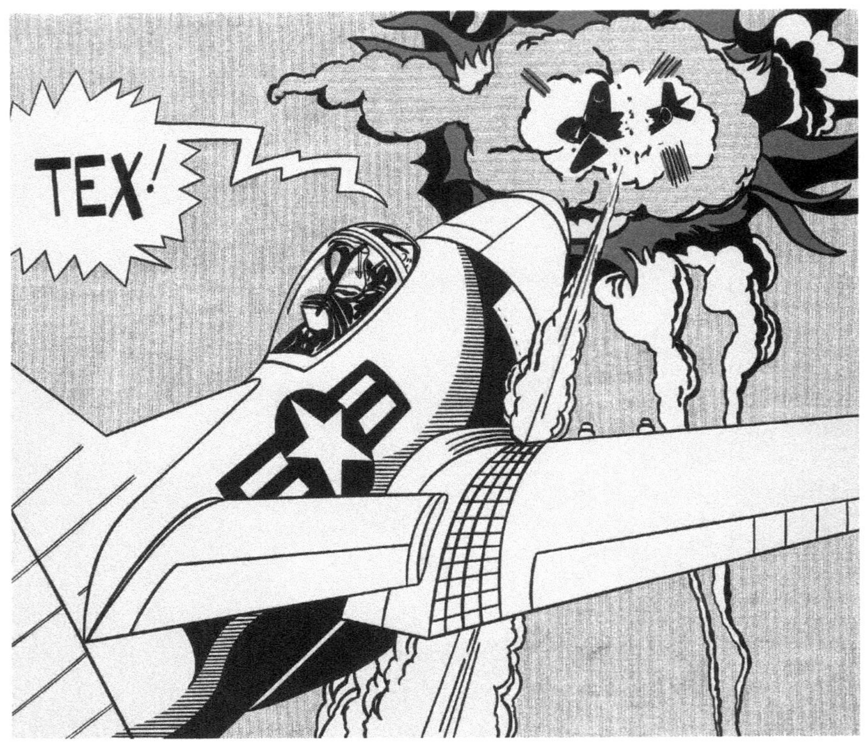

ILL. 30   *Roy Lichtenstein,* TEX!, *1962. Oil, magna and graphite on canvas, 172.7 × 203.2 cm.*
Christie's Images Limited.
© PICTORIGHT, AMSTERDAM. ©IMAGE 2018 CHRISTIE'S IMAGES, LONDON /
SCALA, FLORENCE

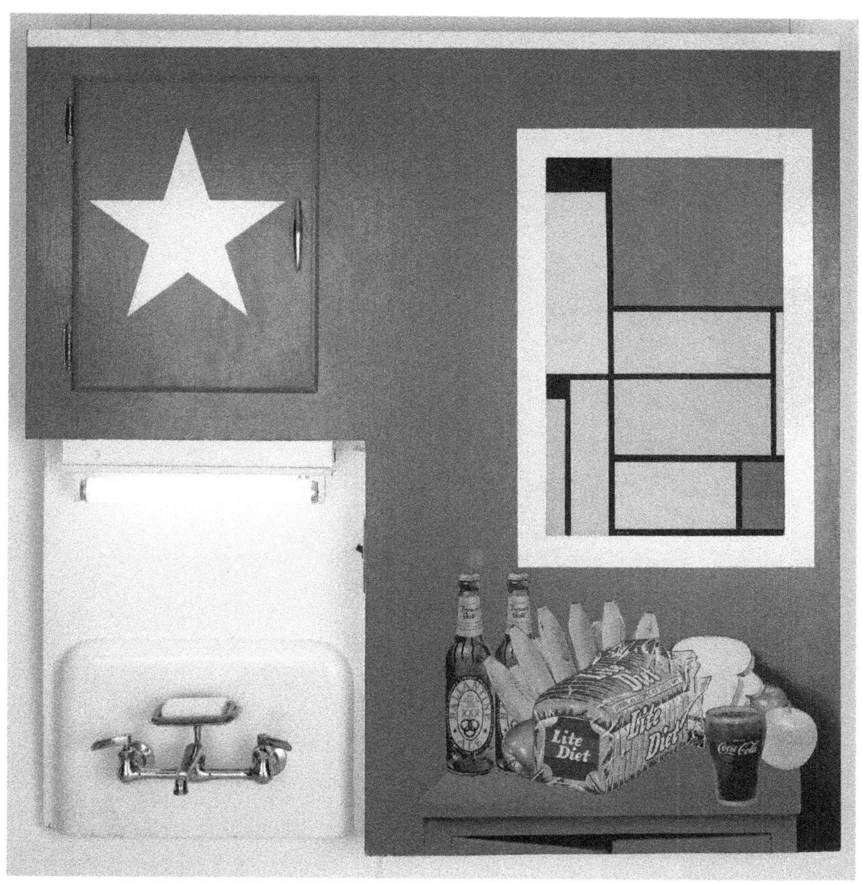

ILL. 31   *Tom Wesselmann,* Still Life #20, *1962. Mixed media, overall: 104.14 × 121.92 × 13.97 cm.*
Albright-Knox Art Gallery, Buffalo, New York, USA. Gift of Seymour H. Knox Jr., 1962.
© 2018 ESTATE OF TOM WESSELMANN / PICTORIGHT, AMSTERDAM. ©IMAGE
2018 ALBRIGHT-KNOX ART GALLERY, BUFFALO / ART RESOURCE / SCALA,
FLORENCE

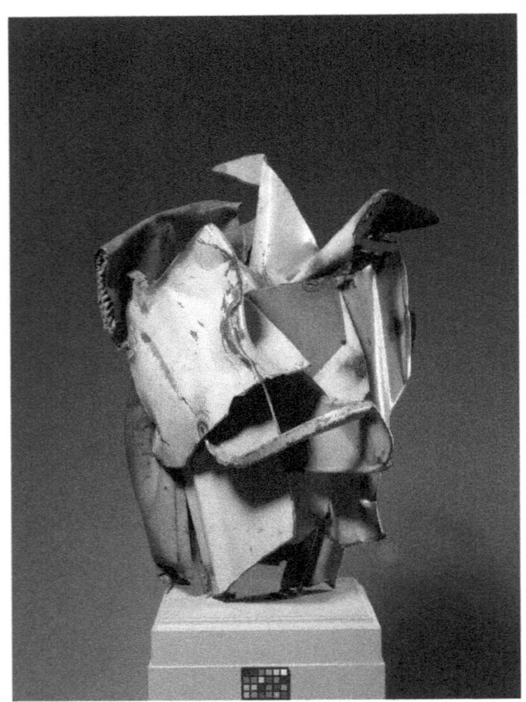

ILL. 32   *John Chamberlain, Untitled, c. 1958–59. Painted and welded metal, overall: 82.4 × 67.3 × 61 cm. Cleveland Museum of Art, OH, USA. Andrew R. and Martha Holden Jennings Fund, 1973.*
© JOHN CHAMBERLAIN / PICTORIGHT, AMSTERDAM. ©IMAGE CLEVELAND MUSEUM OF ART, OH / BRIDGEMAN IMAGES, LONDON

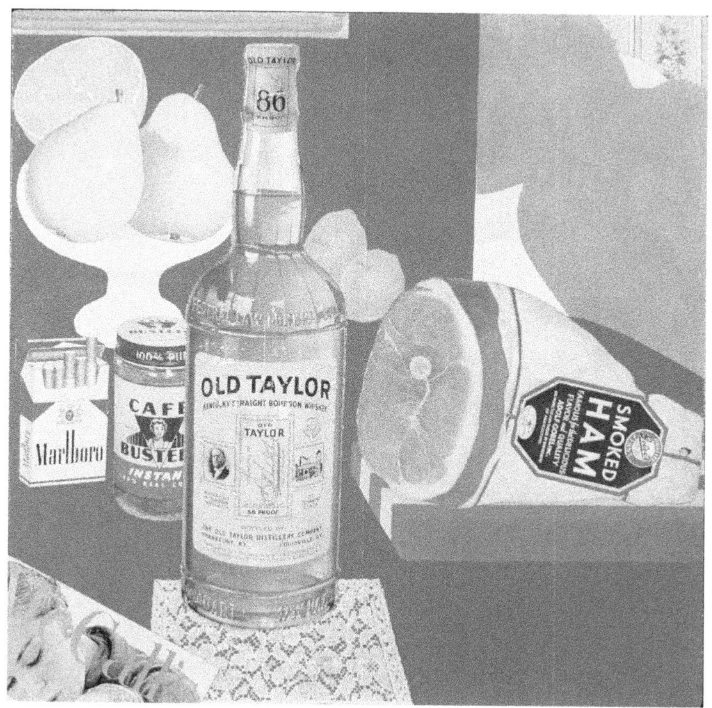

ILL. 33 *Tom Wesselmann,* Still Life No. 1, *1962. Collage on canvas. Galerie Nierendorf, Berlin, Germany.*
© 2018 ESTATE OF TOM WESSELMANN / PICTORIGHT, AMSTERDAM. ©IMAGE GALERIE NIERENDORF, BERLIN / BRIDGEMAN IMAGES, LONDON

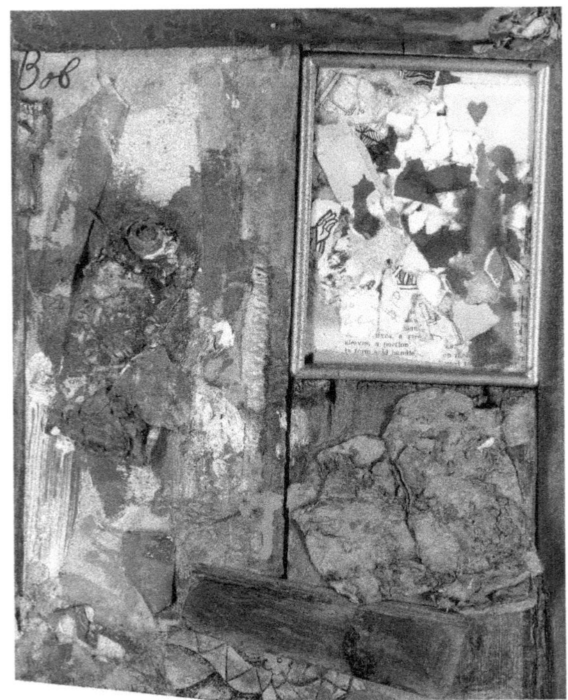

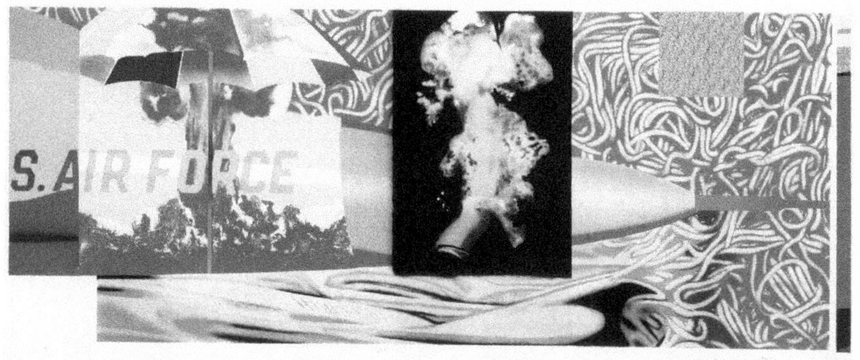

ILL. 35   *James Rosenquist,* F-111 (North, South, East and West), *1974. Four-part lithograph and screenprint in colours on Arches paper. Printed in 1974 at Styria Studio, New York, 92.7 × 190.6 cm. Shown here is one of the four parts. Private Collection.*
Note: Created nearly a decade after the painting of the same title. James Rosenquist began to paint the original 86-foot-long *F-111* in 1964, designed as 23 panels, to wrap around the four walls of the Leo Castelli Gallery in Manhattan, NY, where it was displayed in 1965. The original painting is included in the collection of the Museum of Modern Art, New York, USA.

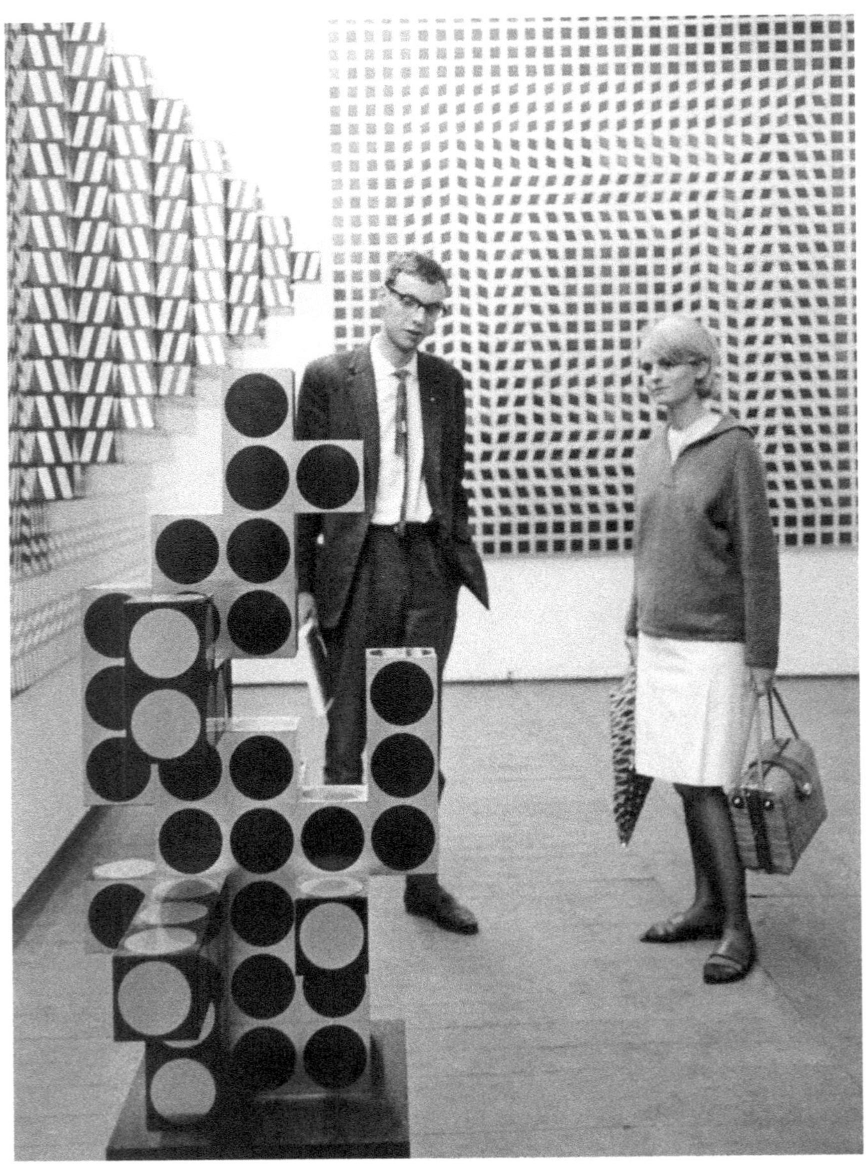

ILL. 36   *Visitors next to works by artist Victor Vasarely at the documenta III art exhibition in Kassel on 30 June 1964. Black and white photograph, by Roland Witschel.*
©IMAGE DPA PICTURE ALLIANCE / ALAMY STOCK PHOTO

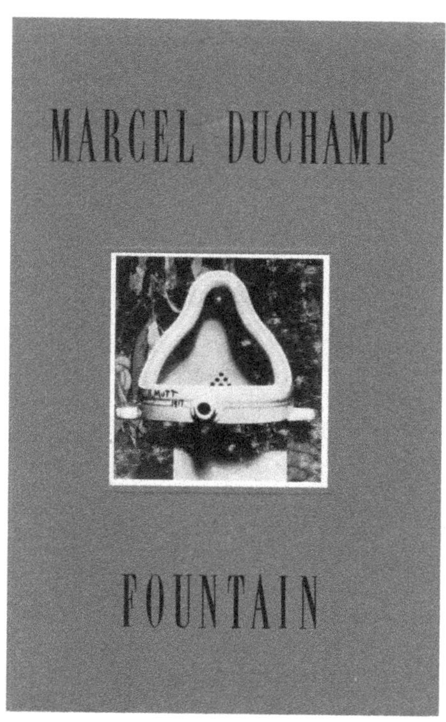

ILL. 37   *Marcel Duchamp,* Fountain, *1917.*
Displayed and photographed by Alfred
Stieglitz at his 291 Art Gallery after the
1917 Society of Independent Artists
exhibit. The original photo has been
lost. Here seen on the cover of William
A. Camfield's book Marcel Duchamp:
Fountain. *Published by Houston Fine*
Art Press, 1989, with an introduction by
Walter Hops. Private Collection.
©ARTWORK PICTORIGHT,
AMSTERDAM. ©IMAGE PRIVATE
COLLECTION / BRIDGEMAN
IMAGES, LONDON